AF328408

Guillermo Kuitca

LUND HUMPHRIES | CONTEMPORARY PAINTERS

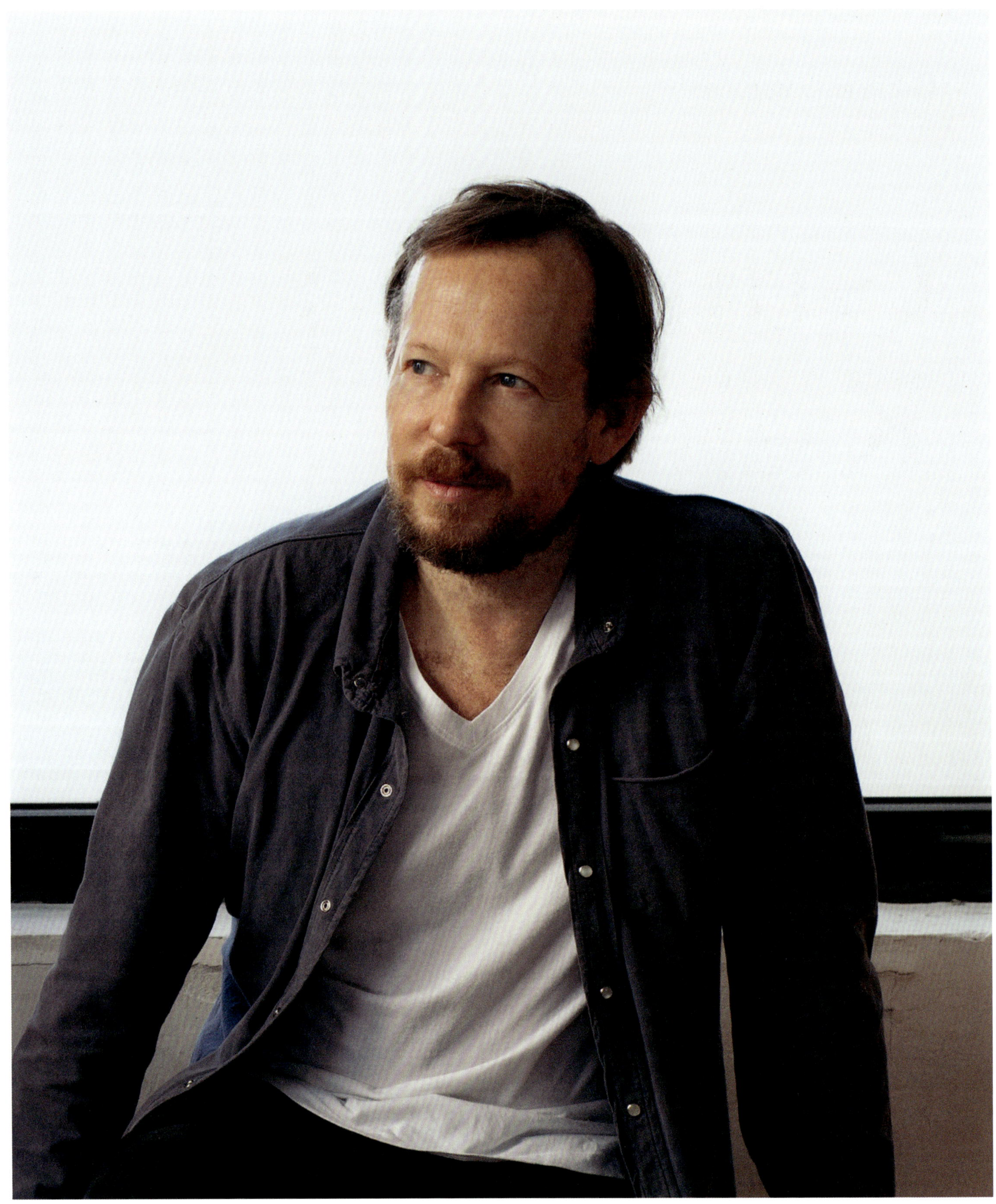

Raphael Rubinstein

Guillermo Kuitca

LUND HUMPHRIES | CONTEMPORARY PAINTERS

Contemporary Painters Series
Series Editor: Barry Schwabsky

The Contemporary Painters Series is a curated series of accessible, authoritative and highly illustrated monographs on the world's leading living painters, which locates painting as a vibrant and vital part of contemporary art.

The series is edited by American art critic Barry Schwabsky, supported by an international advisory board with a specialist interest in contemporary painting. It aims to redefine 'painting' in the contemporary context as work that is done within the conventions and history of painting, but which may incorporate other materials or techniques.

Advisory Board
Paco Barragán, independent curator and arts writer and Contributing Editor of *Artpulse*
Tony Godfrey, freelance writer and curator based in the Philippines
David Pagel, Los Angeles-based art critic, curator and writer
Ida Panicelli, former Editor-in-Chief of *Artforum*
Simon Rees, former Director of the Govett-Brewster Art Gallery/Len Lye Centre, New Zealand
Beatrix Ruf, former Director of the Stedelijk Museum, Amsterdam
Philip Tinari, Director of the Ullens Center for Contemporary Art, Beijing
Gilda Williams, art critic, writer, lecturer and London correspondent for *Artforum*
John Yau, poet, art critic and curator

Also available in the series:
Amy Sillman by Valerie Smith
Bernard Frize by David Rhodes
Etel Adnan by Kaelen Wilson-Goldie
Ding Yi by Tony Godfrey and Kaimei Wang
Jim Shaw by David Pagel
Lois Dodd by Faye Hirsch
Mary Weatherford by Suzanne Hudson
Neo Rauch by Michael Glover
Philip Taaffe by John Yau
Tal R. by Martin Herbert
Thomas Nozkowski by John Yau
Verne Dawson by John Hutchinson

Contents

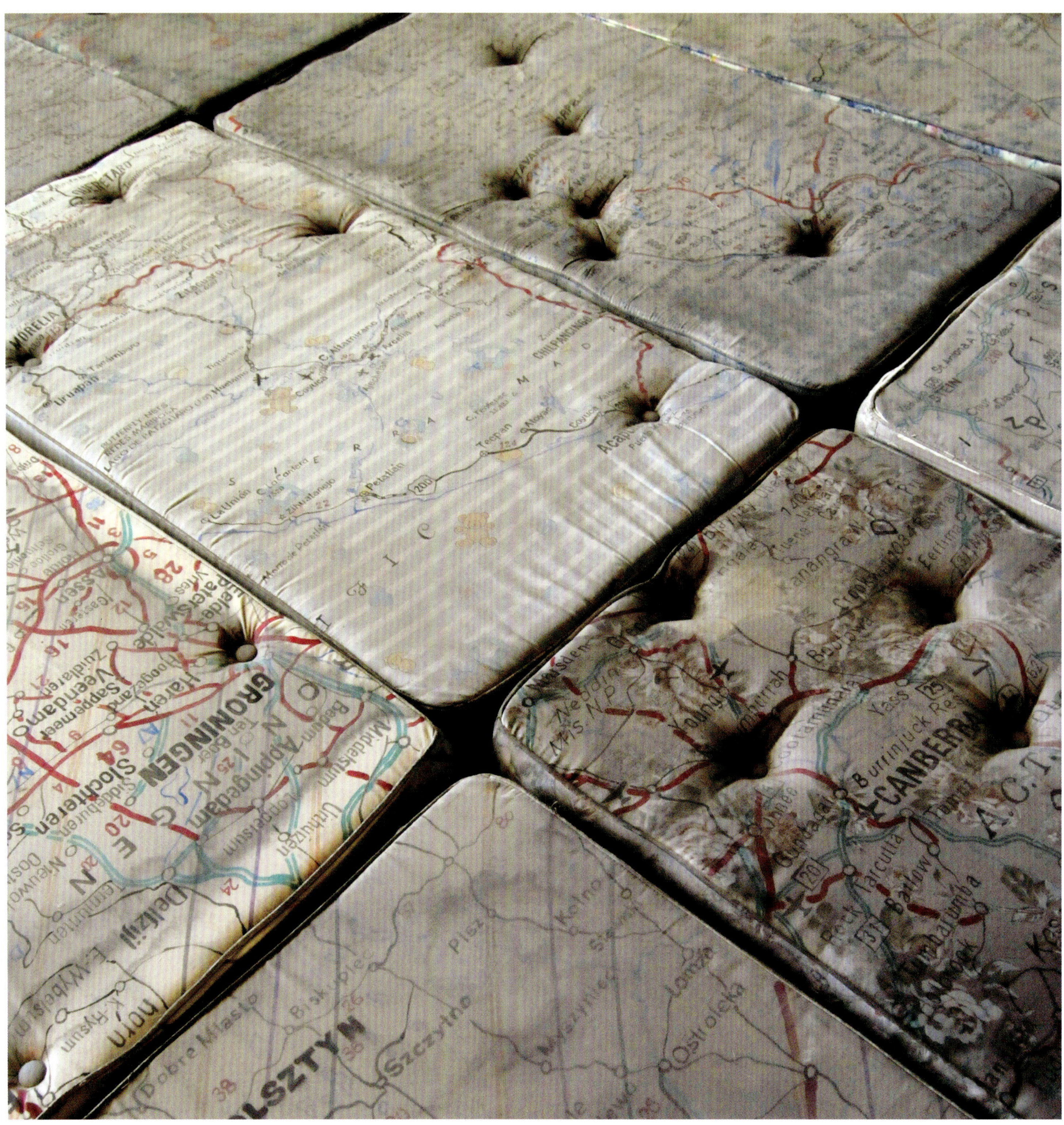

1. *Le Sacre*   1992 (detail)

Acrylic on 54 mattresses with wood and brass legs
120 × 60 × 20 cm each (47 ¼ × 23 ⅝ × 7 ⅞ in each)
Museum of Fine Arts Houston

Foreword

When Guillermo Kuitca (b.1961) began to appear prominently on the international art scene in around 1990, it was because the Argentinian artist, whose country had only emerged from a dark period of dictatorship in 1983, had managed to overcome (or at least avoid) one of the chief challenges facing painters at that moment. As Raphael Rubinstein writes here, Kuitca had 'found a way to escape the endgame mentality that had afflicted so much serious painting, and, just as importantly, did so without having to revert to older styles'. Since then, Kuitca has continued to explore new territories. Again, Rubinstein puts it best: 'For nearly four decades he has led us through an atlas of spaces, places of sleep and spectacle, places of death and diversion, places of tenderness and travel. His muses are to be found amid buildings and maps, in the disciplines of architecture and cartography.' Exploring the origins of Kuitca's art, Rubinstein reveals surprising sources of influence, such as Pina Bausch (1940–2009), whose work moved the young painter so much when he saw it in Buenos Aires in 1980 that he followed her company back to their headquarters in Wuppertal, Germany. There he witnessed first-hand the strength with which she pursued her art in an unfriendly environment. By contrast, he was less than impressed by the expressionist trend in painting at the time, seeking something 'more distant and speculative'. Neither figurative in any traditional sense nor exactly abstract, Kuitca's work often employs diagrammatic forms (maps, floor plans, seating plans for theaters) to convey its oblique scenarios, conjuring memory and longing. Borrowing a phrase from Jorge Luis Borges (1899–1986), Rubinstein describes Kuitca's oeuvre as a 'garden of forking paths'. With this astute critic as a guide, one is happy to remain lost among its teeming bifurcations.

Barry Schwabsky

2. Del 1 al 30,000   1980

Ink on canvas
100 × 200 cm (39 ⅜ × 78 ¼ in)
Collection of Mary and Jaime Kuitca, Buenos Aires

1   A Certain Version of History

In 1980, when, at the age of 19, Guillermo Kuitca sat down to make a work directly about the victims of Argentina's 'Dirty War', the country was still under the rule of the military dictatorship that had seized power in 1976. Since that time, the military had waged a brutal campaign against suspected leftists that involved death squads, torture centers and clandestine prisons. This repression eventually led to the deaths of more than 30,000 Argentineans and the traumatizing of countless survivors. Although Kuitca's family was not directly affected by the Dirty War, the nightmarish atmosphere of the period, in which people were constantly being 'disappeared' from the streets of Buenos Aires and anyone who raised their voice in protest risked imprisonment or death, overshadowed his teenage years. By 1980, the frequency of disappearances had diminished but the country was still under an extremely repressive dictatorship and would remain so until 1983, when the generals who ran the country relinquished power after the debacle of the Malvinas or Falklands War.

The work Kuitca embarked on, titled *Del 1 al 30,000* (fig.2), was a large canvas on which he used a pen to write out in tightly packed lines all numbers from 1 to 30,000. He would never again take on the subject of Argentinean politics so directly, nor would he pursue this kind of conceptual work. It is as if by addressing this difficult subject at the outset of his career he liberated his subsequent work from any obligation to do so. At the same time, *Del 1 al 30,000* can be seen as a valedictory gesture toward the anti-painting aesthetic of the 1970s, a period when video, performance art, land art and a variety of conceptual practices were seen as more relevant to contemporary life than the supposedly obsolete medium of painting.

If there is one theme that runs through all of Kuitca's work, even to the point of obsession, it is space. He is a painter of architectural space, cartographic space, even celestial space, and all of his paintings are marked by the constant interplay of structure and void. Crucially, space is exactly what is missing from *Del 1 al 30,000*. This sequence of numbers not only lacks pictorial space, it rejects the notion that art need engage space in any form whatsoever. As such, it follows the rejection of illusionistic space that dominated so much art of the preceding decades, whether by means of 'flat' painting or by embracing the real space of minimalist sculpture, performance and land art or by choosing the conceptual realm of words and numbers. In 1980, this situation was about to change as younger artists around the world, Kuitca among them, rescued the medium of painting from its marginalized status, often through figurative styles that privileged emotional content, national identities and early 20th-century painting styles. Like so many artists of his generation, Kuitca was not scared of illusionistic space. For young artists who were emerging *c*.1980, the lure of pictorial space, and the lure of the medium of painting, both equally forbidden during the previous decade, were irresistible.

Given the difficulty of seeing much modern art in Buenos Aires – even the work of Argentine modernists like the Madí Group of abstract painters was rarely shown in local museums or galleries when Kuitca was growing up – Kuitca relied heavily on publications. 'I was as influenced by art books as I was by art I saw',[1] he recently remarked. A prodigy when it came to art, Kuitca undertook a nine-year period of private studies with Surrealist-influenced Ahuva Szlimowicz at the age of nine. Szlimowicz discouraged him from attending Buenos Aires's School of Fine Arts. He also studied with another Argentine artist, Victor Chab (b.1930). When he was 19, Kuitca was admitted to the art history program at the University of Buenos Aires but never attended any classes. No doubt he was more excited by his art-world activities – that same year, thanks to collectors Marion Eppinger and Jorge Helft, who were among his earliest supporters, he was given a large solo exhibition at Buenos Aires's Fundación San Telmo.

While access to contemporary art was not as easy in Buenos Aires *c*.1980 as it was in European capitals, there was a deep history of modernist art in Argentina, and its art scene was increasingly connected to the wider world. In the 1960s, the promoter of Argentine avant-garde culture, Guido Di Tella (1931–2001), neatly summed up the relationship of Argentine art to international developments: 'We took up impressionism when it was finished in Europe; we did Cubism a couple of decades later, but we did geometric art only a little later and some say we did it a little before Europe; informalism, two or three years later and the pop movement two or three hours later.'[2] This dynamic continued in the early 1980s, when the figurative style of the Italian Transavanguardia painters was warmly embraced by many young artists in Buenos Aires.

Surprisingly, the transformation that Kuitca underwent in the early 1980s, a process that led him to embrace representational painting, was sparked not by his exposure to the Neo-Expressionist painting that was then emerging in Europe and North America but by his encounter with the work of German choreographer–dancer Pina Bausch (1940–2009). After being struck by photographs of Bausch's productions in a book he came across at the Buenos Aires branch of the Goethe Institute (as a culture-hungry teenager, Kuitca frequented both the Goethe Institute and the French Cultural Services to gain access to international books and periodicals), Kuitca soon after attended a performance by Bausch's Tanztheater Wuppertal when the company came to Buenos Aires.

Fusing dance and theater, Bausch was a controversial figure whose productions mixed beauty and violence, sudden emotion and bruising repetition, elegance and awkwardness. Kuitca was so awed by her work that he followed the company back to Wuppertal, where he befriended several of the dancers and saw more of Bausch's work. He responded to Bausch's rejection of any conventional dance movements.

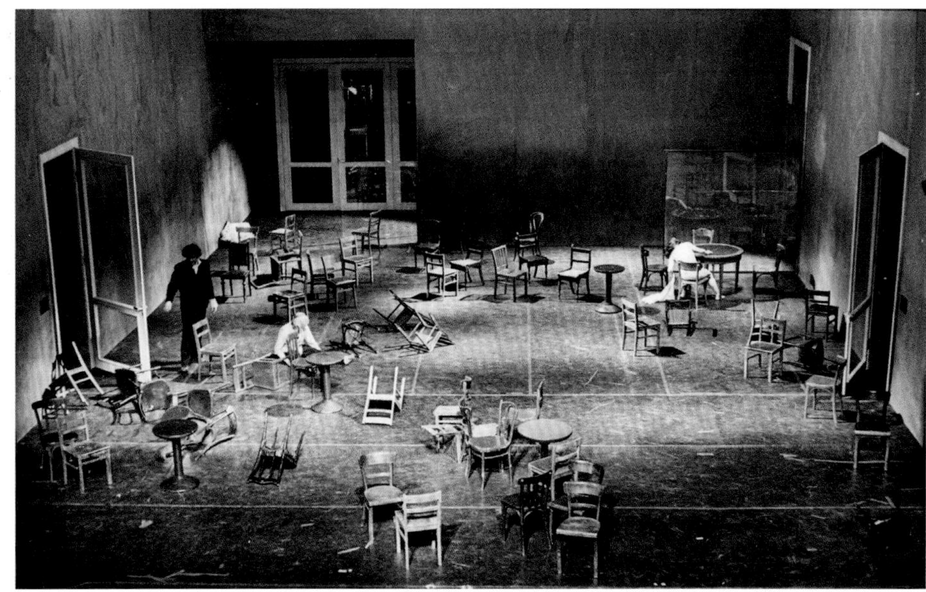

'The company was made up of dancers who had given up dance, and I felt like a painter who had given up painting', he later said of himself.[3] In pieces like *Café Müller* (1978, fig.3) and *Arien* (1979), Bausch created self-contained worlds, dream-like (and sometimes nightmarish) places where men and women enacted intense rituals amid the everyday (chairs and tables that evoked cheap restaurants or dancehalls) and extravagant effects (immense piles of roses, stages flooded with water). Her productions were thrilling without being narrative, glamorous without relying on artifice. Their subject matter was left unspecified, while their content was never less than intense.[4] Having never visited the United States (apart from a trip with his parents when he was eight years old) or Europe, Kuitca reacted to Bausch's work with a sense of total identification: 'It was exactly the type of art I was looking for.' Among the productions he saw was *Bandoneón* (1980), a tango-filled piece inspired by Bausch's visit to Buenos Aires. As he later recalled:

> What made the biggest impression on me was seeing that the members of the company kept working in a completely hostile environment. The place couldn't have been darker, more bourgeois, grayer and, nevertheless, the creative energy was overwhelming. I was there when the audience threw bananas and lettuce during that performance of *Bandoneón*. I saw the reaction of a scandalized audience. That stayed with me. Clearly, it wasn't necessary to live in a place where you fit it.[5]

On his way back to Argentina in 1981, Kuitca passed through London where he saw *A New Spirit in Painting* at the Royal Academy of Arts, one of the first

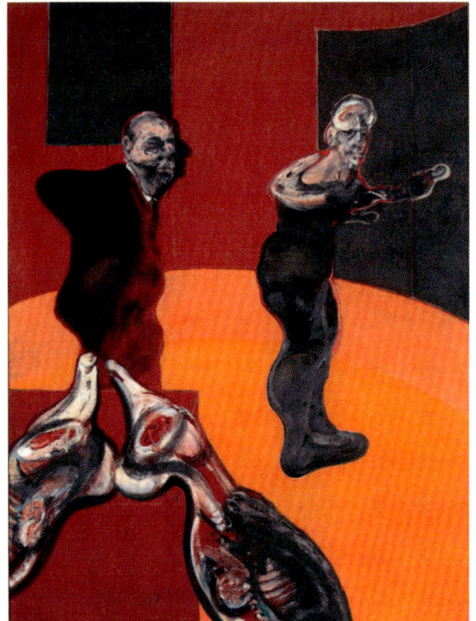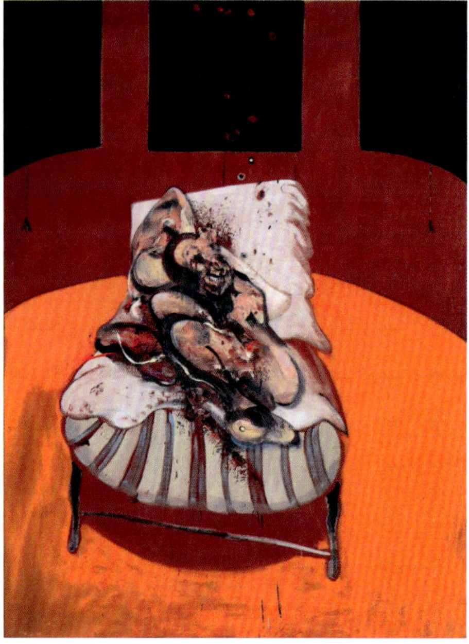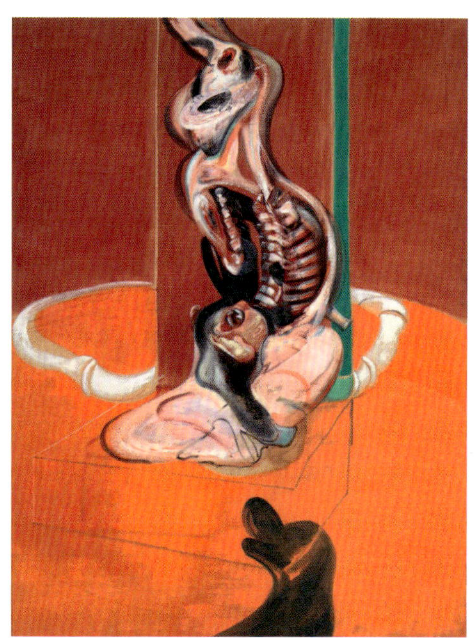

international exhibitions devoted to Neo-Expressionism. 'The artists' studios are full of paint pots again and an abandoned easel in an art school has become a rare sight. Wherever you look in Europe or America you find artists who have rediscovered the sheer joy of painting', declared curator Christos M. Joachimides (1932–2017).[6] Kuitca took note of the renewed energy in figurative painting, and no doubt soaked up the selection of Francis Bacon (1909–92) canvases (several of which featured figures on uncovered mattresses, a motif that would become central to Kuitca's work), but his enthusiasm was tempered. He 'didn't feel very identified with such expressionist work . . . I saw my work as more distant and speculative. I didn't feel that urgent need to paint. I didn't go with the pictorial explosion.'[7] Returning to Buenos Aires, for the moment he believed that his future lay not in painting but in theater. In collaboration with his friend and theater director Carlos Ianni, Kuitca mounted a piece in 1982 titled *Nadie olvida nada* (Nobody Forgets Nothing) featuring a collage of texts (written or assembled by Ianni) and Bausch-influenced scenes. It was at this point, after a year of barely painting at all, that Kuitca took up the brush again in a series also titled *Nadie olvida nada*.

In contrast to the extravagant paintings then popular in New York, Rome and Berlin, the *Nadie olvida nada* paintings of 1982 were markedly impoverished. Executed with house paint on old doors and stray pieces of wood salvaged from the artist's dilapidated studio, they avoided traditional fine-art materials. Renouncing any sign of virtuosity, the figures themselves are simply, even crudely painted. Typically, the *Nadie olvida nada* paintings feature groups of figures, usually, thanks to their skirts and long hair, identifiably female. Their backs are nearly always turned to the viewer and

4. Francis Bacon, *Three Studies for a Crucifixion*   1962

Oil with sand on canvas
Triptych: 198.1 × 144.8 cm each (78 × 57 in each)
Solomon R. Guggenheim Museum, New York

their arms are not visible. Delineated as economically as possible, the faceless figures are quasi-modular. They could be children at play or ghosts of the disappeared. They could be anyone or, as the title suggests, no one.

If *Nadie olvida nada* marks the beginning of Kuitca's painting career, it is also the beginning of painting itself, a zero-degree starting point where painting has been reduced to its most basic state. In one *Nadie olvida nada* (fig.5) against a background of loosely brushed violet and rust brown eight figures in bareback black dresses turn their backs to us. They have neither arms nor feet. Perhaps they are standing in a pool of water. They could be playing some child's game, or they could be lined up to be shot. In another work in the series, painted on a tall narrow door, a single armless and footless figure, sketched in white outline, hovers over a small empty bed (fig.6). The bright yellow blanket on the bed explodes amid the surrounding mess of dirty gray, brown and red brushstrokes. Another painting, more carefully executed, features only a single bed with a carefully turned-down blanket (fig.7).

In the context of the political climate in Argentina it is hard not to see these paintings as memorials to the missing victims of the Dirty War and, at the same time, as depictions of the emotional toll such events have on individuals, and society as a whole. Even before the end of military rule the question of forgetting and remembering had begun to preoccupy Argentineans. At the time Kuitca was making these works, the Mothers of the Plaza de Mayo, a group of women wearing white headscarves whose children had been kidnapped and in most cases murdered by the government, had for years been protesting every week in front of the Casa Rosada, Argentina's presidential palace. They clearly had not forgotten anything, nor had the rest of Argentina, but almost no one was willing or brave enough to articulate the memory of the missing.

When he looked back a decade later at the beds in *Nadie olvida nada*, Kuitca noted how they coincided with the Falklands or Malvinas War, but explained them in purely personal terms.

> At the time of la Guerra de las Malvinas I started painting little beds. . . . at that time I was going through a depression; what I wanted to convey in my work was that my hand and brush did not move at all; the painting was the result of the canvas moving. What it painted was hardly a sketch. My hand was not strong enough to grasp the brush firmly.[8]

Throughout his career, Kuitca has resisted interpretations of his paintings as being about specific historical subjects. His work is most frequently associated with two subjects: political repression (particularly in Argentina) and the Holocaust. It is understandable that an artist would not want his or her work to be narrowly interpreted. In interviews, Kuitca does his best to discourage such readings. For instance, in this exchange with curator Mari Carmen Ramírez:

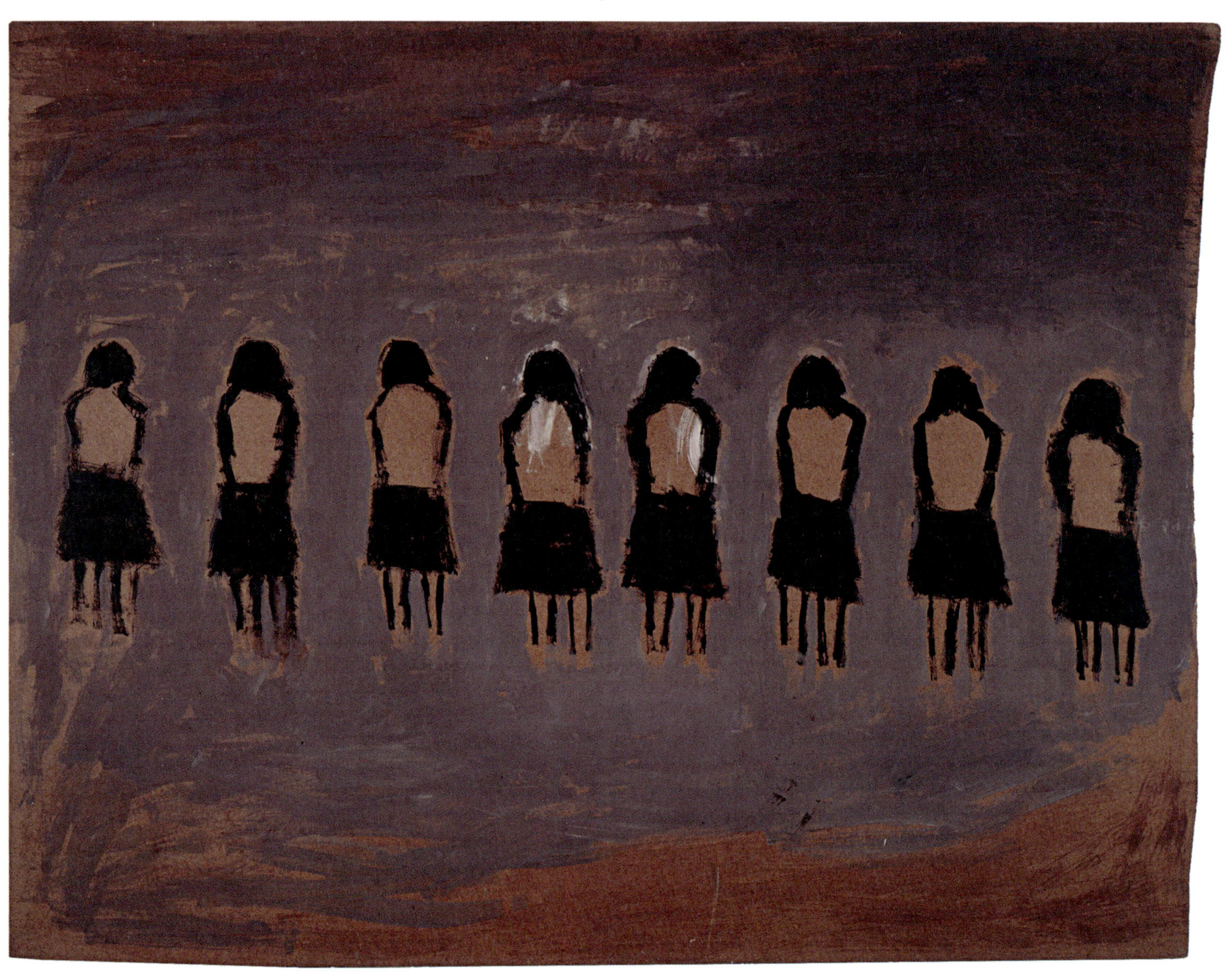

5. Nadie olvida nada   1982

Acrylic on wood
24 x 30 cm (9½ × 11 ¾ in)
Private collection, Buenos Aires

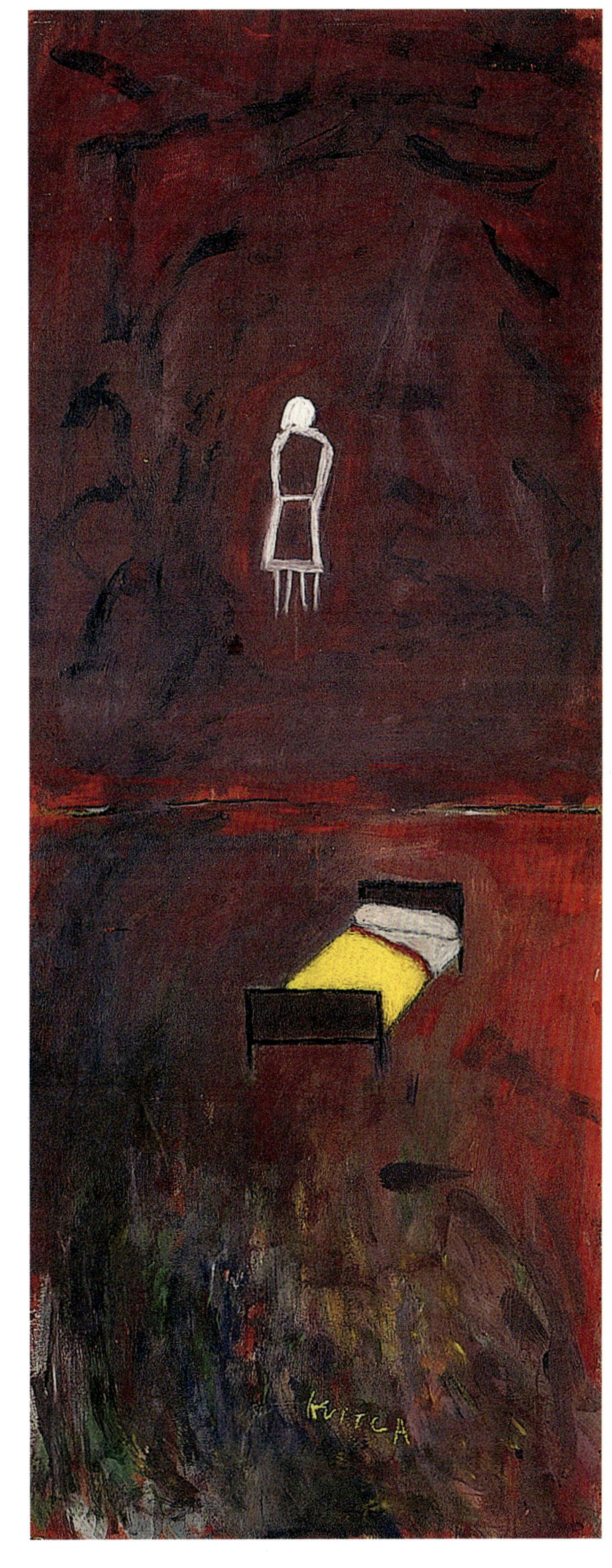

6. Nadie olvida nada   1982

Acrylic on wood
140 × 52 cm (54 ½ × 20 ¼ in)
Balanz Collection

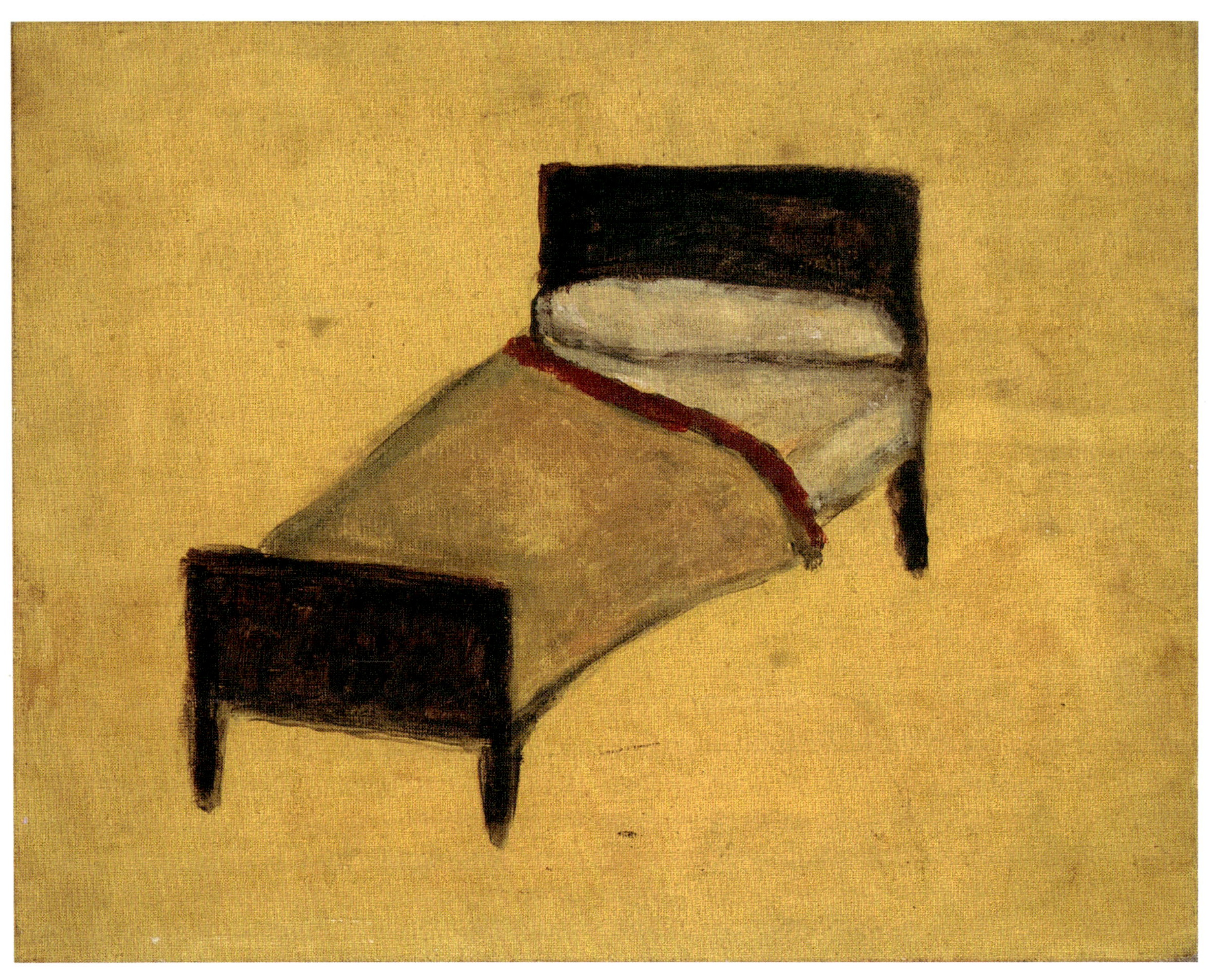

7. Nadie olvida nada   1982

Acrylic on canvas-covered hardboard
140 × 52 cm (54 ½ × 20 ¼ in)
Collection of the artist

MCR: Some critics have related some of your work to the Holocaust, but you
have rejected any kind of reference on your work.
GK: Exactly. The fact that I am Argentinean with a Jewish background does
not mean that my work addresses the subject. So yes, I have tried to protect the
abstract nature of my work.[9]

When during her extensive interviews with the artist, Graciela Speranza notes
that Kuitca's work is too autonomous and allusive to be subsumed by interpretations
linking it to the Holocaust, the Dirty War or, with his *Tablada Suite* of the early 1990s,
oppressive social control, Kuitca articulates his response to such readings. While they
are contrary to his intentions and he wants no part of them, he also accepts them:

> Why deny, for instance, that those beds—as I once read—could be in a
> concentration camp? Or why should I deny that the history of Argentina's
> dictatorship is also lying there? I tend to discourage that kind of reading because
> I know that it forces my work, it invades it and stifles it, but, on the other hand,
> I feel ridiculous when I categorically deny it. In the end, I can't deny that there
> is in my art a political vision of the world, a certain vision of history. It's that
> I can't formulate that vision in any other way but as my work formulates it.[10]

When it comes to the significance of *Nadie olvida nada*, Kuitca is less categorical,
but he still denies intentionally making a political work. 'I accept the version that this
series [*Nadie olvida nada*] was touched by the Argentine experience, by the Malvinas,
by the social and historical context, but, when I used that title, I wasn't thinking about
that, but instead, myself standing in Wuppertal, watching *Bandoneón*.'[11]

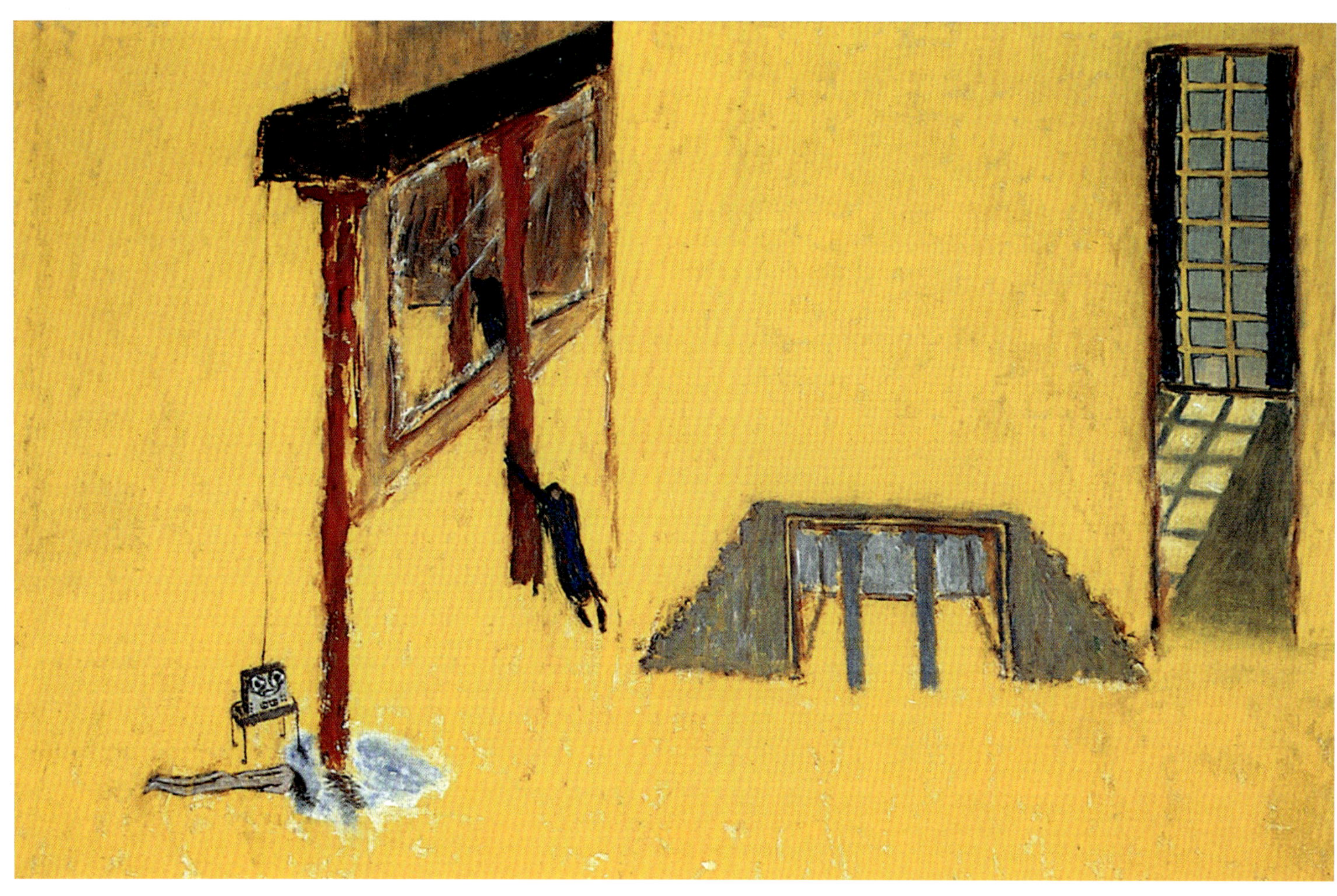

8. El mar dulce   1983

Acrylic on canvas
130 × 200 cm (51 ³⁄₁₆ × 78 ¾ in)
Private collection

2   The Painter as Dramaturge

Surprisingly quickly the impoverished mode of *Nadie olvida nada* gave way to an
opulent manner in which expressionistically painted figures appeared on immense,
dramatically appointed stages. Here, the influence of Pina Bausch was explicit.
The paintings often employed the same motifs Kuitca had seen in Tanztheater
productions: jumbled chairs and table as props, stages flooded with water, spaces that
dwarfed the figures (Bausch liked to open up theaters so that the spaces extended
back as far as possible). More directly, he based some of his *El mar dulce* (Freshwater
Sea) paintings on photographs he had taken of a theater piece he and Carlos Ianni
had presented at Buenos Aires's Teatro Planeta in 1984. In the early 1980s, Kuitca's
activity in the theater was flowing directly into his painting, but the painting would
soon so totally absorb him that he would turn away from the actual theater.

A transitional painting on wood carries the title *Nadie olvida nada* but instead of the
clumsy figures who dominate the rest of the series it depicts an enormous red interior
with two small figures: a child in a bed being viciously beaten by a club-wielding
female adult. The violence seems even more terrible because the figures are so small
and off-center. Brutal violence is everywhere, the painting reminds us, and not just in
the stories that make the front page of newspapers or that fill protest art. The effect is
not unlike the disappearing legs in Pieter Breugel the Elder's *Landscape with the Fall of
Icarus* (*c*.1555), a painting that W.H. Auden in his famous 1938 poem *Musée des Beaux
Arts* found emblematic of how the world so easily turns away from human suffering.

The architectural setting was crucial. As Kuitca explained to Graciela Speranza
in 1997, 'The figures were no longer floating in a space without perspective, as they
were in the paintings of *Nadie olvida nada* of 1982. On the contrary, they were inside
a space demarcated by three walls. From that moment on, I never again painted
any figure without some spatial reference.'[12] In the *El mar dulce* paintings (figs 8
and 9), which depict enormous theater stages on which small isolated figures enact
ritualistic actions, the spatial configurations are complex and, in theatrical terms,
unconventional. Imposing staircases lead to unseen or nonexistent spaces, small
rooms in the wings are occupied by figures having sex or engaging in more enigmatic
pursuits. In one painting, three naked men pose in front of a mirror; in another, what
look like cloaked skeletons (but may be just emaciated women) gather around a coffee
table. Often narrow black doorways, usually in pairs, are cut into the rear wall, too
small and too far away to offer any hope of exit.

Prominent in many of the *El mar dulce* paintings is a still from the famous Odessa
Steps sequence in Sergei Eisenstein's movie *The Battleship Potemkin* (1925). The image

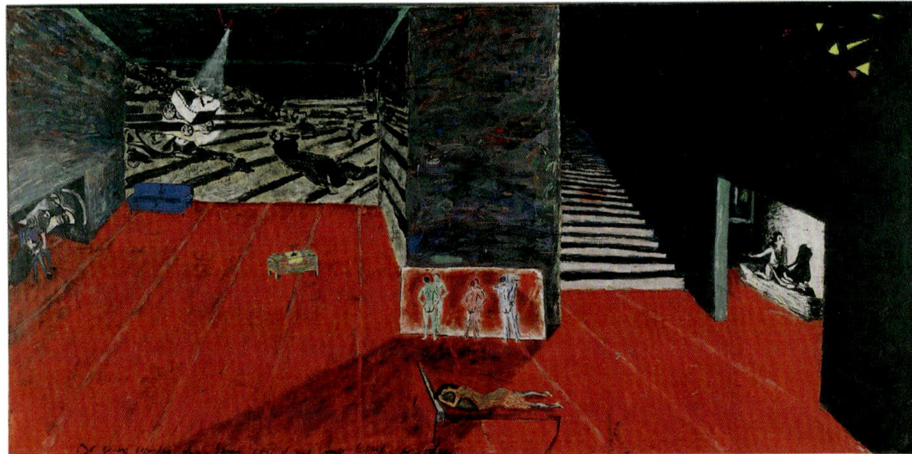

9. El mar dulce 1984

Acrylic on paper mounted on canvas
170 × 310 cm (67 × 122 in)
Solita Cohen Collection

Kuitca chose is of baby carriage hurtling down the steps amid a massacre.[13] It is perhaps no accident that another shot from the same sequence – a close-up of the infant's nanny screaming in horror – features prominently in a number of paintings by Francis Bacon, one of Kuitca's important early influences. Kuitca's insertion of the Potemkin image is full of paradox and ambiguity. The viewer's first impulse is to take it as a film being projected in the fictive space of the painting, but certain details contradict this reading, foremost the ceiling spotlight that shines a cone of light onto the image, illuminating the baby carriage at its center. If this were an accurate depiction of a film projection, a spotlight would erase the image rather than highlight it. So perhaps this is meant to depict a painting, a giant mural, rather than a projection. Is Kuitca, thus, constructing an allegory about the triumph of painting over cinema? Or is he simply taking gleeful advantage of the fact that anything is possible in a painting? But why this image in the first place? What does Eisenstein's re-creation of an episode from Russian history have to do with the theatrical goings-on here? Is it a symbol of violent repression? An image of threatened childhood? The baby-carriage motif turns up again toward the end of the 1980s in *Odessa* (1987, fig.10) in which a road map of the Odessa region, then part of the Soviet Union but today in Ukraine, is superimposed over the Eisenstein image.

The artist, who speaks eloquently about his work but rarely discloses much in the way of private meaning, has discussed the personal significance of the Eisenstein still. As he explained to Graciela Speranza, 'I don't know much about my family, but I know that my grandparents were from Kiev, and I suppose that like most of the Russian Jews who came to the Río de la Plata, they sailed from Odessa. So, for me, that stroller tumbling down was like my grandparents leaving port. Hence, El mar dulce.' Kuitca's Russian grandparents would have arrived in Buenos Aires via the Río de la Plata estuary, which an early Portuguese explorer dubbed 'El Mar Dulce'. The artist goes on to recount 'an even darker story' that involves the death of his father's infant sister Sophia:

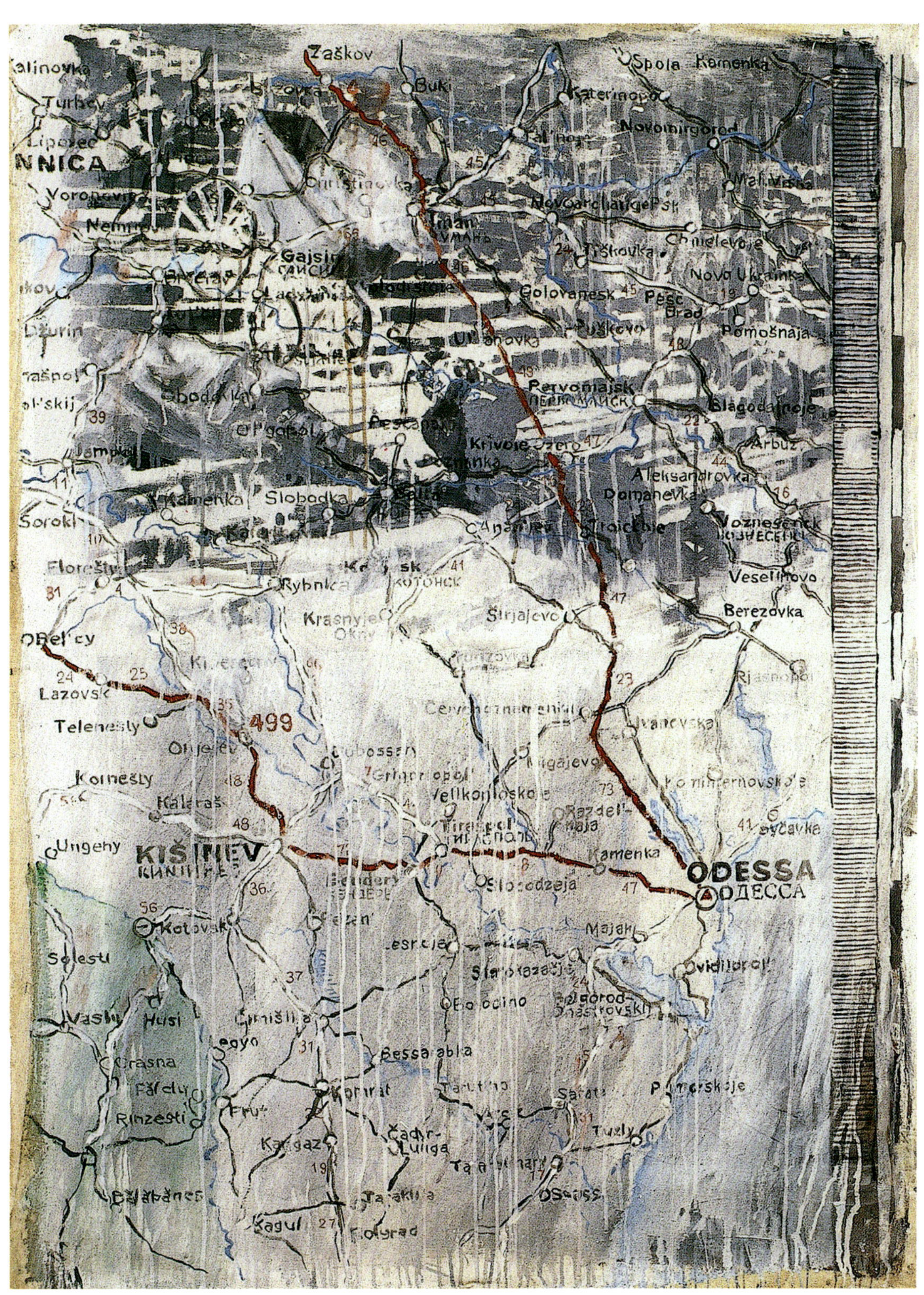

10. Odessa   1987

Acrylic on canvas
125 × 88 cm (49 ³⁄₁₆ × 34 ⅝ in)
Stedelijk Museum, Amsterdam

At some point, I found out that she had died in a horrible domestic accident caused by negligence. The story, no doubt, affected me greatly and, unable to conceive of a more dreadful image, I used the one of the stroller tumbling down the giant staircase. Somehow my family was traveling in that stroller. That was the ship that was bringing my family from Odessa.[14]

Here, in a single image, the artist has conflated the history of his family's immigration and a tragic incident in Russian history. For Kuitca, the powerful image created by Eisenstein to awaken his audience to the cruelty of Tsarist Russia, and, by implication, to the justness of the 1917 Bolshevik Revolution, becomes a metaphorical emblem of family history. He tells a private story through a public image. This is a form of appropriation but very different in motivation from so many other appropriated images in art, from Pop Art through the 'Pictures' artists like Richard Prince (b.1949) and Sherrie Levine (b.1947). Kuitca borrows a modernist icon not in the service of critique or parody but in order to tell a personal story. And yet, he does not exactly 'tell' the story, or only very obliquely. Most viewers will interpret this image as an allusion to cinematic history, to political violence, to Francis Bacon, to the competing languages of painting and film. That there is a more personal association is not spelled out. This indeterminacy, this reticence, this unwillingness to specify meanings and motivations is characteristic of Kuitca's work and, perhaps, the source of much of its power. The open symbolism of his work may be another of the lessons he learned from Pina Bausch. In a 1992 interview, the choreographer explained that her productions 'can only work if we avoid anything explicit—anything where we see something and we all know what it means. We think, oh, this is a sign for that: you know it in your head. But if we avoid this and if the audience are open to experience or feel things, I think there is a possibility of another kind of language.'[15]

In the mid-1980s, along with the *El mar dulce* series, Kuitca produced several related groups of paintings in which we seem to be looking down from a theater balcony at small figures in vast spaces. In *Yo, como el angel* (Me, as the Angel) (1985) a male figure sporting what look like burning wings is caught in a spotlight amid a jumble of overturned chairs and tables that suggest the aftermath of a bar fight or a wild party (fig.11). In *Tres Noches* (Three Nights) (1986) the title is spelled out by a pale pink neon sign that has found its unlikely way into a bedroom in the middle of which is a naked mattress; nearby a woman has wrapped herself around a man, while a seated woman in a black veil watches them. There is a powerful narrative impulse in all of these paintings, but whatever story they may be allowing us to glimpse remains tantalizingly out of reach. For Kuitca it is because we are coming on these scenes too late. As he explained in 1997, 'from the beginning it was clear to me that the story, in the anecdotal sense, had been erased, but what was left was a strong sense that we see a scene in which something had already happened.'[16]

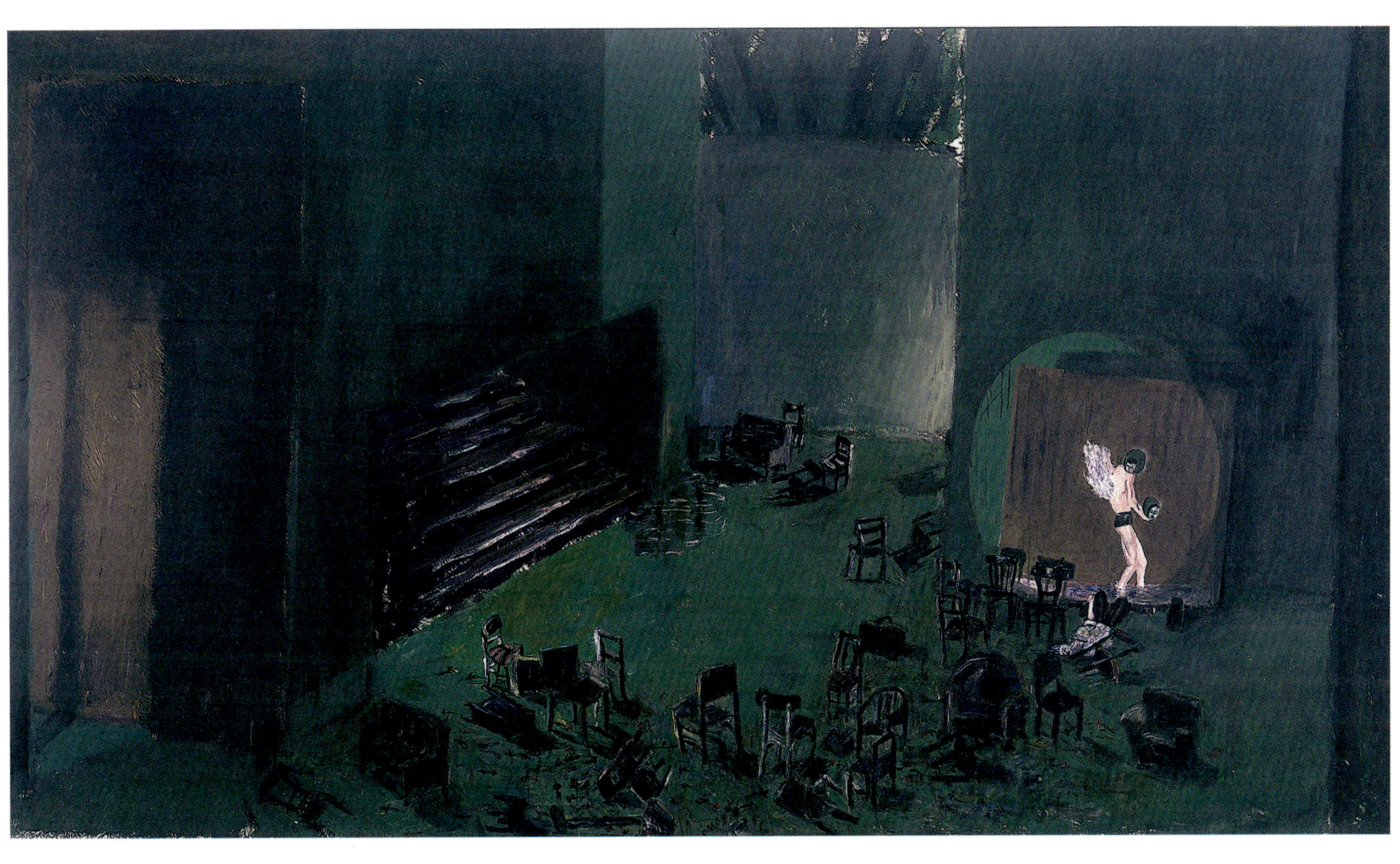

11. Yo, como el ángel   1985

Oil and acrylic on canvas
200 × 340 cm (78 ¾ × 133 ⅞ in)
Private collection, Buenos Aires

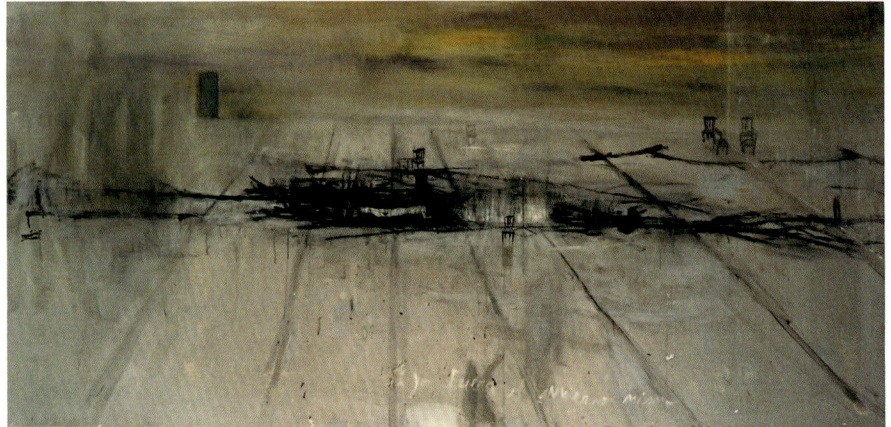

12. Si yo fuera el invierno mismo   1986

Acrylic on canvas
140 × 280 cm (55 × 109 in)
Rosalía and Humberto Ugobono, San Juan, Puerto Rico

The perspective changes in *Si yo fuera el invierno mismo* (If I were the winter itself)
(1986), a wide composition as desolate as its title suggests (fig.12). Spread across the
canvas, which seems to be suffocating under a thin layer of greenish-gray mold, is what
looks like the charred remnants of a collapsed wooden structure. A few chairs stand
unused. On the right edge an enormous mirror or wall blocks the space. What appears
to be a naked body, though one cannot be entirely sure, sprawls amid the charred
wreckage. Kuitca paints a cloudy Turneresque sky where the rear wall of the stage
should be. This is one of the rare occasions when Kuitca allows a hint of landscape
into his art. Although landscapes are presumably implied by the maps he references,
the world of his paintings is strangely devoid of nature. The spaces he depicts are
either interiors or partially enclosed public spaces. The only trace of landscape is in the
empty areas between place names on his map paintings. This apparent lack of interest
in landscape might seem strange given that responding to the natural world was so
central to modern art, from the Impressionists' ventures into the French countryside
to Jackson Pollock's claim that he was nature itself. It might just be a question of
sensibility but it may also have something to do with the fact that toward the close
of the 20th century when Kuitca emerged as a painter ever greater swaths of human
activity were being confined within built environments, whether analog or digital.

The more one studies Kuitca's mid-1980s paintings, which initially seem all about
empty space, the more their wealth of details emerge: a reel-to-reel tape recorder, a
menorah on a table, a Christian cross floating above the action, knocked-over lamps,
microphone stands. Some red and yellow triangles floating in the upper-right corner
of one of the *El mar dulce* paintings puzzled me. I wondered if, perhaps, they were
allusions to the work of Rául Lozza (1911–2008), an Argentine abstract painter whose
'Concrete' work often features similar shapes. When I put this to Kuitca he said that
the presence of those brightly colored geometric forms were probably closer to Bowie
and New Wave design than to Lozza. This candid response suggests several points
worth keeping in mind when looking at Kuitca's work, or, indeed, at any artist's

oeuvre. First, that one should never assume that some visual resemblance is the result of an art-historical reference, conscious or unconscious; second, that artists are open to the visual culture of their time; third, sometimes one has to accept that something in a painting, even by an immensely talented painter, might not have a deep reason behind it – it may be simply the result of a sudden impulse.

This phase of Kuitca's work culminated in a 1986–87 series titled *Siete últimas canciones* (Seven Last Songs). Adapting his title from Richard Strauss's *Four Last Songs*, Kuitca turned from the relatively open theatrical spaces to featureless rooms that feel more like enormous cells or bunkers (fig.13). In one that is painted in a flurry of metallic grays and pinks the color of a polluted sunset (fig.14), a man dressed in black stands before a small fire and a chair. Behind him a ghostly female figure lies on the floor and behind her sits an empty bed surrounded by piles of long-stemmed black roses. A microphone on a stand is placed in front of the bed, as are a few chairs and a line of velvet ropes and stanchions. Two small doors in the far gray wall offer the only possible escape from this bleak scenario. It is like the last scene in a grim tragedy. Mournful and claustrophobic, and painted in a deliberately slapdash manner, all the *Siete últimas canciones* paintings are haunting works. They also marked a kind of double ending for the artist. Following his presentation of them in a Buenos Aires gallery in 1986, he would cease to show in the city where he lived for the next 17 years.

Initially his withdrawal from the Buenos Aires art world was unintentional – he was simply more focused on his accelerating international opportunities – but as the years went by he began to find it interesting to live in one place but show elsewhere, a situation he has referred to as an 'inverted exile'. In 1991, partly in order to reconnect with the local artistic community, he partnered with different Argentinean foundations to create annual workshop–seminars for young Argentine artists. He also soon turned away from painting figures and illusionistic spaces. As he later told Graciela Speranza, 'I didn't know that the word "last" in the title meant "last" in another sense.'[17]

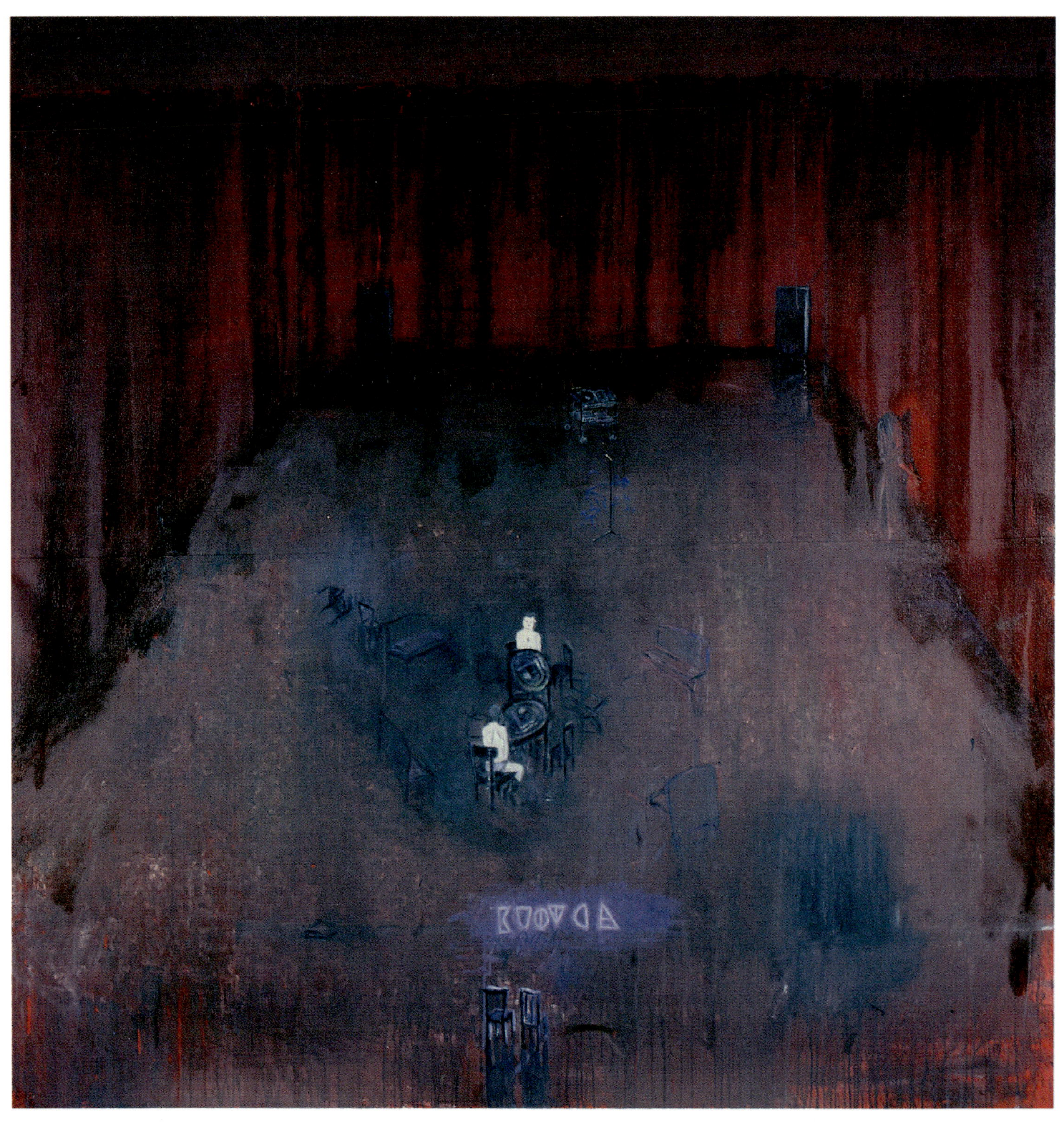

13. Siete últimas canciones   1986

Acrylic on canvas
207 × 200 cm (81 ½ × 78 ¾ in)
Eduardo F. Costantini, Buenos Aires

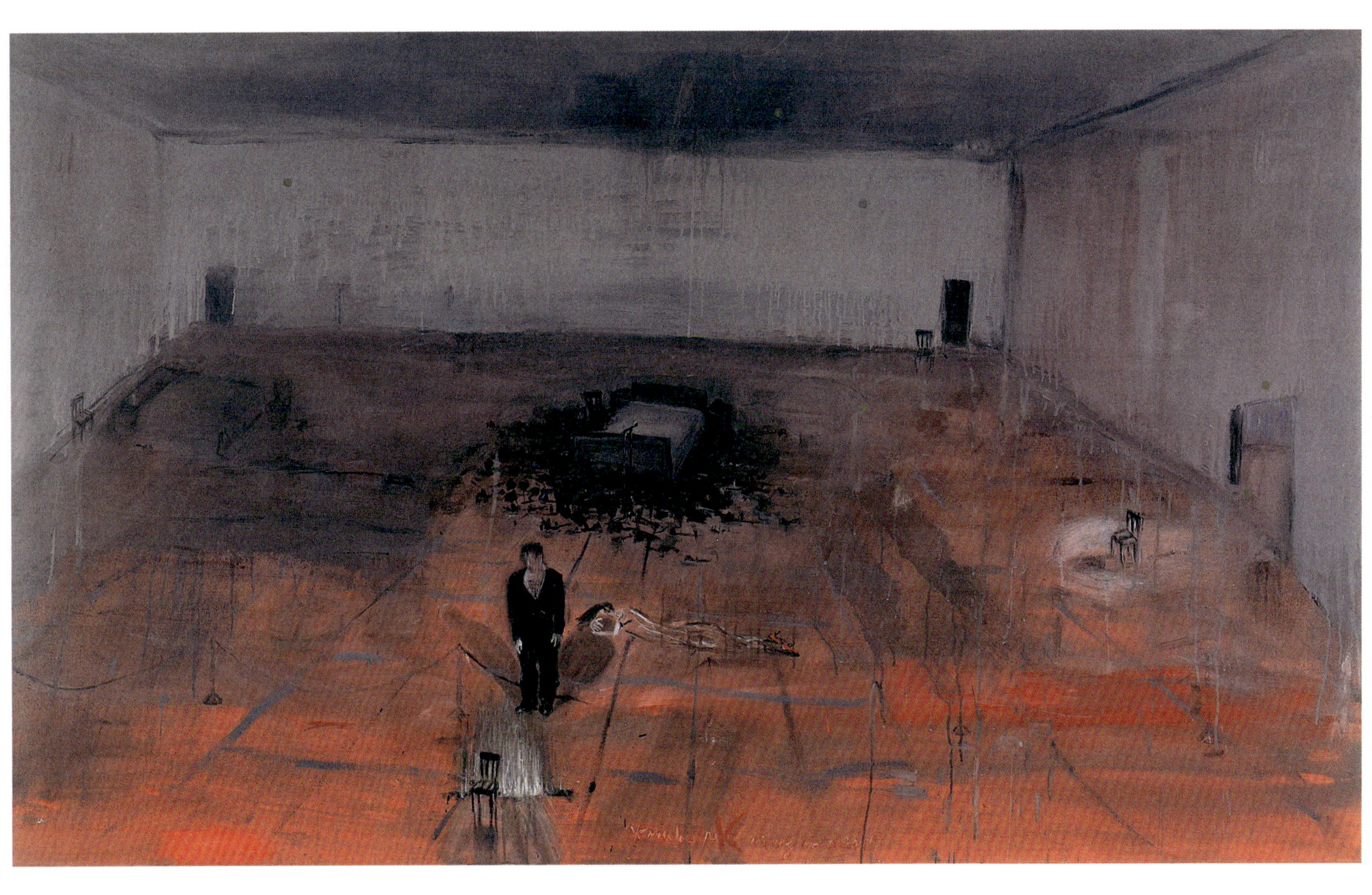

14. Siete últimas canciones   1986

Acrylic on canvas
150 × 190 cm (59 × 74 ¾ in)
Collection MALBA, Museo de Arte Latinoamericano de
Buenos Aires

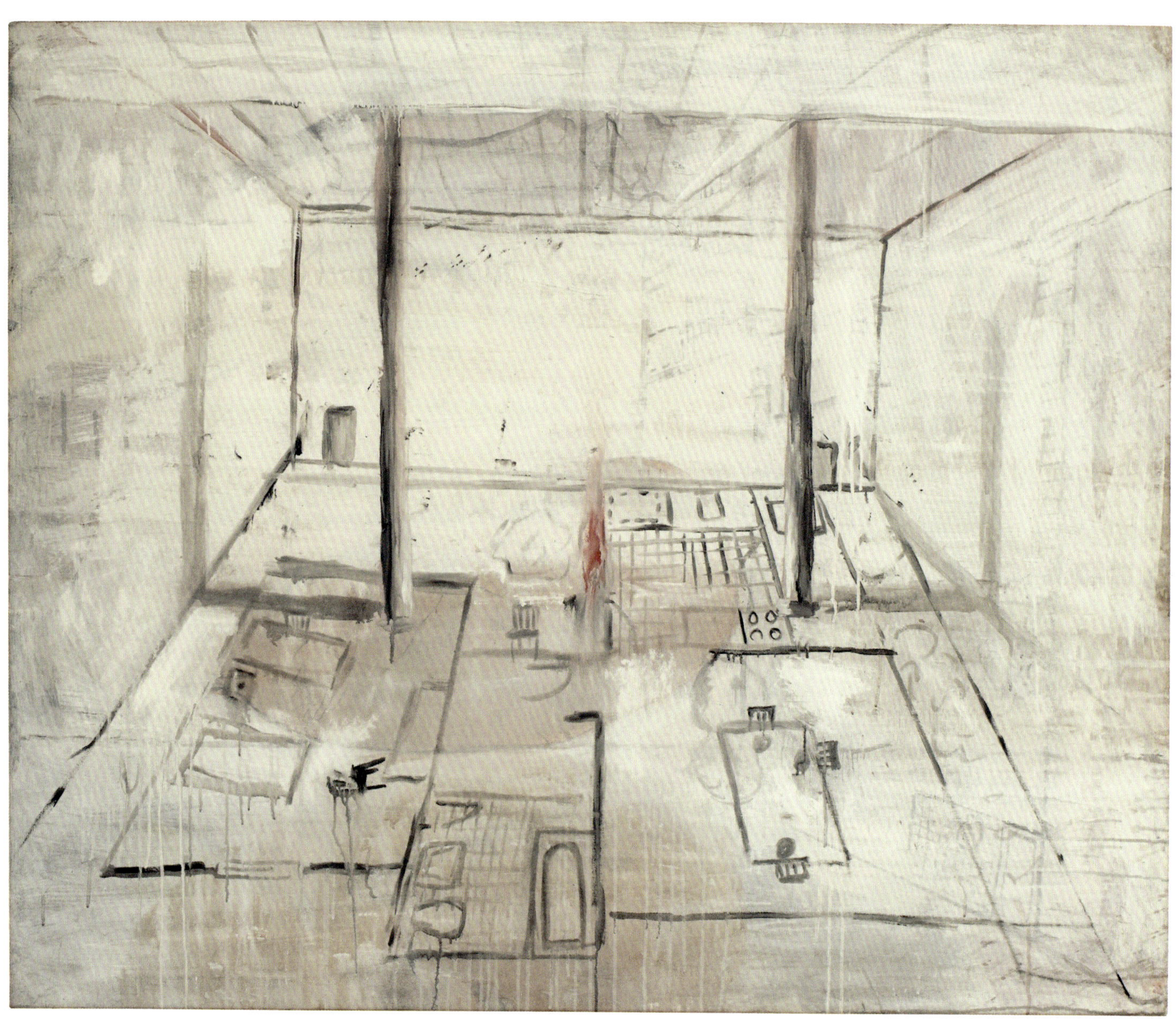

15. Untitled   1987

Acrylic on canvas
122.8 by 142.5 cm (48 ⅜ × 56 ⅛ in)
Private collection, Minneapolis

3 The Pathos of Home

Kuitca remembers 1987 to 1988 as a period of confusion when he did not know what to paint. After *Siete últimas canciones* he experimented with using a projector to make text paintings but that did not hold his attention for long. Eventually he discovered two subjects that would quickly take over his work and transform him as an artist: the house plan and the map. In both these modes, which emerged more or less simultaneously, the deep space of the theater is ironed flat, and the figures and props that littered the vast stages, as well as the cinematic images on the walls, have disappeared. At first glance, there seems to be an absolute break between the Theater Paintings of 1983 to 1986 and the House Plans he made between 1988 and 1993, but as with the earlier shift away from *Nadie olvida nada*, there are several transitional works in which the deep Bauschian space of the theater lingers for a moment. In one untitled 1987 Theater Painting a white house plan spreads across a red stage like a carpet. In a related grisaille painting, also from 1987, a floor plan is sketched onto the floor of a high-ceilinged chamber.

In some ways Kuitca's 1987 to 1988 transformation looks like a classic modernist divestment of figuration and illusionistic space in favor of abstraction and flatness. Yet, obviously, Kuitca's new diagrammatic imagery is too full of precise signification, of schematic representation, to qualify as abstract, even though it is no longer figurative. In effect, Kuitca introduced a third term into the figuration/abstraction binary: the diagrammatic. Although he was not the first artist to employ diagrams (precedents include Francis Picabia's Mechanical Portraits, Marcel Duchamp's Large Glass, Öyvind Fahlström in his politicized Pop cartography and Shusaku Arakawa in his diagram paintings), Kuitca developed diagrammatic painting to a greater degree of richness and complexity. Indeed, it could be argued that when Kuitca began employing diagrammatic imagery in the late 1980s, he had stepped out of art history: a painting of a floor plan or a road map (or any of the other diagrams the artist would later explore, from theater seating charts to cemetery maps) did not come with any artistic baggage. The imagery was almost without style, belonging to no existing fine-art genre. Thus where most other painters had to grapple with influences, with inherited styles, with powerful predecessors, Kuitca found himself in a relatively clear field because the types of images he employed had so little precedent in painting.

Interestingly, the concept of painting as diagram was on the minds of some artists and critics in the late 1980s. In 1989, for instance, independent curator Saul Ostrow organized an exhibition titled *Diagrams and Surrogates* at the New York gallery Shea & Becker that included three artists – Lydia Dona (b.1955), Jonathan Lasker (b.1948)

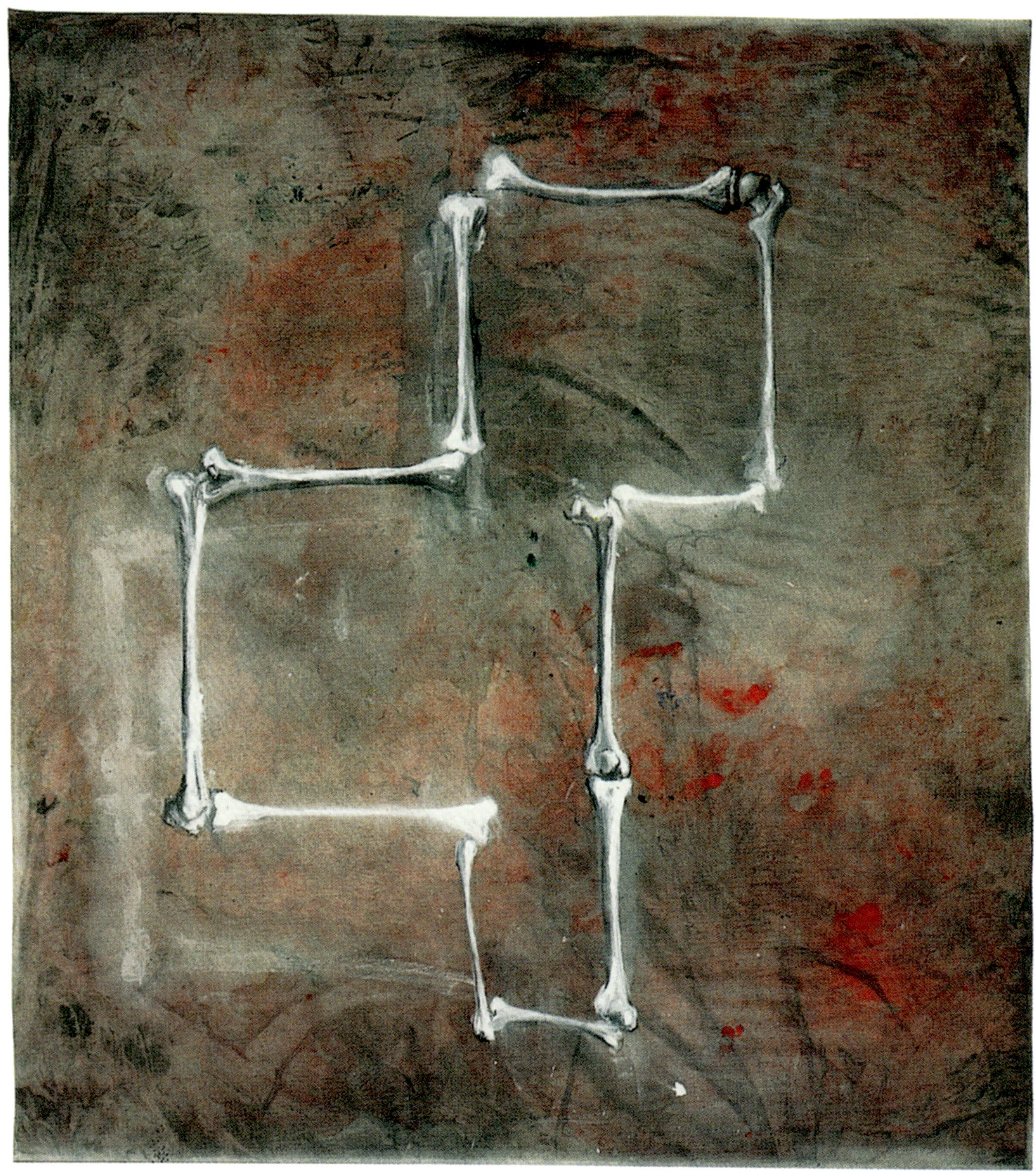

16. Bones Built for Eternity   1990

Acrylic on canvas
160 × 140 cm (63 × 55 ⅛ in)
Gian Enzo Sperone Collection, New York

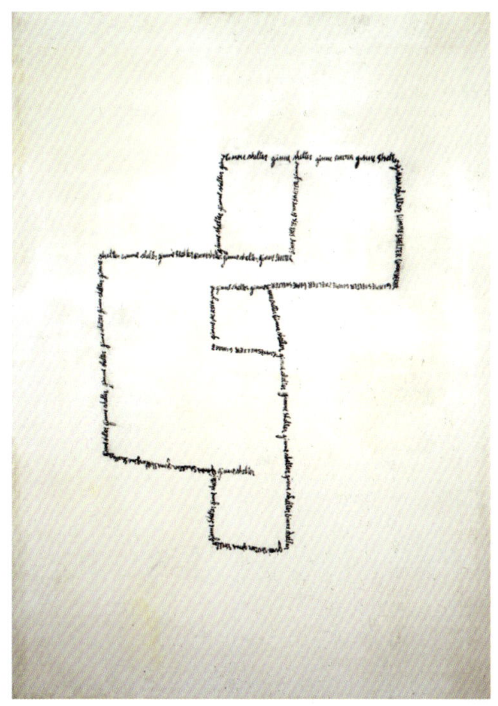

17. Gimme Shelter   1992

Acrylic on canvas
130 × 90 cm (51 × 35 in)
Private collection

18. Corona de espinas   1993

Oil on canvas
198 × 288 cm (78 × 113 ½ in)
Collection of Ron and Ann Pizzutti, Columbus Ohio

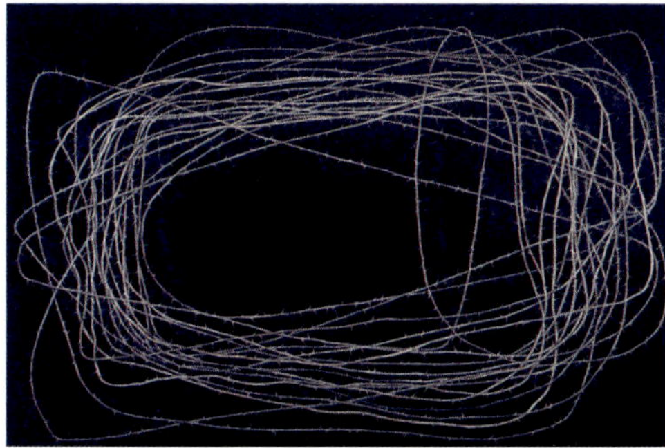

and David Diao (b.1943) – who incorporated diagrammatic elements into their abstract paintings. Peter Halley (b.1953) also approached his paintings as diagrams. What distinguishes Kuitca from these painters is that his diagrams are carriers of information, of visual data. This fact allowed him to bring the world into his paintings, just as, with very different techniques and concerns, Jean-Michel Basquiat (1960–88) did with his proliferating textual transcriptions.

The first house plan painting was based on a diagram the artist found in a do-it-yourself home repair and design manual. He liked that it was an absolutely standard and anonymous design, something he could therefore identify as a 'social module'. The floor plan, with its two bedrooms and a living–dining area, bathroom and kitchen was, Kuitca thought, 'the perfect figure of a typical urban family'.[18] He imagined it inhabited by a mother, father and son.[19] Once he discovered the house plan, it was as if he had simultaneously found an infinitely fascinating subject and an infinitely adaptable form. Made of three abutting, differently sized rectangles, often with additional internal divisions designating rooms and fixtures, Kuitca's apartment plan is a shape almost without qualities. It is certainly not elegant but it is not noticeably awkward or clunky either; it is not centered or symmetrical but it has a simplicity and internal cohesion that anchors it to the larger rectangle of the canvas. To a certain extent, the house plan became for Kuitca what a set of nesting squares had been for Josef Albers (1888–1976). One could also compare the House Plan series to Raymond Queneau's 1947 book *Exercises in Style* in which the French author retells the same anecdote 99 times, each time in a different literary form or manner.

In the early house plans the layouts are rendered in perspective, but soon they flatten out. Once this happens, Kuitca lets his imagination loose. In several paintings, including *Bones Built for Eternity* (fig.16), which appears to be painted on a drop cloth, he uses bones to delineate the house plan. Others are drawn with cursive writing – for example, the words 'Gimme Shelter' (taken from the eponymous film about the Rolling Stones, though not specifically about it, fig.17) – or snakes (*Planta con serpientes*, 1991) or thorns (*Corona de espinas*, fig.18) or filled with lacy underwear patterns (*Lingerie Plan*, 1989). In a number of paintings, the house plan becomes a living body with blood coursing through its veinlike contours and a pumping heart within (*House Plan with Blood Flows*, 1991) or when large tears drip from it (*Planta con gotas*, fig.19). In a painting titled *Disposable House Plan* (1990) the apartment is defecating. Other House Plan paintings become opportunities to experiment with color and texture and the liquid properties of paint. Once the apartment vanishes under a checkerboard grid, another time it is turned into a quilted mattress. It also appears as the palm lines on a human hand, and is overlaid with text in Spanish and English.

Although in a few cases Kuitca painted variants on one theme, the general impression of the ensemble of House Plans is that no two paintings are alike. This seemingly endless diversity could be taken as a comment on how people will personalize even the most anonymous and standard living quarters, but it is also a

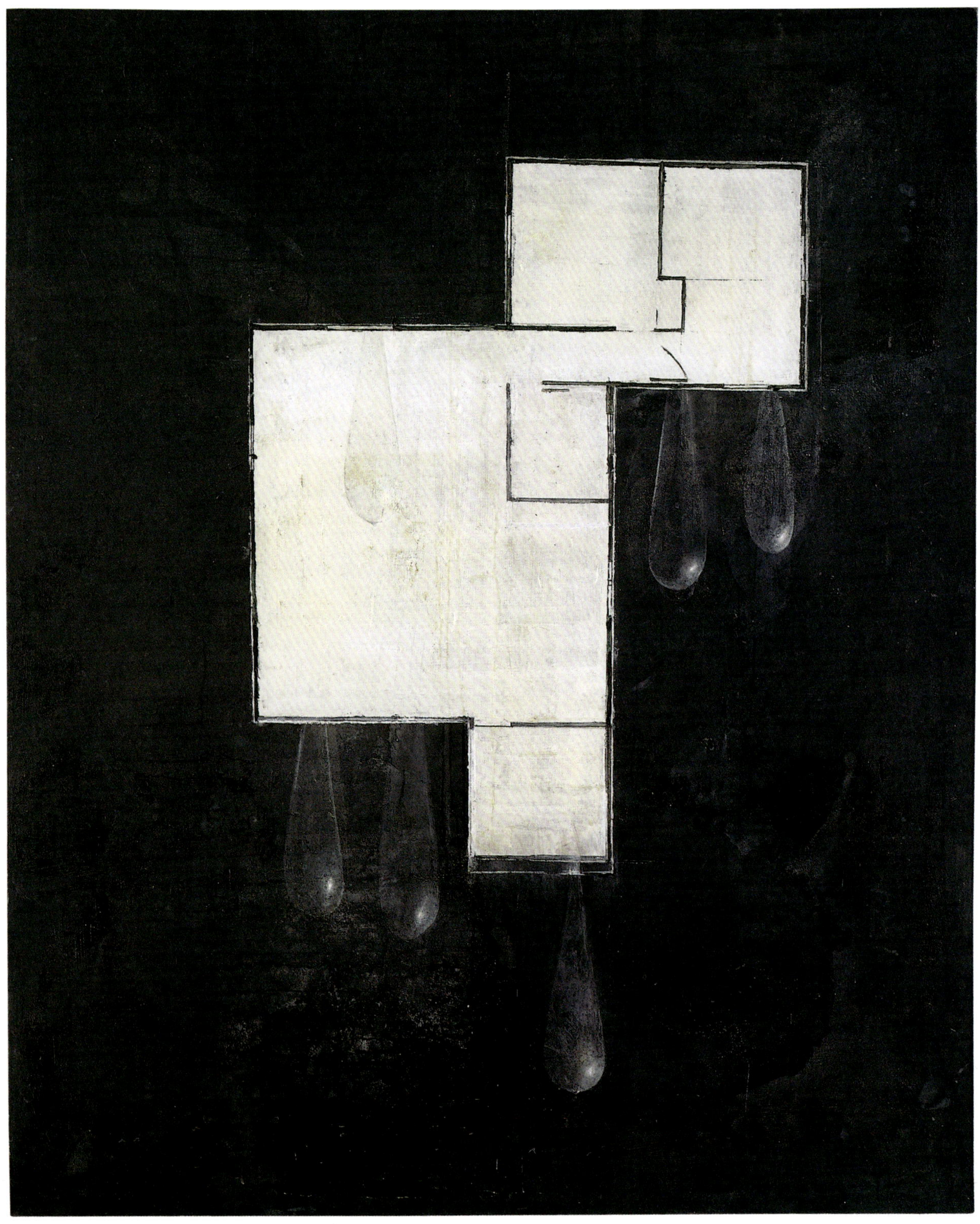

19. House Plan with Tear Drops   1989

Acrylic on canvas
201 × 160 cm (79 × 63 in)
Walker Art Center, Minneapolis

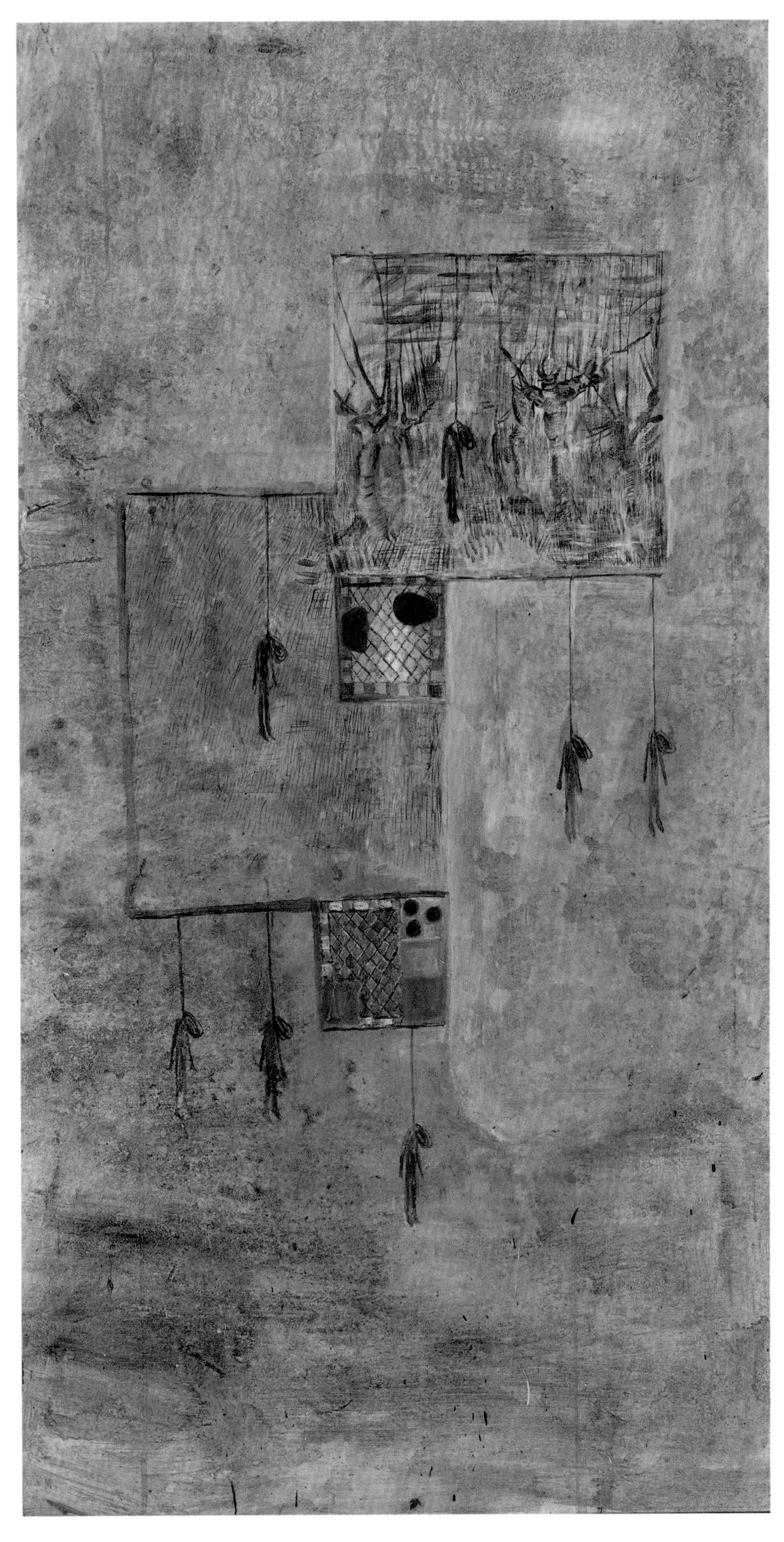

20. Strange Fruit   1989

Mixed media on canvas
198 × 101 cm (77 $^{15}/_{16}$ × 39 ¾ in)
Private collection

declaration of artistic freedom, proof that nothing is out of bounds for this artist, or for any artist. The era of loyalty to one kind of image or one style of painting is over.

Among the House Plans are several that make pointed political statements. In an all-gray 1989 painting seven human figures hang limply from ropes around their necks, their heads lolling to one side. The title, *Strange Fruit* (fig.20), leaves no doubt that it is a painting about lynching, though even without the title the sensation of abject violence is palpable. Most of the House Plan paintings are vertical rectangles, but in some cases Kuitca uses horizontal formats, as in *House Plan with AIDS* (fig.21), a roughly 1.5 m-high by 2.2 m-wide (5 × 7 ¼ foot) canvas in which the floor plan floats above a floral wallpaper pattern on a pale yellow ground. The title invites us to look more closely at the pattern, which interweaves floral images and diagrams of cells (presumably related to the HIV virus). Along the bottom of the painting Kuitca sketches in some floorboards and an uncovered mattress surrounded with long-stem black roses and a single empty chair. Areas of the canvas are stained with reddish-pink paint. At once delicately decorative and ominously funereal, the painting gains additional vulnerability by being painted on very thin, fragile cotton fabric. It is worth recalling that in 1987, the year in which it was painted, about half a decade into the epidemic, AZT, the first drug to treat AIDS, was approved in the United States, and New York playwright Larry Kramer (b.1935) launched the AIDS Coalition to Unleash Power (ACT UP), an activist group that included many artists. The way in which the virus pervades the entire painting, effortlessly passing through the walls of the apartment plan, is a reminder that in 2019, as in 1987, AIDS is a disease that can touch anyone anywhere.

In several House Plan paintings Kuitca gives this family abode a religious dimension with the title *L'Enfance du Christ*, sometimes painting the words directly onto the picture. Drawing, as so often in his work, on the history of European classical music, Kuitca takes the title from French composer Hector Berlioz's (1803–69) oratorio. In one *Enfance du Christ* painting he multiplies the apartment plan three times (the Holy Trinity, one presumes). Religion also turns up, if one is to believe the artist, in the bathroom fixtures of the house plans. In an interview with Kuitca, Lacanian analyst Josefina Ayerza remarks that she has always seen masklike faces in the House Plan bathrooms, to which Kuitca replies, 'The bathroom became a mask because of the WC, the sink, and the bathtub. Three features, like the holy family. I think the WC is the son, and the bathtub is the mother of course, so the sink is left for the father.'[20]

While this remark about bathroom fixtures might have been made half in jest, explicit Catholic imagery appears in other Kuitca paintings, such as the many canvases with thorns either wound into crownlike shapes or delineating city streets. It might seem odd for an artist from a Jewish family to employ Christian iconography, though no artist steeped in the history of Western art, whatever his or her religious background, can fully avoid the symbolism that dominated European art for centuries. What is more, Kuitca grew up in a deeply Catholic country – until 1994, the

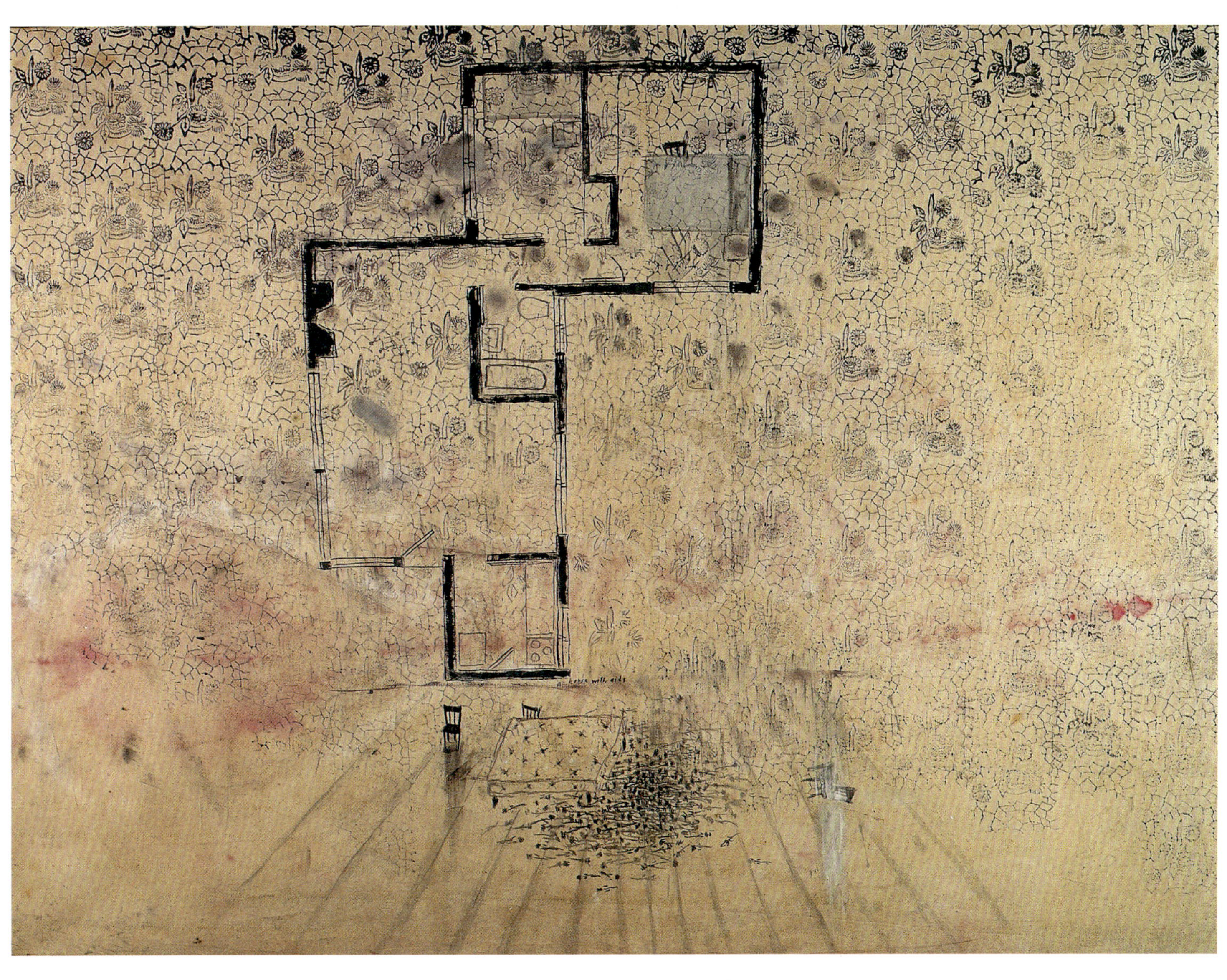

21. House Plan with AIDS   1987

Acrylic on canvas
157 × 214 cm (61 ¹³⁄₁₆ × 84 ¼ in)
Collection of Jorge Helft, Paris

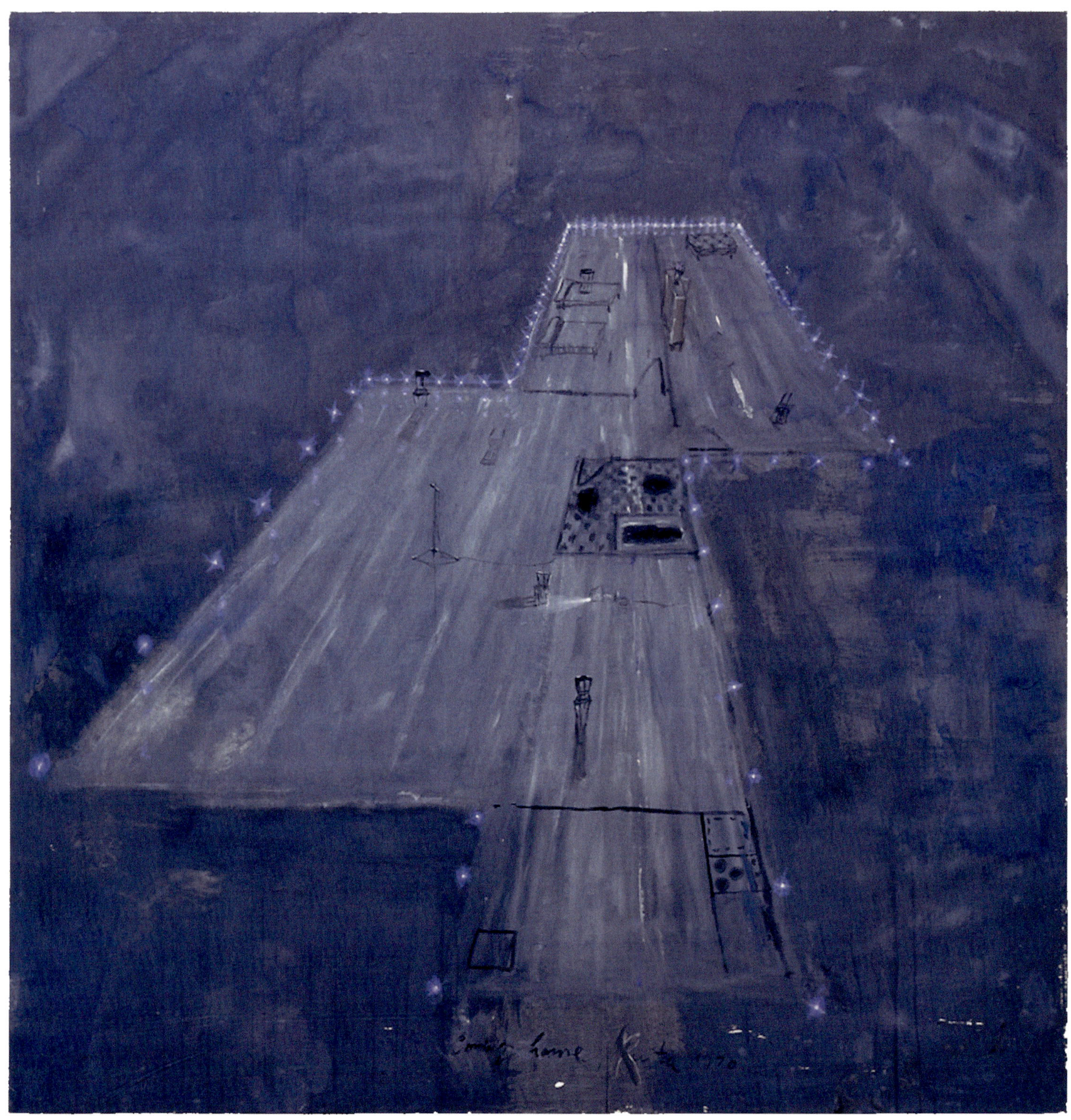

22. Coming Home   1992

Acrylic on canvas
198 × 188 cm (78 × 74 in)
Collection of Josefina Ayerza, New York

Argentine Constitution required that the president be a Roman Catholic. According to Lynn Zelevansky (b.1947), who curated an exhibition of Kuitca's work that traveled to several U.S. museums in 1991 and 1992, it was the example of Frida Kahlo (1907–54) that inspired Kuitca's use of Christian images:

> Kuitca saw her [Kahlo's] work for the first time in Madrid in the early eighties, and she became a major influence, providing him with a means of integrating indigenous Latin American and specifically Catholic imagery into his art. As a Jew, Kuitca initially felt that Catholic symbols were not his to use, and it took time for him to introduce them into his paintings.[21]

Initially it comes as a surprise to learn that Kahlo was so important to Kuitca. They seem to be so different as artists: one is an obsessively autobiographical figurative painter, the other an artist who reveals little to nothing about his life in his art and, at least since 1987, usually constructs his paintings from dry technical diagrams; one is famous as an icon of her Mexican identity, the other has largely avoided any specifically Latin-American imagery. For instance, Kuitca has almost never used Buenos Aires or any part of South America in his Map Paintings (see Chapter 4).

Despite his occasional raids of conventional imagery (Catholic or otherwise) and his sometime plunges into topical subjects, Kuitca prefers to fashion his own iconography, as beautifully demonstrated in several 1989 paintings titled *Coming Home* (fig.22). If the Map Paintings, which are the focus of the next chapter, symbolize travel and the House Plans represent its opposite, these two states – voyaging and staying put – are elegantly reconciled in the *Coming Home* works. In each one Kuitca outlines his standard apartment floor plan – seen in perspective rather than his usual blueprint style – with tiny bursts of purple that resemble the lights along an airport runway. Countless parallel streaks of white paint on the floor plan convey a sense of speed and the ground rushing up to meet the plane. Like all great metaphors, it is instantly understood and deeply resonant. Anyone who has traveled abroad knows the relief of arriving, the sense of being home the moment the wheels touch ground. We experience this sensation because we carry an image of home with us wherever we go. Places never exist for us in isolation; in our mental life they overlay one another. Our bodies may be limited to a single location at a time but our minds can easily be in two places at once. Maybe they always are. *Coming Home* is less a fanciful metaphor than a piece of psychic realism.

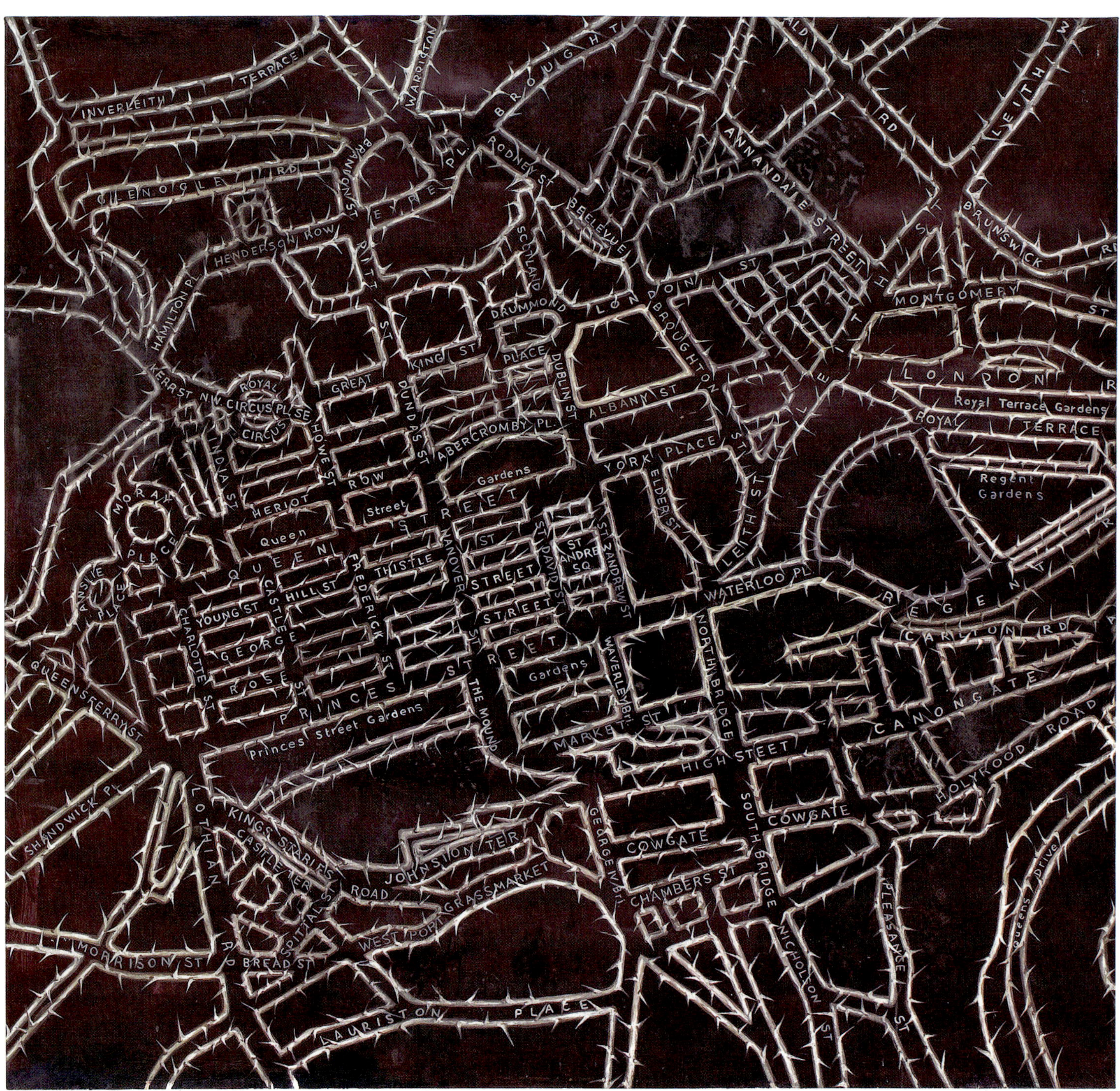

23. Town of Thorns   1991

Oil on canvas
197.5 × 203.5 cm (77 ¾ × 80 ⅛ in)
Private collection

4   Cartographic Dreams

Kuitca has connected his discovery of maps to the fact that he was traveling a lot in the late 1980s. (It was around this time that his career widened in scope with museum exhibitions throughout Europe. Kuitca's first New York solo show was in 1990, with Annina Nosei, who had helped launch Jean-Michel Basquiat's career in the early 1980s; he subsequently moved to the New York–Rome gallery Sperone Westwater.) Like anyone finding himself in unfamiliar cities, he often had to consult maps, so they naturally became part of his everyday life. His first map painting was of Prague, a city he had visited in 1985. In the Czech capital he had bought a thick guidebook from which he had ripped out a street map that, for some reason, he had kept after the trip. The resulting painting, *Prague* (1987), is unlike all the subsequent street-map paintings in that it includes tourist-friendly drawings of major monuments and sites. *Prague* is also uncharacteristic of the Map Paintings because it depicts a city that the artist had actually visited. Generally Kuitca preferred to use maps of cities he had never seen, and also places that were not popular tourist destinations. Thus, you will not find Map Paintings of Paris or London or Rome, nor paintings of cities the artist was familiar with, such as Buenos Aires and New York.

Nonetheless, it seems appropriate that the first street map is of Prague, Kafka's city. Kafkaesque echoes have long been inescapable in Kuitca's work, from the early paintings and drawings where he plays with the first letter of his family name, to his many paintings of vast forbidding architectural plans and more private scenes of isolation and alienation. As Robert Alter eloquently explains in *Imagined Cities: Urban Experience and the Language of the Novel*, 'the unfriendly, untidy city of *The Trial* is, in sum, a place of constricting interiors, baffling streets, and narrow lanes, where neighborhoods often seem telescoped into each other, and where the bureaucratic orderliness of the office is contiguous with a horrific junk room.'[22] His characterization of 'the spooky anonymous city of *The Trial*'[23] could well be applied to the street plans and house plans that constitute the fictional fragmented metropolis of Kuitcaville.

As with the House Plan paintings, Kuitca often substituted the plain lines of the original with unexpected, symbolically charged motifs. In *Town of Thorns* (fig.23), the streets of what seem to be a provincial English town judging by the street names are delineated by thorny vines, painted white against a somber ground. For several other paintings, including an untitled 1995 painting that is recognizably San Francisco, he substitutes bones, turning the cities into vast, neatly ordered ossuaries (fig.24). In 1991 he devoted a large, over-2.8-by-3.7-m (9 ¼ × 12 ¼ foot) canvas to an unidentifiable city – all street names have been erased – constructed wholly out of

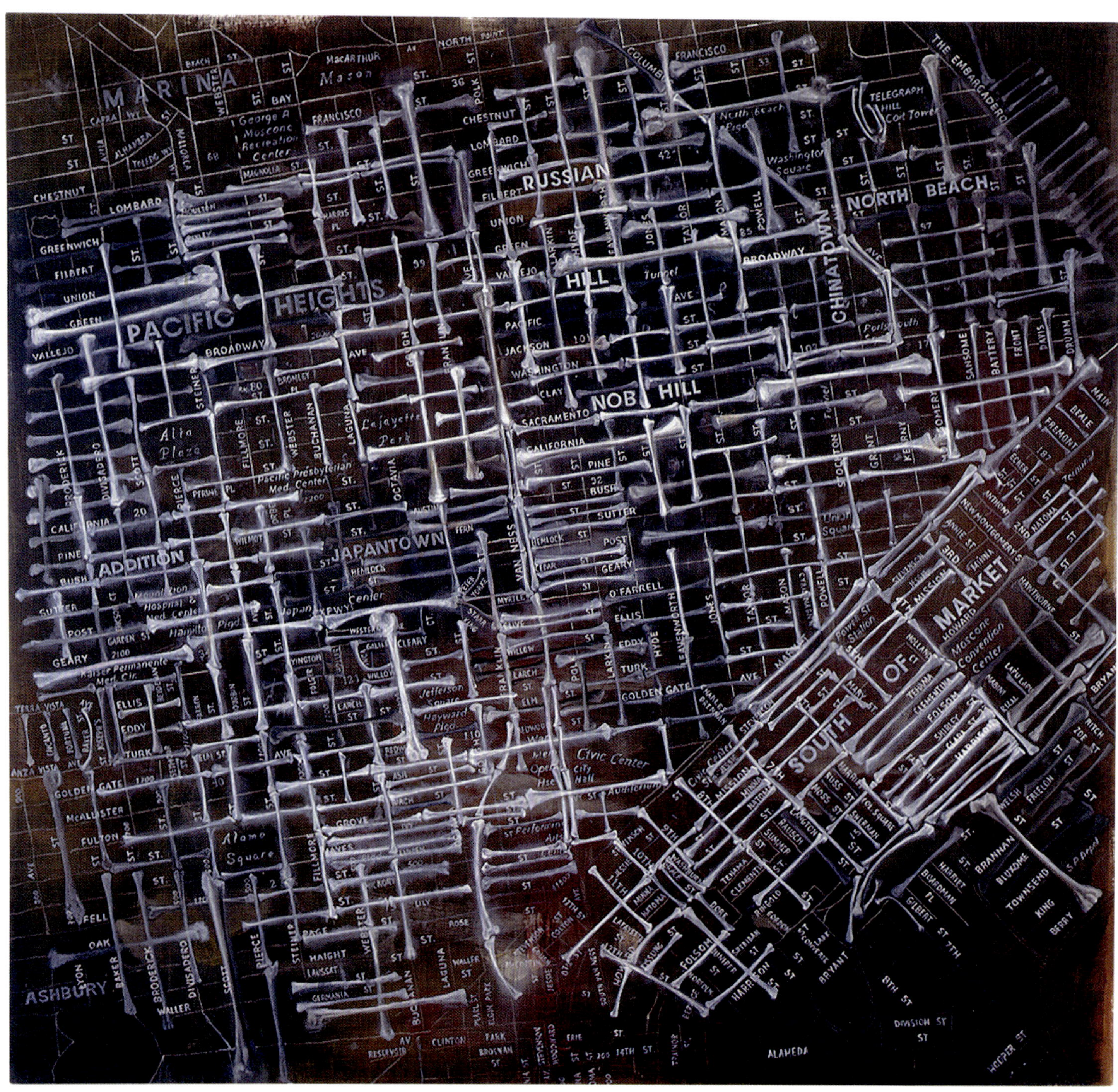

24. Untitled   1995

Oil and acrylic on canvas
193 × 200.7 cm (76 × 79 in)
Collection of Frances Bowes

hypodermic syringes (fig.25). As in other street-map paintings, sections of the city are partially obscured by dark stains that suggest cloud cover. One of the most dramatic instances of this effect comes in an untitled 1992 painting in the collection of New York's Museum of Modern Art where cloudlike smears of gray obscure most of a vast city (an unidentified Zurich) (fig.26). The image feels like nothing so much as a bombsight view. The all-gray palette of the painting contributes to this effect, evoking familiar aerial footage and photographs from Second World War bombing runs. The grisaille color scheme also suggests Gerhard Richter's *Stadtbilder*, gray-scale aerial views of cities the German artist (b.1932) painted in the late 1960s.

About two years into working with maps, Kuitca began to make some of his cartographic paintings not on conventional stretched canvases but on small, specially constructed beds. For each bed, Kuitca selected a different patterned fabric, which he covered with grayish acrylic paint to make the beds look old and soiled. As with nearly all his cartographic work, the map imagery was hand-painted by the artist's assistants. The first of these works was a trio of beds he made in 1989 for the São Paulo Biennial. Gradually the number of these bed paintings grew and the artist began to present them as installations. He also started painting on specially made mattresses, sometimes made from vinyl rather than the cotton fabric used for the beds, that could be hung on the wall. An important feature of all these works are the upholstery buttons sewn into the mattresses (a tricky technique involving waxed string that his assistants had to master). Rather than being regularly spaced out, the buttons on Kuitca's mattresses are irregularly distributed, usually corresponding to the geographical features. While not meant to be descriptive, these indentations are unintentionally full of associations, from bullet holes to bodily orifices. For some viewers, they also connect to the Lacanian concept of *point de capiton*, usually translated as 'quilting point' or 'anchoring point'. Mattress buttons are used to prevent the stuffing from moving around over time; in Lacanian thought, the *point de capiton* is what prevents slippage between signifier and signified. Jacques Lacan (1901–81), who held that the unconscious was structured like a language, believed that a certain minimum number of such stabilizing points were 'necessary for a person to be called normal', and that 'when they are not established, or when they give way' the result is psychosis.[24] While Kuitca was not thinking about Lacan when he began incorporating upholstery buttons into his work, he grew up and lived in a city famously full of psychoanalysis enthusiasts, among them quite a few Lacanians.[25]

As with the airport runway–apartment plan conjunction in *Coming Home* (see fig.22), the overlaying of a map onto a bed makes a single powerful image from two disparate entities. On the one hand, a symbol of intimacy and stasis, the place where we feel ourselves furthest removed from the world, from the realm of the social, of politics, of others; on the other hand, a representation of intimacy's opposite, the wide world of strangers and unknown places and geopolitical divisions and travel. The bed is also a symbol of vulnerability, the site of birth, sex and death, as well as of dreams. The

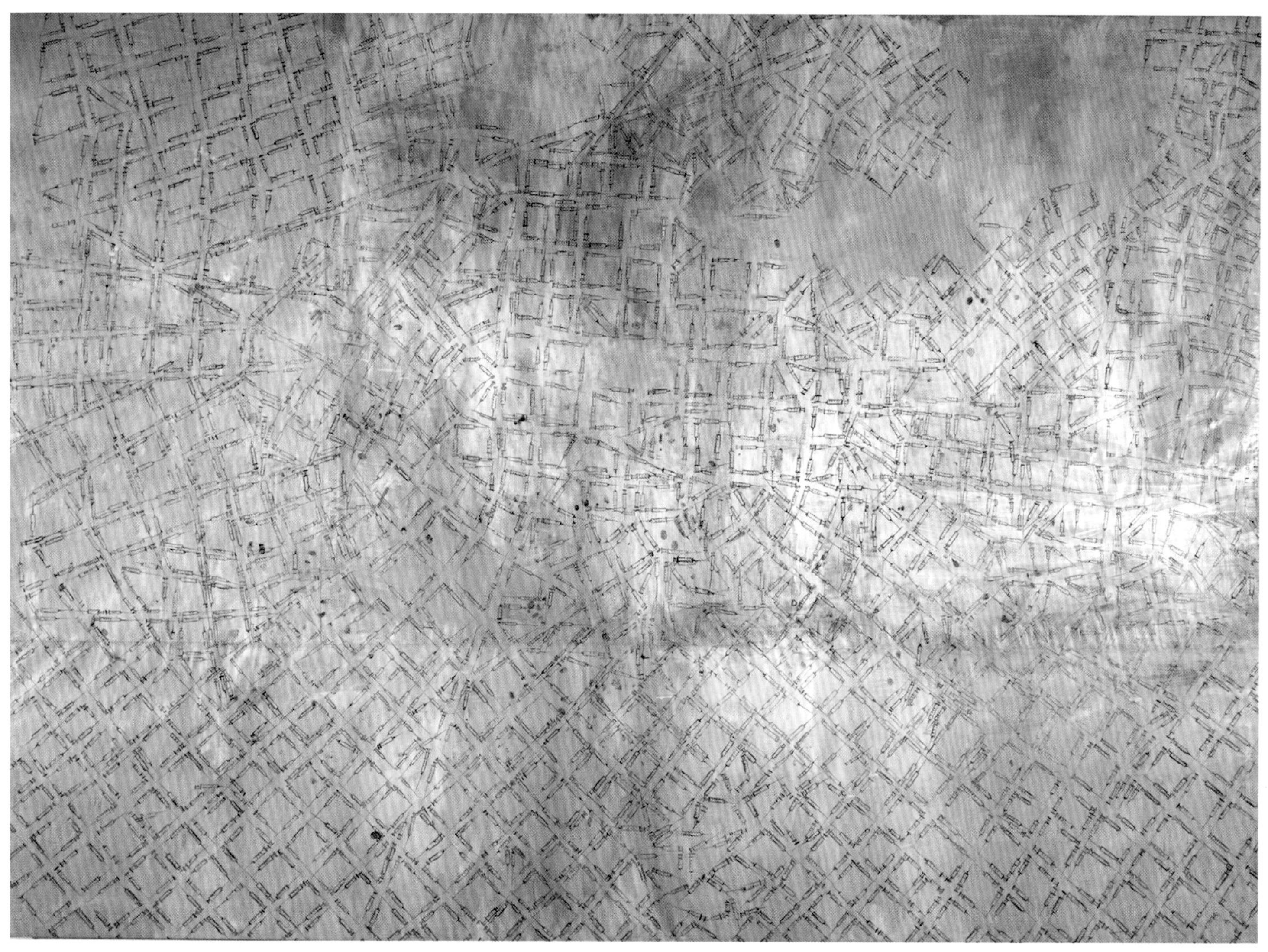

25. Untitled   1991

Acrylic on canvas
282 × 373 cm (111 × 146 ⅞ in)
La Caixa, Barcelona

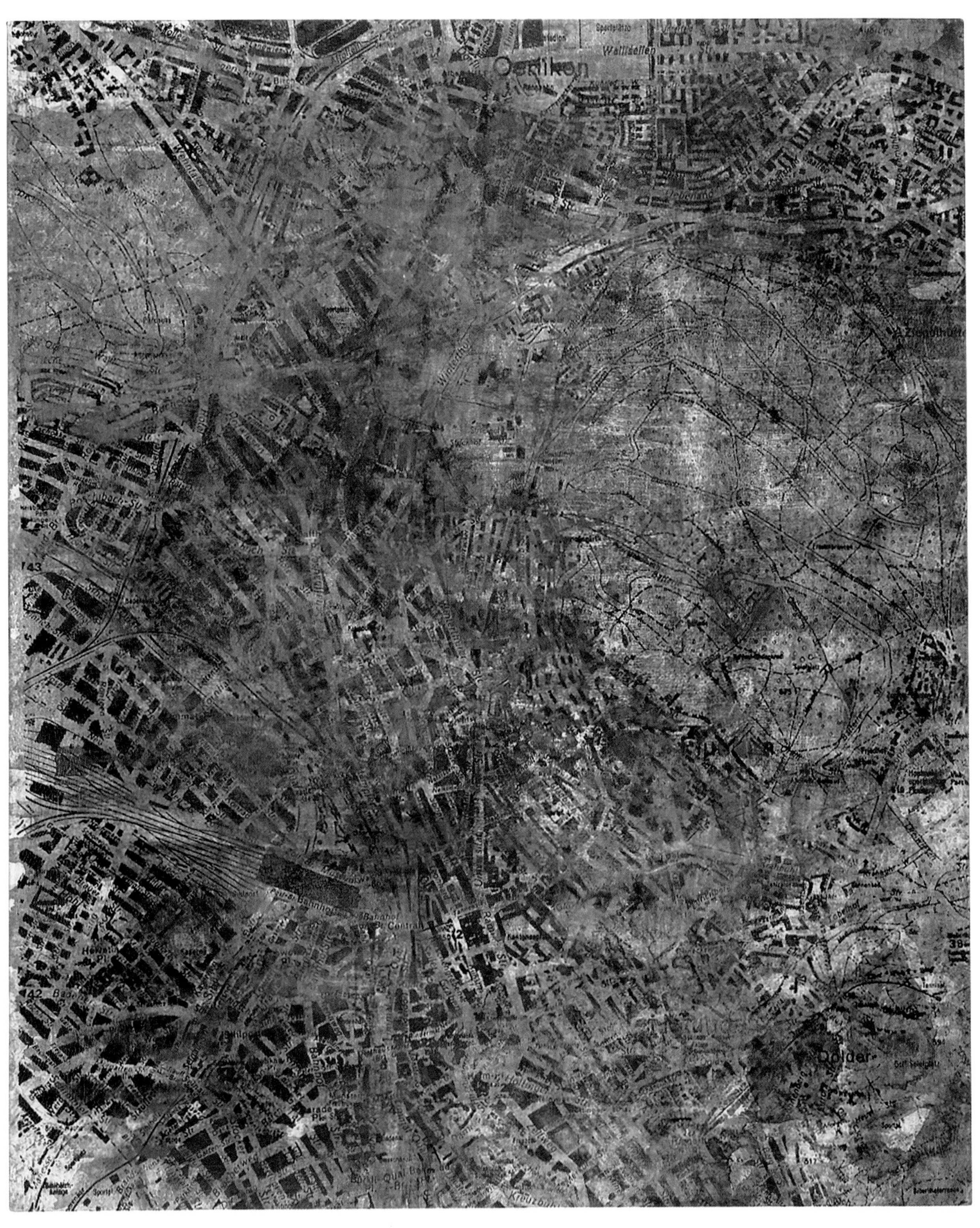

26. Untitled   1991

Mixed media on canvas
223.5 × 180.3 cm (88 × 71 in)
The Metropolitan Museum of Art, New York

diminutive size of Kuitca's beds, which are often taken to be children's beds, contributes to this sense of vulnerability. Here it is important to note the artist's insistence that he did not mean them to be seen as child-size beds: 'They aren't really "little beds" but regular beds seen from afar, only that when they are close, in front of us, they keep the size they had at a distance.'[26] This fascination with suggesting distance by making things smaller was already evident in the tiny figures in the Theater Paintings (see pp 19–27).

In 1992, Kuitca presented an assembly of 20 painted beds, mostly with road maps from Central Europe, at *documenta* in Kassel, Germany (this work is now in the collection of Tate Modern, London). That same year he created a second, larger group of 80 beds that included maps from Mexico, Australia and China. For a 2000 exhibition at the Cartier Foundation in Paris, he reduced the number of beds to 54. Now owned by the Museum of Fine Arts, Houston, this ensemble remained untitled until 2010 when the artist named it *Le Sacre* (fig.28). The title is usually taken to be an allusion to Stravinsky's ballet *Le Sacre du Printemps* (The Rite of Spring, 1913), but in fact the title owes a greater debt to Cuban writer Alejo Carpentier's *La consagración de la primavera* (The Consecration of Spring), a politically charged 1978 novel inspired by Stravinsky's *Le Sacre du Printemps*. The novel tracks the life of its heroine, a dancer in Diaghilev's Ballets Russes, from the Russian Revolution to Castro's Cuba, where she seeks to stage a radical version of Stravinsky's ballet. As the artist remarked to me in Buenos Aires in 2019, it is also Carpentier's novel and not Stravinsky's score that he was alluding to when he used the title *La consagración de la primavera* for a series of paintings in the early 1980s. He was also well aware of Pina Bausch's 1975 piece *Das Frühlingsopfer* (The Rite of Spring) that he had seen in Buenos Aires in 1980.

At the time he began the maps, Kuitca was not particularly aware of artists who had used map imagery before him, neither Jasper Johns (b.1930), who vibrantly rendered the United States in 1961, nor Alighiero e Boetti (1940–94), an Italian artist he would later come to admire, nor Swedish artist Öyvind Fahlström (1928–76). 'I felt that I had discovered maps, that I was the first man to see a map,' he recalled.[27] No doubt he was more aware, in 1989, of how the map of Europe was literally being redrawn with the collapse of Communism. Nowhere was this more dramatic than in Germany, which was the subject of many of Kuitca's early Map Paintings. For his part, the artist has explained his preference for maps of Germany because even as a child he had loved the sound of German place names. 'I probably never evoked a place, but just the name of the place. There wasn't, for me, a real city or a historical experience of a city behind those names. It's a kind of childhood desire,' he explained in 1997.[28] (Of course just because the artist doesn't associate 'a real city or a historical experience of a city' with a name on a map does not mean that viewers cannot make such associations. In some fundamental way the place names on Kuitca's maps are multivalent, open to diverse interpretations.) Similarly, he was not interested in the functionality of maps, telling Mari Carmen Ramírez, 'I mostly thought of maps as a device to get lost and not to find your way. A map is a device that allows you to get your bearings, but to me they served as the opposite.'[29]

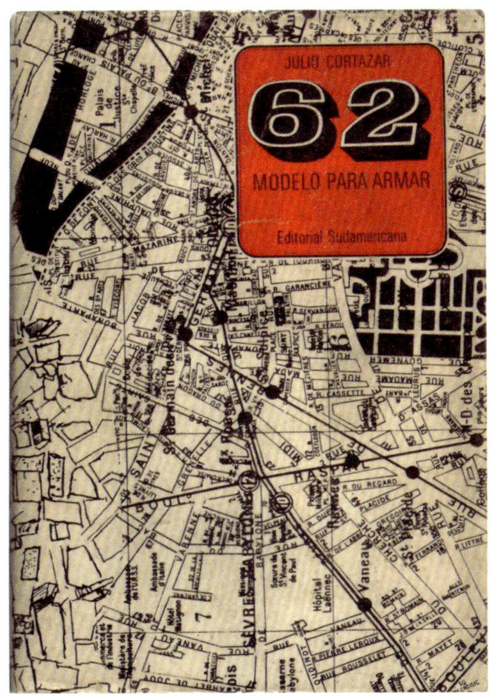

27. Cover of the first edition of Julio Cortázar's *62 Modelo para armar* (62: A Model Kit), 1968.

The experience of being lost in a city, of wandering its streets and immersing oneself in its crowds and its desolation, has been an essential part of the modern experience from Baudelaire's *flâneur* to the artists who became 'painters of modern life' to devotees of the Situationist *dérive*. Argentine literature is particularly rich in depictions of *flânerie* and the labyrinthine character of city life: the seedy urban landscapes in the work of Roberto Arlt (1900–42); Jorge Luis Borges, who declared in a poem 'My soul is in the streets of Buenos Aires'; the lyrical geography in Julio Cortázar's (1914–84) *Hopscotch* where the protagonist and his lover search for each other through the streets of Paris; the slums at the center of the novel *La villa* (Shantytown) by César Aira (b.1949). In a striking visual-literary foreshadowing of Kuitca's Map Paintings, the cover of the first edition of Cortázar's deconstructive 1968 novel *62: Modelo para armar* (62: A Model Kit) features the details of a Paris street map that could easily serve as a template for one of Kuitca's paintings (fig.27).

It is easier, Kuitca knows, to dream about someplace you have never been than about familiar territory. The most extreme instance of such dreaming might be *Heaven* (1992) in which Kuitca painted a crowded astronomical star map, punctuated with numerous upholstery buttons, onto shiny black vinyl. Armed with a stack of maps in his Buenos Aires studio – many of them purchased at a Rand McNally map store he frequented on his visits to New York City – Kuitca engaged in a kind of reverse exoticism. For centuries, Europeans enjoyed fevered romantic dreams about the distant lands of the Americas, Africa and Asia, savoring the names of fabulous-sounding locations. A classic expression of this cartographic romanticism is W.J. Turner's 1916 poem *Romance*, which recalls the effect the names of two Ecuadorian mountains had on the young poet (1889–1946): 'When I was but thirteen or so/ I went into a golden land,/ Chimborazo, Cotopaxi/ Took me by the hand.' For Kuitca, a Latin-American artist working at a moment when the Anglo-European art world is finally becoming global, the names of obscure towns in Europe and North America are fair game, connected to a 'childhood desire' not unlike W.J. Turner's imperialist fantasy. Kuitca's maps of nations and cities in Europe and North America are, among many other things, an anti-imperialist gesture in the spirit of Joaquín Torres-García's famous 1943 upside down map of the Americas.

Selecting European and North American maps was a highly conscious decision on Kuitca's part. When he was invited to participate in the 1992 *documenta*, perhaps the most prestigious exhibition in the world, he thought carefully about the work he would present:

I didn't want to expressly appear with maps of Latin America. What I wanted to do was to revert the idea of 'orientalism', because for me, Kassel and all those cities represented the unknown, and those names inspired some kind of fascination in me. I tried to use maps of Central Europe, not Mediterranean Europe, but maps that had mainly Germany, Poland, Czechoslovakia, using

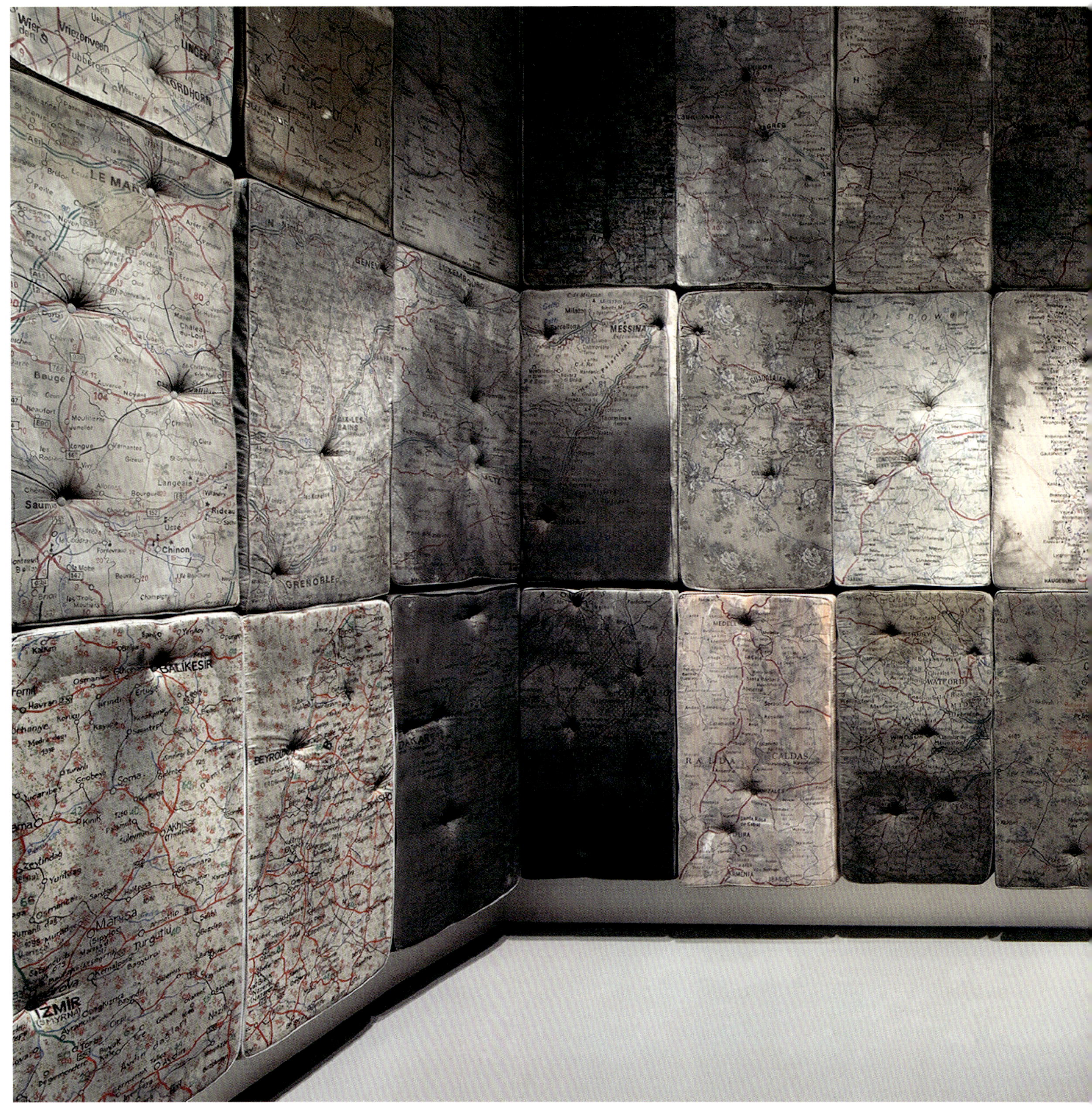

28. Le Sacre (detail) 1992

Acrylic on 54 mattresses with wood and brass legs
120 × 60 × 20 cm each (47 ¼ × 23 ⅝ × 7 ⅞ in each)
Museum of Fine Arts Houston

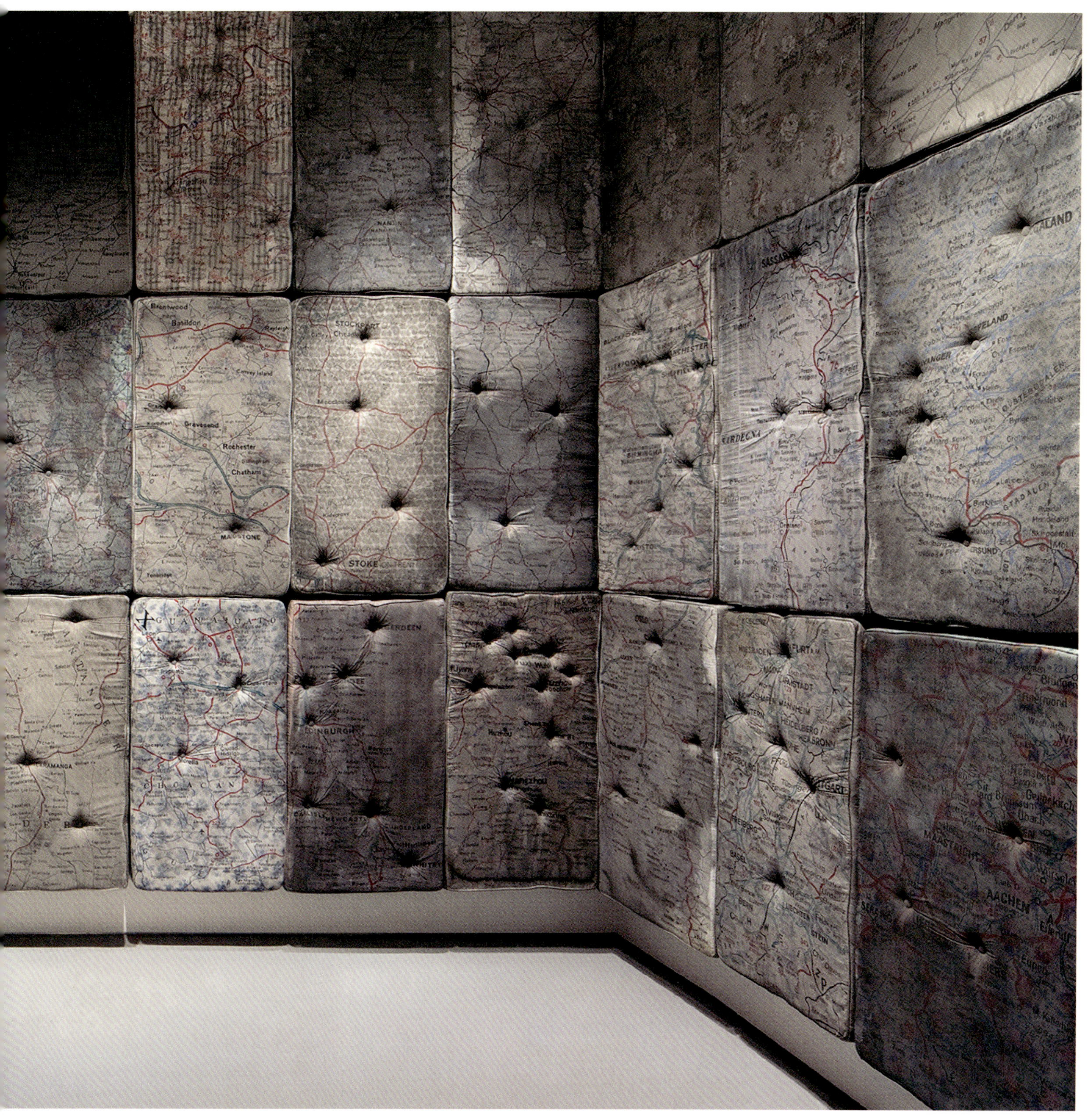

arbitrary sectors, fragmented cuts. What I wanted to do was not determine my identity based on geography, or if I did, determine it based on a geography that was foreign to me.[30]

This was at a time when, following the 1989 *Magiciens de la Terre* exhibition at the Centre Pompidou, the contemporary art world, so long dominated by Western Europe and North America, felt the first stirrings of globalism. As often happens in the early phases of such cultural exchanges, there was an emphasis on exoticism and otherness of the new arrivals. In the case of the Latin-American artists who were being invited to exhibitions (such as Kuitca, and Mexican painter Julio Galàn, 1958–2006), their work was often presented, especially in the United States, as embodying the cliché of 'magical realism'. An instance of this is the exhibition *The Art of the Fantastic: Latin America, 1920–1987*, which traveled to museums in the United States and Mexico. Kuitca, who was included in *The Art of the Fantastic*, recalls what it was like:

> My first participations in international exhibitions in the United States were thought 'from a magical realism point of view', or something of the sort. But think about it, how much of my work has to do with that? Nothing! Though there'd always be someone who would interpret it along those lines. Any Latin American artist can corroborate that from way before Documenta and even afterwards, this was the underlying basis of the approaches.[31]

The pitfalls of being linked to Argentine identity (or, indeed, any national identity) are highlighted at the beginning of Cortázar's *Hopscotch* (first published as *Rayuela* in 1963). The book's epigraph from French writer Jacques Vaché (1895–1919) reads 'Rien ne vous tue un homme comme d'être obligé de représenter un pays' (Nothing kills a man like being obliged to represent a country).

The experience of looking at one of Kuitca's Map Paintings is very different from looking at an actual map. We do not consult his work to know where we are or how to get to where we want to go, or to figure out the distance between Rochester and Buffalo, or to understand where Fukushima or Fallujah or Ferguson (Missouri) are located. And yet, these are 'actual maps' that conceivably could be used to answer questions about geography. Being copied onto a canvas in acrylic or oil paint with various effects, subtle or dramatic, with the artistic touches that make the painting identifiable as the work of a particular artist, does not make these city plans and road maps any less maps. Because of their size they may not be practical to use, but they are still maps, even when Kuitca introduces delirious elements (as when every town on a map carries the same name). A painting of an apple can never be an apple but a painting of a map is still a map. So, we are aware, at some level, of the reality of the image, the fact that it is functional, that it conveys information, that it is doing something alongside its status as a representation of something in the world. And,

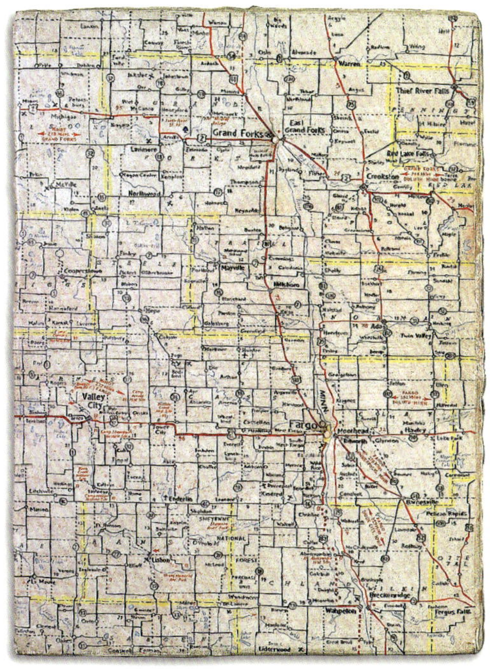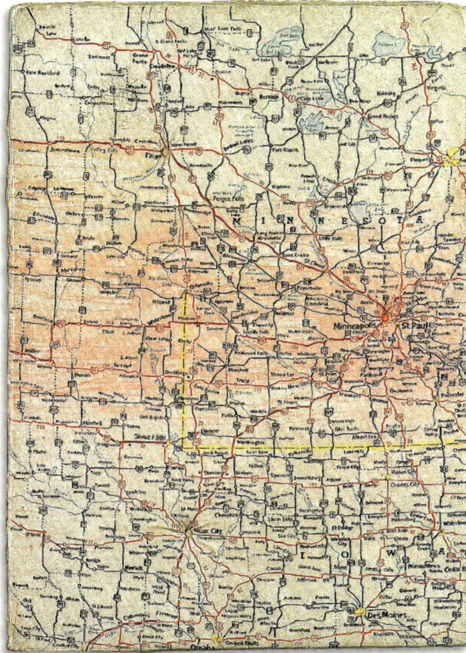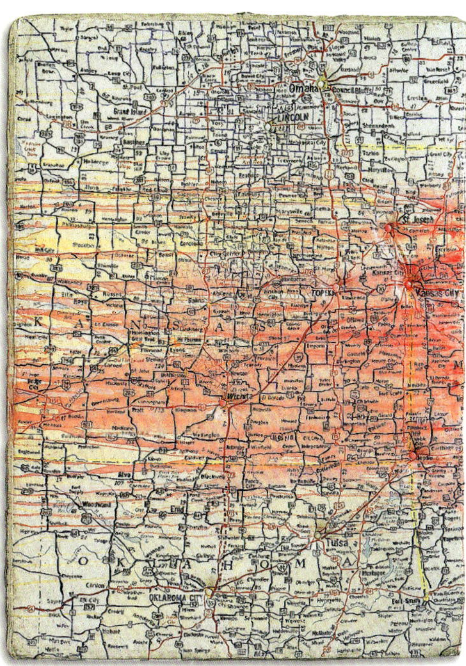

29. Untitled 1990

Mixed media on mattresses
Three parts, each 198 × 140 cm, overall 198 × 437 cm
(three parts, each 78 × 55 ⅛ in, overall 78 × 172 in)
Private collection

as with any work of art, we bring to it our own personal experience. I, for instance, look differently at an untitled 1990 painting on three wall-mounted mattresses (fig.29) that includes my birthplace (Lawrence, Kansas) than someone with no connection to that place.

We may also project ourselves into the paintings, trace with our eyes a route through the territory or city being depicted. Of course, this is what happens with most paintings: we project ourselves into the fictive spaces they create and let our eyes graze over their surfaces. What is different in the Map Paintings is that this movement is explicitly guided: we follow roads from town to town, turn corners in cities. And yet our visual itineraries are not so straightforward; how we absorb these paintings is different from the way we read a map. Kuitca is constantly introducing irregularities, glitches that interfere with a purely cartographic experience. The most blatantly disruptive elements are the buttons in the mattress maps, but all of the Map Paintings feature imperfections, frequently in the form of smudged areas, that proclaim 'this is a work of art, not a map'.

The smudge or smear is, in fact, one of Kuitca's most characteristic moves. From the beginning he has incorporated error into his work. If one effect of these mistakes is to distinguish his maps and architectural plans from their technical-drawing sources, another is to suggest that perception is imperfect, and that things tend to fall apart, especially things made by human beings. In his later work, images are subjected to increasing breakdown: dissolved by water, torn apart by unseen forces; entropy is everywhere.

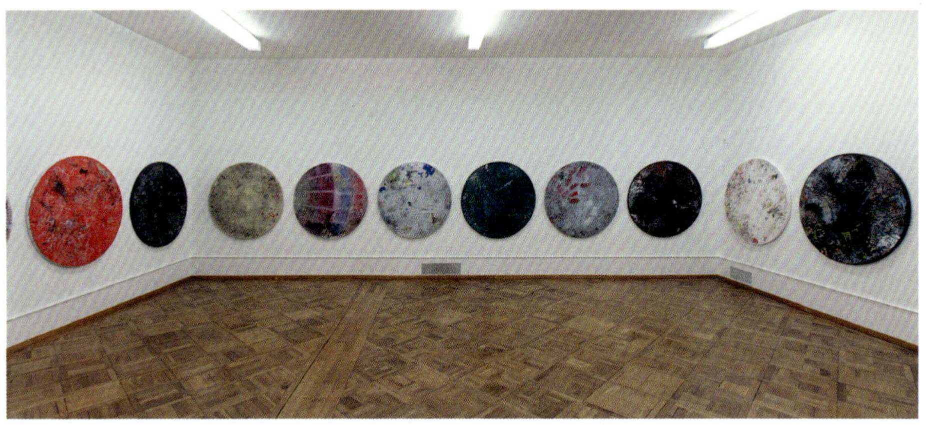

30. Diarios, installation view of *Guillermo Kuitca* exhibition, Centre Pasquart, Biel, 2017

In the case of Kuitca's *San Juan de la Cruz* paintings, in which he renames most of the towns on a given map after the Spanish poet–saint, we find ourselves on the endless ouroboros from one San Juan de la Cruz to the next (fig.31). As well as being powerful models of solipsism, the *San Juan de la Cruz* paintings conjure up uncanny narratives in which characters vainly attempt to escape some preordained fate or find themselves caught in the same endless story. These paintings come up in a revealing conversation between Kuitca and Josefina Ayerza:

> JA: We seem to be talking about solitude.
> GK: Solitude seems to be a very important subject in my work. It's in the idea of being isolated in the midst of all these people and places. Do you remember those paintings that I did where the same city name is repeated many times? Whatever road you took, you ended up at a place called San Juan de la Cruz or Hannover.
> JA: This is similar to the idea of trauma, in that trauma always returns you to the same experience.
> GK: Trauma? My God, that is absolutely what I did.[32]

Ayerza's psychoanalytical reading of the *San Juan de la Cruz* series invites us to understand the paintings as models of some kind. For her, Kuitca's works can be seen as diagrams of trauma and its aftermath. The closed circular structure of the San Juan de la Cruz paintings recurs some ten years later in the Conveyor Belt Paintings. It also finds an echo – more conceptual than visual – in the 2002 paintings Kuitca made in homage to Wagner's *Der Ring des Nibelungen* (Ring Cycle, see p. 86), a series of operas that center on a ring and are usually referred to as a 'cycle'. Circular motifs appear in a number of individual paintings, such as the stadium in *The Tablada Suite V* (1992) and the numerous *Corona de espinas* (Crown of Thorns) paintings, some of which are modeled on rollercoasters. One might also include the *Diarios* (Diaries) – tondo canvases on which Kuitca accumulates notations and sketches over many months – in the category of circular structures (fig.30).

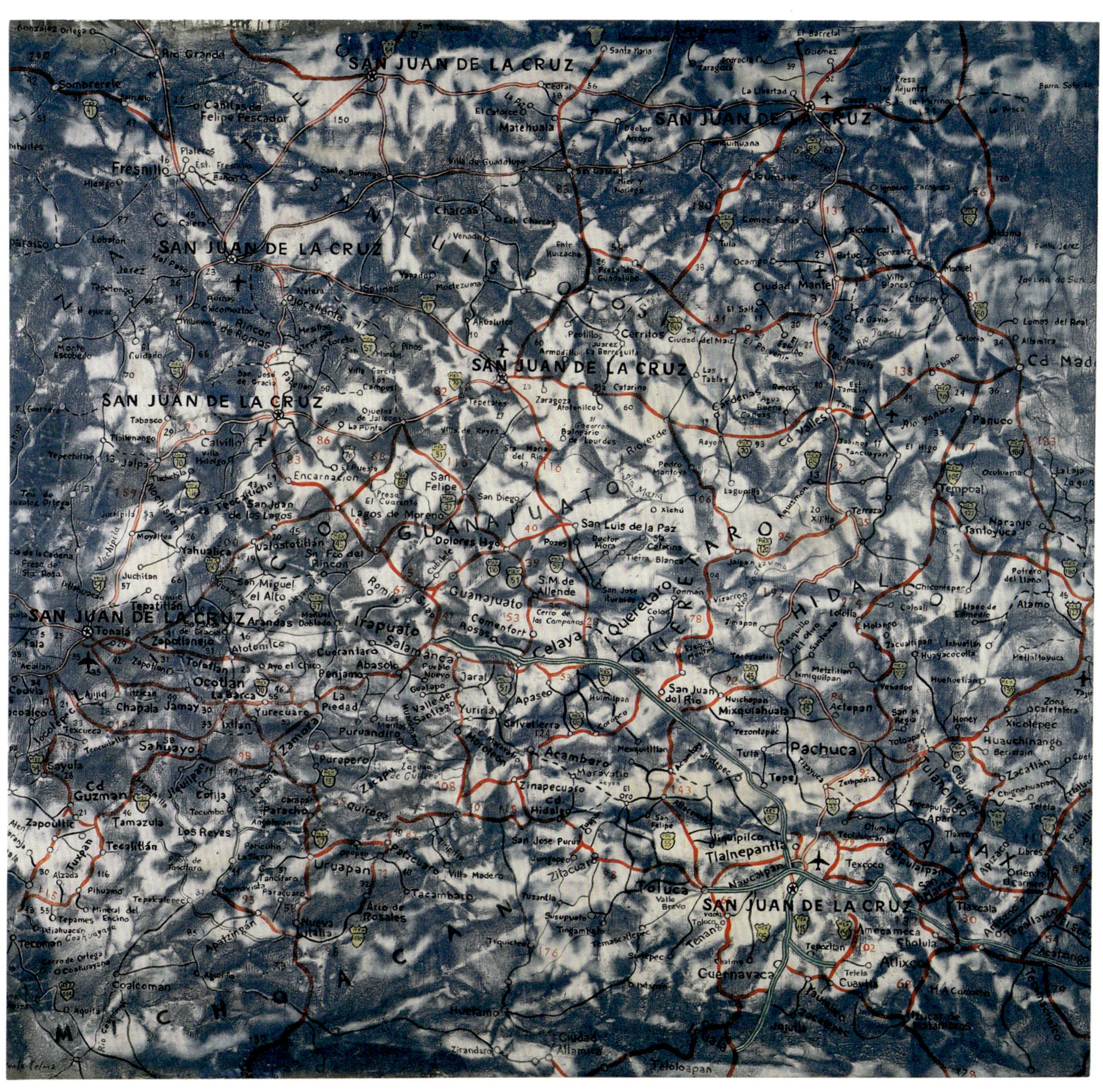

31. San Juan de la Cruz   1991

Acrylic on canvas
198.1 × 203.2 cm (78 × 80 in)
Private collection, New York

At one point in their extensive conversations, Graciela Speranza comments on how Kuitca's work seems to chart increasing distances, from bed, to home, city, nation and outer space. Kuitca denies that the sequence of progressive distancing in his work was deliberate, at least not initially. He then tells Speranza that the first time he noticed this reverse zoom effect was in his painting *Coming* (1987, fig.32) in which images are distributed in a grid.

> I organized my work like a path, starting at the bed as an origin, going on to the apartment floor plan, then to the images of some buildings, then to the city plan—Hamburg in this case—with these same buildings, then the same buildings seen far away and, finally, the typical road map in which Hamburg appears along with other European cities.

In a second version of *Coming*, also made in 1989, Kuitca eliminates the identifying labels. (Both paintings play with the double meaning of the word 'coming' by including splatters of white paint that look like semen, a device Kuitca borrowed from a 1975 work by Gilbert & George that was also titled *Coming*.) Nothing tells us that this is Hamburg. In the city maps that followed, the cities are rarely identified. Similarly, he never included the dotted lines that mark the borders between nations. 'What interested me was that uniform, homogenous panning, and acknowledging borders would have destroyed the idea.'[33] For those who might see in Kuitca's erasure of national borders a utopian message, the artist's explanation of a purely visual desire ('that uniform, homogenous panning') would be discouraging, but who is to say if, underneath Kuitca's dislike of dotted lines there lies a rejection of nationalism, of political territoriality.

32. Coming   1988

Acrylic on canvas
140 x 100 cm (55 × 39 ½ in)
La Caixa, Barcelona

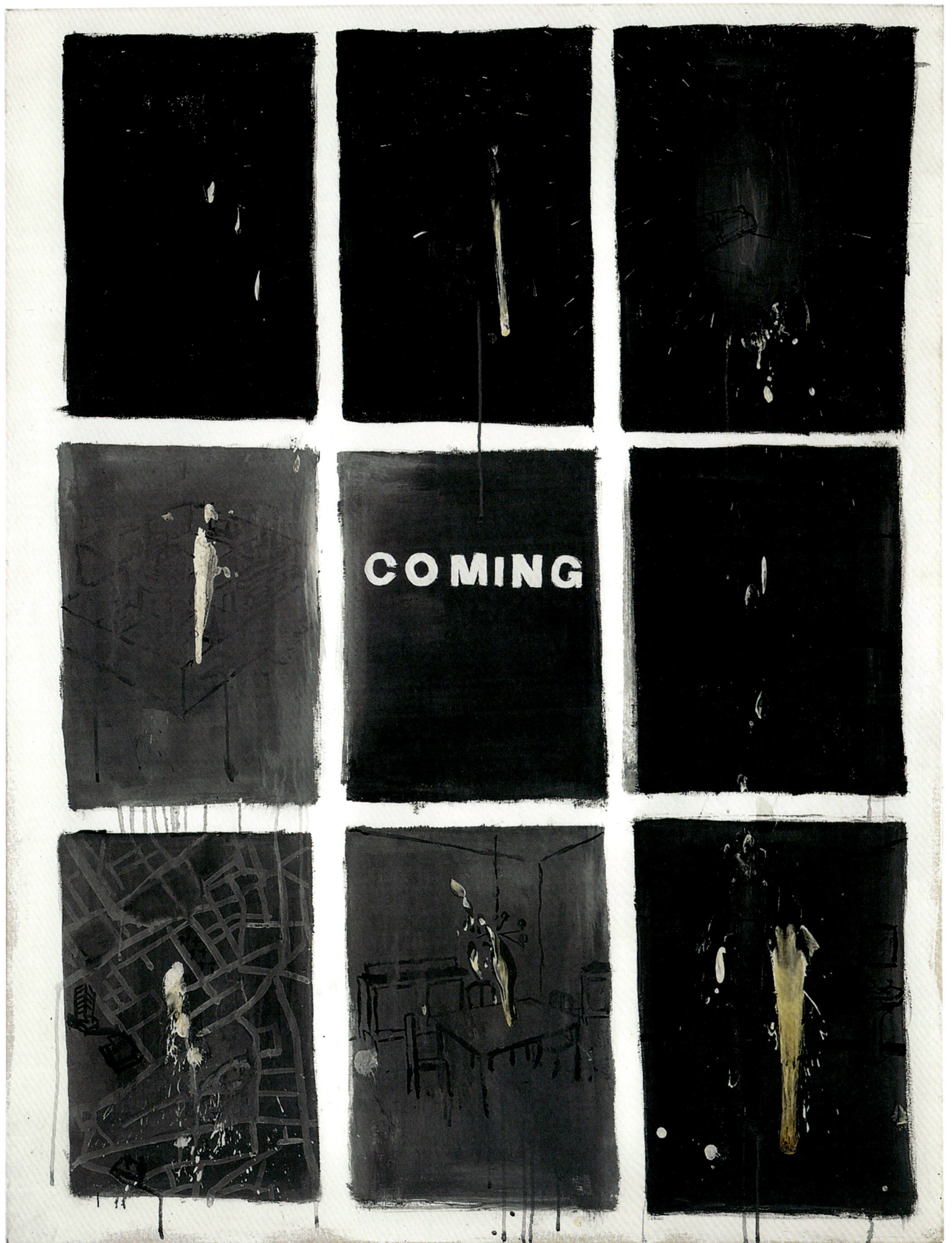

COMING

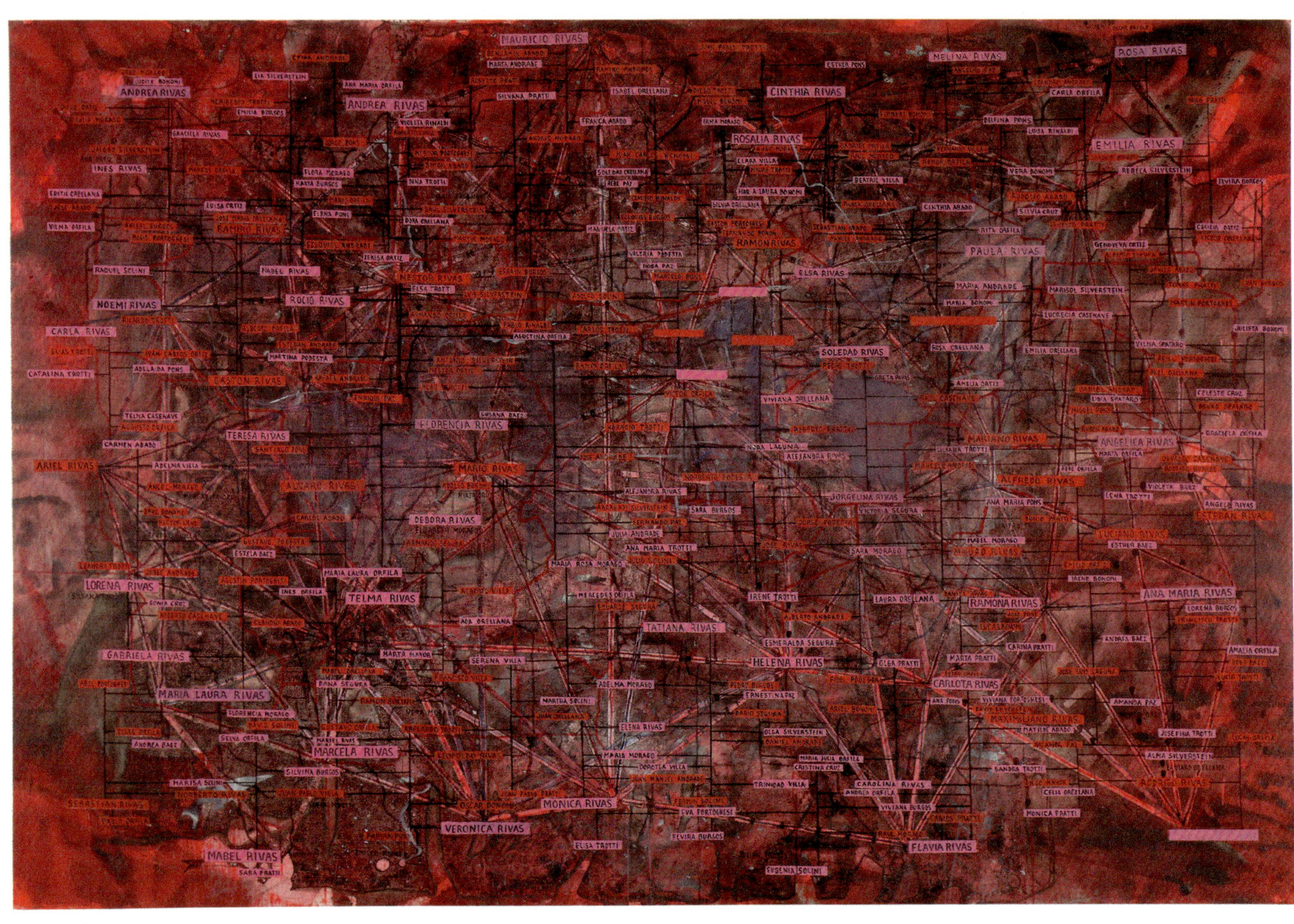

33. People on Fire   1993

Mixed media on canvas
193 × 279.4 cm (76 × 110 in)
North Carolina Museum of Art, Raleigh

5   Discovering the Diagram

In the early 1990s, the maps and house plans, which had appeared more or less simultaneously around 1987, gradually vanished from Kuitca's paintings. As he explained later:

> I abandoned the maps in 1992–93, although I painted maps again many years later. That was the worst decision of my career. To become well-known for something and abandon it right away [he laughs]. No, I feel that I follow my own logic. I find it very hard to do what others want from me. That doesn't make me purer or put me above anything. What happens is that I could never understand what that anonymous entity made up of spectators, collectors, curators and critics could possibly want. I haven't the faintest idea of what they may want from me, so that if I didn't have my own interests, I couldn't even do my job.[34]

Although he continued making Map Paintings through 1992, including the epic *Le Sacre* (see fig.28), a new direction announced itself in 1991 with *The Tablada Suite*. Unlike the Map and House Plan Paintings – both sprawling, open-ended bodies of work – *The Tablada Suite* was conceived and executed according to a strict plan: ten works each showing the plan of some public institution, drawn in graphite on a pale ground. Relying solely on penciled lines, they are in essence giant drawings executed on canvas. Even though Kuitca had been relying on diagrammatic imagery in the Maps and House Plans, the act of renouncing the brush and all the physicality of paint was a brave step. Confronted with the austerity of *The Tablada Suite* the viewer must set aside certain expectations of what a painting should be. To make the grounds, each of which is a different variety of what the artist saw as 'institutional' colors, Kuitca used everyday house paint, in part because he wanted the paintings to look as if they had been drawn on a wall.

A notable quality of the works forming *The Tablada Suite*, which were made with only the most basic of tools (pen and ruler), are the fingerprints and smudges pervading their surfaces. Rather than being calculated effects, these features are the result of the artist's graphite-covered hands touching the surface of the painting as he worked, and the fact that he never cleaned his hands during the process. Nonetheless, he was aware of the contrast between the precision of the plans he was drawing and the messiness of his method, which clearly distinguishes the paintings from technical drawings. A final stage in *The Tablada Suite* involved applying a heavy coat of varnish to the painting. For the artist, this varnish 'was like a plastic seal, so that even though there is dirt under this layer, it is washable. The varnish, as if it were a window, sets up a very clear separation between the piece and the gaze.'[35] Here, perhaps, is another trace of Francis Bacon's influence on Kuitca: the British painter was famous for insisting that his canvases be exhibited under glass and in heavy gilt frames.[36]

Named after a Jewish cemetery in Buenos Aires – El Cementerio Israelita de la Tablada is actually the largest Jewish cemetery in South America – *The Tablada Suite* includes, along with the layout of a cemetery, plans of a theater, two stadiums, a hospital, a prison, an archive, a convention center, a hotel and, dropping a fictional structure among nine real-world locations, the Starship Enterprise from *Star Trek* (figs 34 and 35). Ironically, the 'real' structures, while loosely inspired by actual plans, are largely invented, while the fictional one most closely follows a pre-existing design. As this list reveals, it was not only the materials and technique that changed from the House Plans to *The Tablada Suite* but also the scale and nature of the paintings' sources. Instead of the small, private, domestic space of a family apartment, *The Tablada Suite* examines the designs of large, public, institutional spaces. In shifting from the intimate realm of private dwellings to the impersonal domain of institutions Kuitca inevitably invites us to think about how such structures affect us, to ponder our relationship to larger entities such as medicine, law, sports, entertainment, business, religion – all the systems and ideologies that constitute a society, and that define an individual in the eyes of that society.

By turning his attention as a painter to the visualization of social and political subjects, Kuitca contributed to, and influenced, an emerging tendency in contemporary painting. In New York in the mid-1980s, influenced by the ideas of Michel Foucault (1926–84), Gilles Deleuze (1925–95) and Jean Baudrillard (1929–2007), artists such as Peter Halley were making paintings in which the language of modernist abstraction was used to comment on the impact of emerging technologies on social structures. For Halley it was obvious that 'the history of abstract art is the history of a real progression in the social. It is the history of the organization of the compartmentalized spaces and the formal systems that make up the abstract world.'[37] In the late 1990s, Julie Mehretu (b.1970) introduced an array of diagrammatic architectural motifs into her work. Describing the development of her work in 2002, Mehretu cited the same kind of source material that Kuitca had pioneered: 'The paintings occurred in an intangible no-place: a blank terrain, an abstracted map space. As I continued to work I needed a context for the marks, the characters. By combining many types of architectural plans and drawings I tried to create a metaphoric, tectonic view of structural history.'[38] As the 1990s progressed, more and more painters (such as Matthew Ritchie [b.1989] and Toba Khedoori [b.1964]) adopted a diagrammatic approach. In part thanks to Kuitca's pioneering works such as *The Tablada Suite*, the diagram became recognized as suitable material for painting.

One thing that set Kuitca apart from many of his contemporaries who tackled social subjects through painting in the 1980s and 1990s is that his work was largely devoid of self-reflexivity. Unlike Halley, for instance, he did not seem to be interested in engaging in critiques of abstraction, nor of painting tout court. Instead, the viability of the medium was assumed, which left the artist free to explore a wide range of subject matter. (In a later body of work, the Cubistoid Paintings, Kuitca did make the medium of painting, and the history of abstraction, central to his project.) One commentator, Olga Viso, makes the intriguing suggestion that the true context for Kuitca's work in the 1990s was not to be found in the realm of painting. For Viso, his works of the time are closer to the 'sculptural practices' of Rachel Whiteread (b.1963), Miroslaw Balka (b.1958), Doris Salcedo (b.1958), Robert Gober (b.1954) and Juan Muñoz (1953–2001), artists with whom he frequently exhibited.[39]

In essence, Kuitca found a way to escape the endgame mentality that had afflicted so much serious painting, and, just as importantly, did so without having to revert to older styles. If the two dominant modes of painting in the 1980s were Neo-Expressionism, which frequently relied on historical pastiche, and a critique-driven abstraction, Kuitca, almost singlehandedly, introduced a third option: a painting practice that was representational without being backward-looking and rigorous without being self-referential. His success in navigating his way out of postmodernist aesthetics depended in no small part on a sense of mission he felt as a painter, a sense that the medium of painting could be a vehicle for something more than continual reexamination of its own past, or worrying about its current commodification. In 1994, just after the completion of *The Tablada Suite*, Kuitca wrote to curator Lynne Cooke of the 'personal responsibility' he felt 'to comment in my works on the human condition'. His ambition as an artist, he explained, was 'to give order to everything that surrounds me. To try to understand the world in which I live.'[40]

Shortly after beginning *The Tablada Suite*, Kuitca embarked on a separate series: *People on Fire* (fig.33). The diagrammatic reference in these paintings comes not from architecture or cartography but from genealogy. Each painting contains the names of individuals connected by clusters of lines and organized into structures that suggest flow charts or family trees, as well as maps; one painting distributes names around the plan of a stadium. The names are mostly invented or taken from a Buenos Aires phone book, although occasionally the artist transposed existing genealogical charts, such as an elaborate English family tree that features Virginia Woolf and Julia Margaret Cameron among dozens of other names. There is something unsettling about these clusters of floating names, seemingly severed from all references, from any context. We expect a name to refer to a person, not to a point in space. And what does 'people on fire' actually mean? Souls burning in Hell? Self-immolating protestors? A metaphoric expression of passion? The artist has commented on how elements from the Maps and House Plans were carried over and transformed:

A strange thing happened, as if the series had gotten crossed. The architectural plan that before had been strictly related to the family unit appears, in *The*

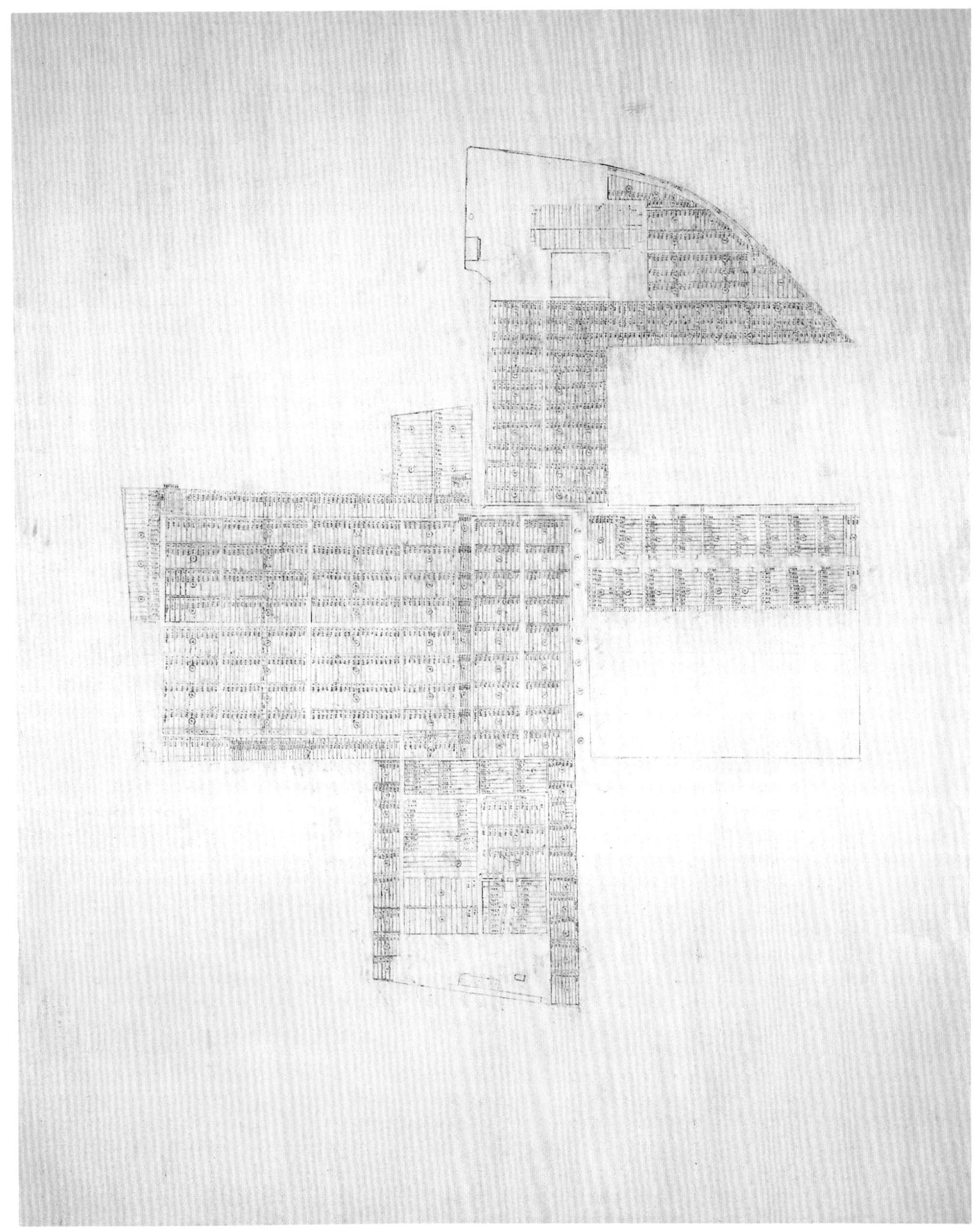

34. The Tablada Suite I   1991

Acrylic and graphite on canvas
239 × 190 cm (94 ⅛ × 74 ¾ in)
Milwaukee Art Museum

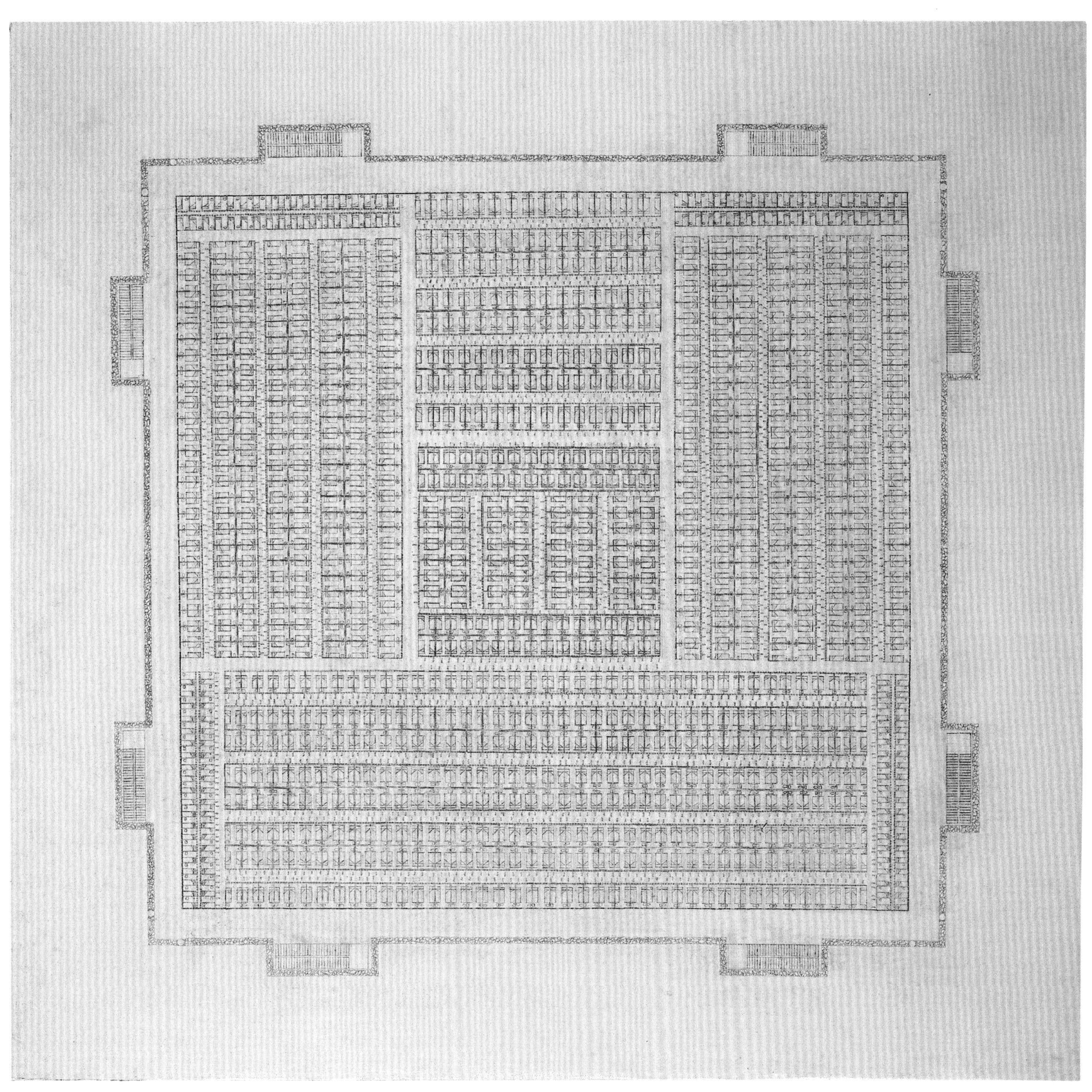

35. The Tablada Suite VI   1992

Acrylic and graphite on canvas
200 × 200 cm (78 ¾ × 78 ¾ in)
Albright Knox Art Gallery, Buffalo, New York

Tablada Suite, in the middle of a wider social context. In *People on Fire*, on the other hand, the map . . . becomes a kind of genealogical tree and that which had been connected to a wider social situation moves closer to a more familiar order. The floor plans opened up to a more institutional order and the maps folded into a more private version.'[41]

This all sounds very calculated, as if the artist had planned it, but, as nearly always with Kuitca, there was no plan, no conscious intention. As he recently remarked, 'My paintings never come from ideas, good or bad, but from intuition.'[42] Certainly, chance frequently plays a role in his work, as exemplified by how the Starship Enterprise made it into *The Tablada Suite*: 'I was trying to find something different for this Suite, and on a sidewalk in New York I stumbled upon an envelope lying there with the plans for the spaceship in the film *Star Trek*.'[43] The series that followed *The Tablada Suite* was also sparked by a chance encounter, again in a foreign city.

During a visit to London in 1993, as he was buying tickets for a play in Covent Garden, Kuitca noticed the seating chart for the theater. Unlike the seating charts he was familiar with, which showed the theater from above (he had used one such plan of Carnegie Hall in *The Tablada Suite*), this chart depicted the seats as seen from the stage, from an actor's point of view. In his mid-1980s paintings, Kuitca had depicted the stage from the point of view of the audience. What would happen, he wondered, if he made a 180-degree rotation? To facilitate this series he bought a copy of *The Complete Guide to London's West End Theaters*, which was illustrated with many such charts.

The resulting series of paintings feature the seats and balconies and boxes of London theaters presented in large schematic compositions flooded with color that seems to bleed out of its designated area (figs 36, 37 and 38). In a few paintings, Kuitca uses pixel-like shapes to spell out lines from famous plays, such as Lady Macbeth's plea, 'Come, thick night', in the seats. When he presented these mostly untitled paintings at Sperone Westwater Gallery in 1995, he titled the show *Puro Teatro*. Initially he had some doubts about the title because, as he later observed, 'in Spanish it's an expression that means something like "it's all lies". This idea doesn't interest me as much as that it's just theater.'[44]

Following the exuberant *Puro Teatro* paintings, Kuitca's palette turned subdued and somber for his next body of work, which includes the *Poema Pedagógico* paintings as well as related untitled canvases. Drawn almost exclusively with graphite on white grounds or with white pencils on black grounds, these paintings have a ghostly, fugitive quality, suggesting X-rays, MRI imagery or photograms (figs 39, 40, 41 and 42). They can also evoke ephemeral drawing a child might make with metal shavings and a magnet, or debris floating on water. They continue Kuitca's passion for architectural plans, but something unexpected has happened. In place of the carefully organized structures of *The Tablada Suite* we see irregular, jittery, fragmented shapes. On close examination it is evident that these donut-like ovals and shaky grids are composed of small geometric units, little separate strips of squares. It is as if the artist had disassembled the meticulous institutional plans of his earlier paintings and asked a small child to put them back together. In fact, the irregularity of these paintings is due to the fact that Kuitca made them while wearing a blindfold. Using small stencils to guide his hand, he found a way of turning modular geometric units into very unmodular, non-geometric shapes. Subsequently, he introduced more chromatic activity into this process, as in an untitled 1997 painting (fig.45) where the fragments are rendered in colored pencil against a dark ground.

When Kuitca donned a blindfold in his studio he was following an avant-garde tradition that includes Pinot Gallizio's (1902–64) epic abstraction *La Notte Cieca* (1962), American artist William Anastasi (b.1933), who began making drawings wearing a blindfold or with his eyes closed in 1963; and French artist Noël Dolla (b.1945), whose 'Chernobyl' paintings were made with one eye covered and one hand tied behind his back. For each of these artists, the constraint of their vision was a means to make a dramatically different kind of work from what they accomplished when fully sighted, yet it was also a way to discover what of theirs might persist under such conditions. If the viewer is unaware of Kuitca's preceding works, of the architectural origins of the modular stenciled units, the *Poema Pedagógico* paintings might seem like abstractions, a kind of Agnes Martin (1912–2014) on speed. The artist himself was well aware that he was straying into the zone of the abstract. 'It was a relief to think that I could be an abstract painter', he told Graciela Speranza. 'I tried to continue that work from the logic of an abstract painter, but I felt trapped, because I gradually became aware that there was very little that I could do before a figurative effect would pop up. I ended up exhausted.'[45]

Following this near brush with abstraction, Kuitca took off his blindfold and renewed his engagement with the built world, yet the coherence and stability that had characterized his early 1990s work was not to be regained. As he remarked later to Speranza, 'after *The Tablada Suite* the plans began to come apart'. This dissolution is clearly visible in the *Neufert Suite*, a series Kuitca worked on in 1998 and 1999. Inspired by Ernst Neufert's classic 1970 reference book *Architects' Data*, commonly referred to as 'The Neufert', these paintings deploy details from mostly unidentified architectural plans. An unfinished quality pervades the paintings, with parts of some plans left inexplicably empty and carefully drawn designs that abruptly stop in the middle of a row of rooms.

Although pencil lines are evident in some of the works, they rely mostly on oil paint. After the austerity of *The Tablada Suite* with its graphite lines and smooth varnished surfaces, and the drawing-based works that followed it, the Neufert paintings mark a return to a more painterly mode. In some paintings, patches of color – yellow, orange, green – appear, as if the artist had started to color in a plan but was interrupted before he could finish. In others, Kuitca manipulates value to give the illusion of three-dimensionality to conglomerations of schematic designs. In one untitled almost 190 cm² (29 ½ in²) painting from 1998, it looks as if the artist has fused together fragments of a dozen different building plans to create a dense composition that suggests aerial views of a decayed labyrinth or a shantytown (fig.46). It could also depict some eccentric piece of outsider architecture where the owner just kept adding room after room to the point of madness.

When the first of these works were shown at Sperone Westwater in 1998, Kuitca contributed a brief preface to the accompanying catalogue in which he noted the inevitable divergence at the heart of the series: 'I was always fascinated by the Neufert, that architectural catalogue where the world is completely organized, measured, calculated. Taken to painting, any project with that cataloguing spirit becomes totally absurd. Painting produces an enormous referential arbitrariness, while architecture does just the opposite.'[46]

Defining painting as absurd and arbitrary in comparison with architecture, Kuitca situates his work in opposition to the utopian, rationalist strain in modernist painting, from the Bauhaus and De Stijl to postwar Concrete art movements in Europe and South America. It is no accident that Ernst Neufert himself was a product of the Bauhaus. What distinguishes Kuitca's implicit critique of modernist idealism from previous challenges to the idea that art can be successfully harnessed to utopian projects is that rather than offering a counter model (in the manner of, say, gestural abstraction) he discovers the irrational *within* the rational. In striking ways, Kuitca's subversion of Neufert's orderly world resembles the architectural interventions of Gordon Matta-Clark (1943–78) – they are the painterly equivalent of tunneling through a disused apartment building or slicing into a suburban family home, what Matta-Clark called 'anarchitecture'.

Kuitca was not the only artist in the mid-1990s to evoke the unconscious of institutional architecture. In 1995, Mike Kelley (b.1954) presented *Towards a Utopian Arts Complex* at Metro Pictures in New York, an exhibition centered on *Educational Complex*, a large tabletop model of all the schools Kelley had attended in his life, from a Detroit elementary school to a university art school, with some spaces left deliberately empty. Informed by a controversial psychological condition called Repressed Memory Syndrome in which victims were supposedly able to recover the memories of traumatic events with the help of psychologists, Kelley pretended to explain the 'perversity' of his own artistic practice through 'repressed' aspects of his educational experiences. But within this satirical response to a pop psychology phenomenon, Kelley had a larger point to make. As he later explained: 'In utopian projects, moral and aesthetic dimensions are presented, often openly and dramatically, as mirrors of each other. Of course, my project is a perversion of such an attitude: I present an obviously dystopian architecture, reflecting our true, chaotic social conditions, rather than some idealized dream of wholeness.'[47]

Throughout the 1990s, Kuitca's deconstructive treatment of architecture via painting was part of a prolonged assault by artists, philosophers (and a few architects) on what they viewed as the unexamined ideologies of modernist architecture. Just as Foucault had

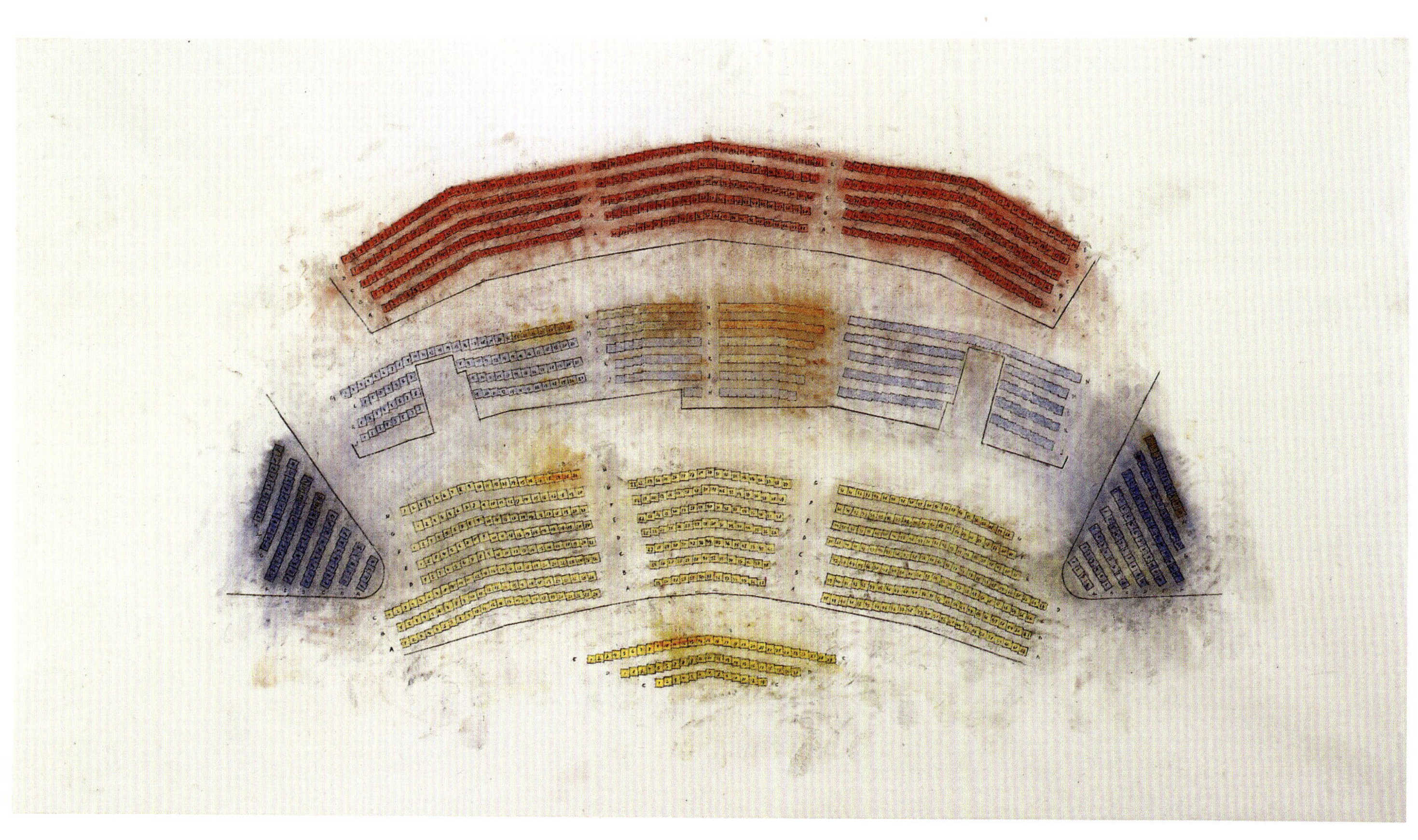

36. Untitled (Puro Teatro)　1995

Mixed media on canvas
190.5 × 144 cm (75 × 56 $^{11}/_{16}$ in)
Private collection, New York

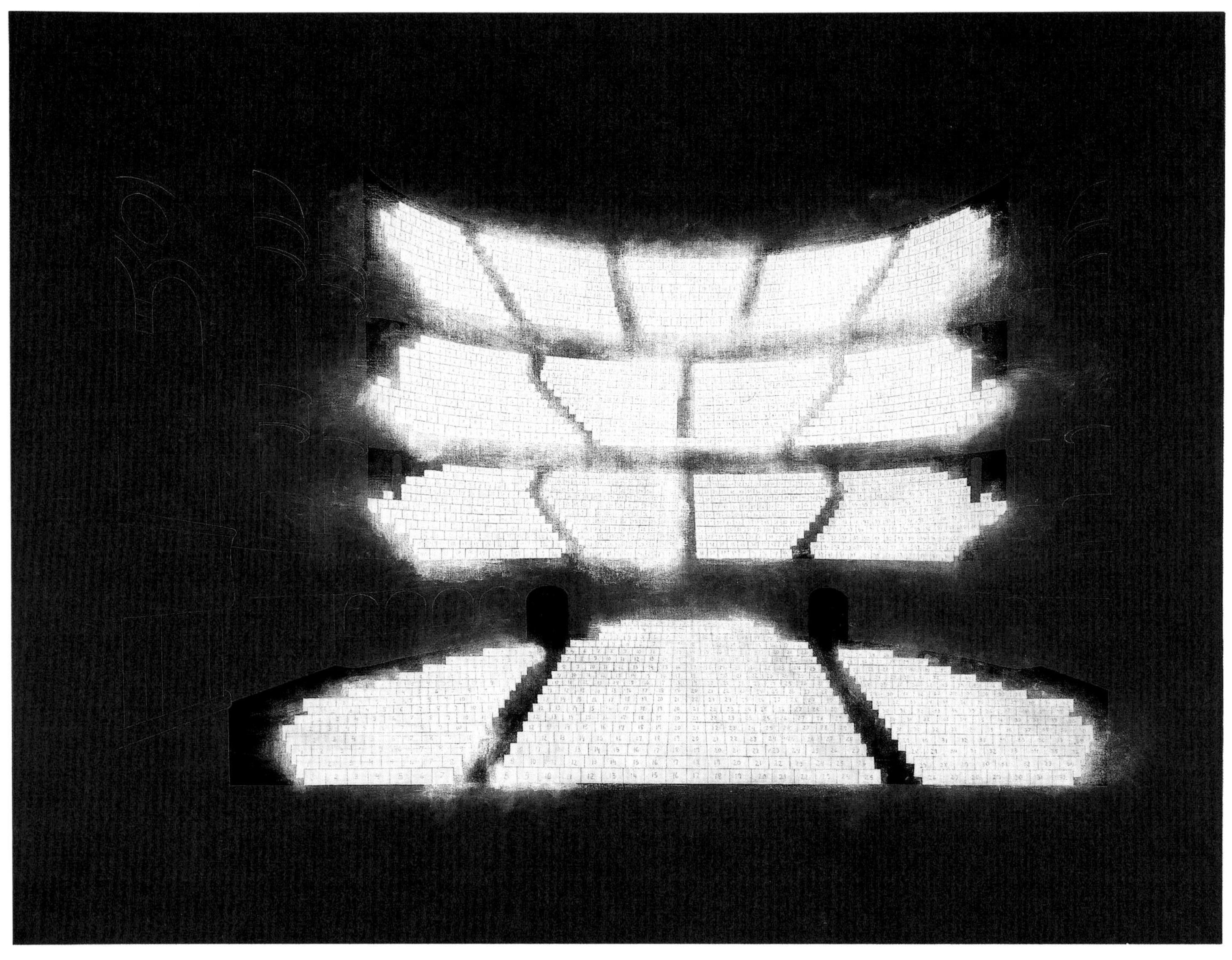

37. Untitled   1995

Chalk and acrylic on canvas
108.3 × 233.7 cm (71 × 92 in)
The Art Institute of Chicago

64

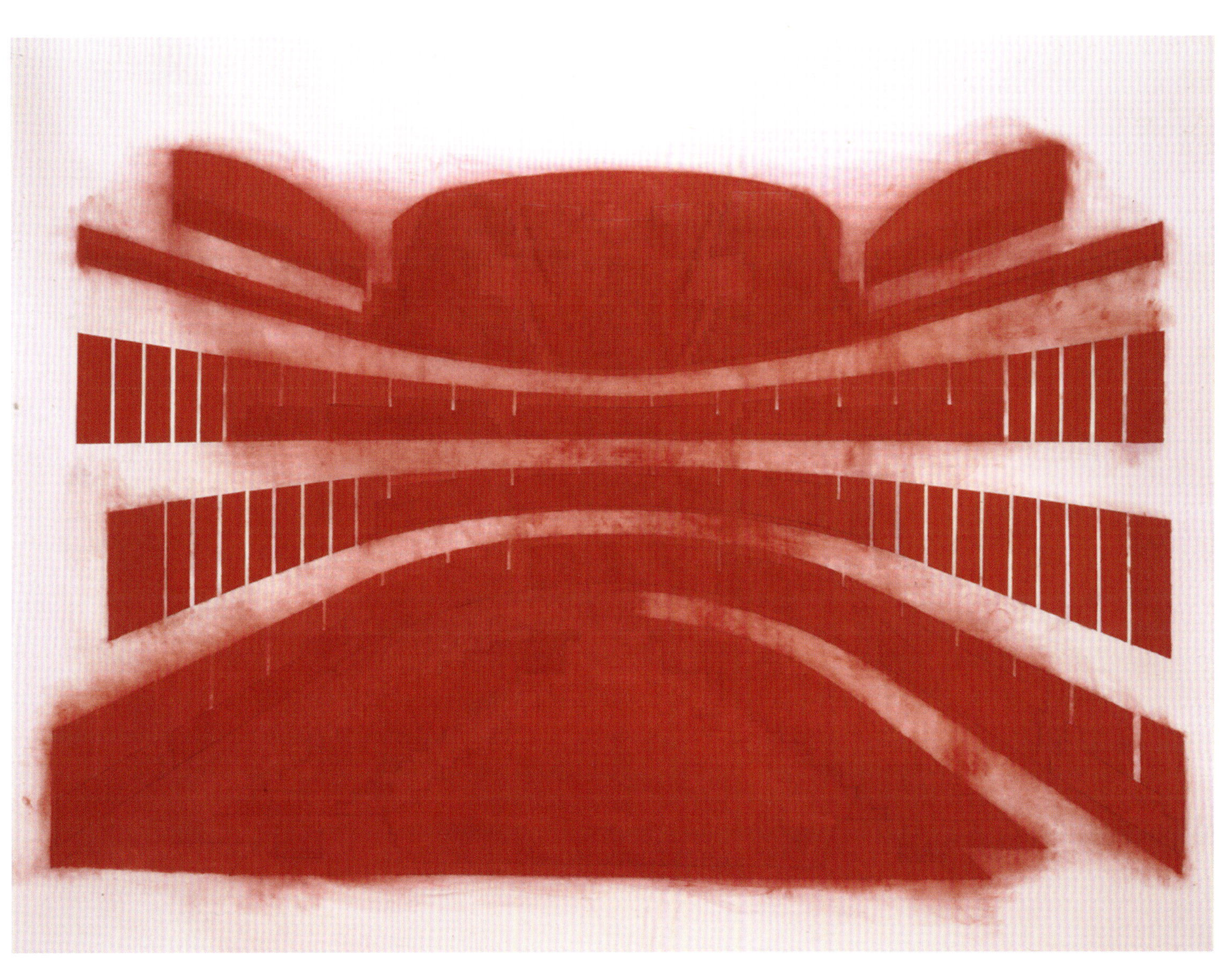

38. Mozart da Ponte I   1995

Mixed media on canvas
108.3 × 233.8 cm (71 × 92 ⅛ in)
Hirshhorn Museum and Sculpture Garden, Washington D.C.

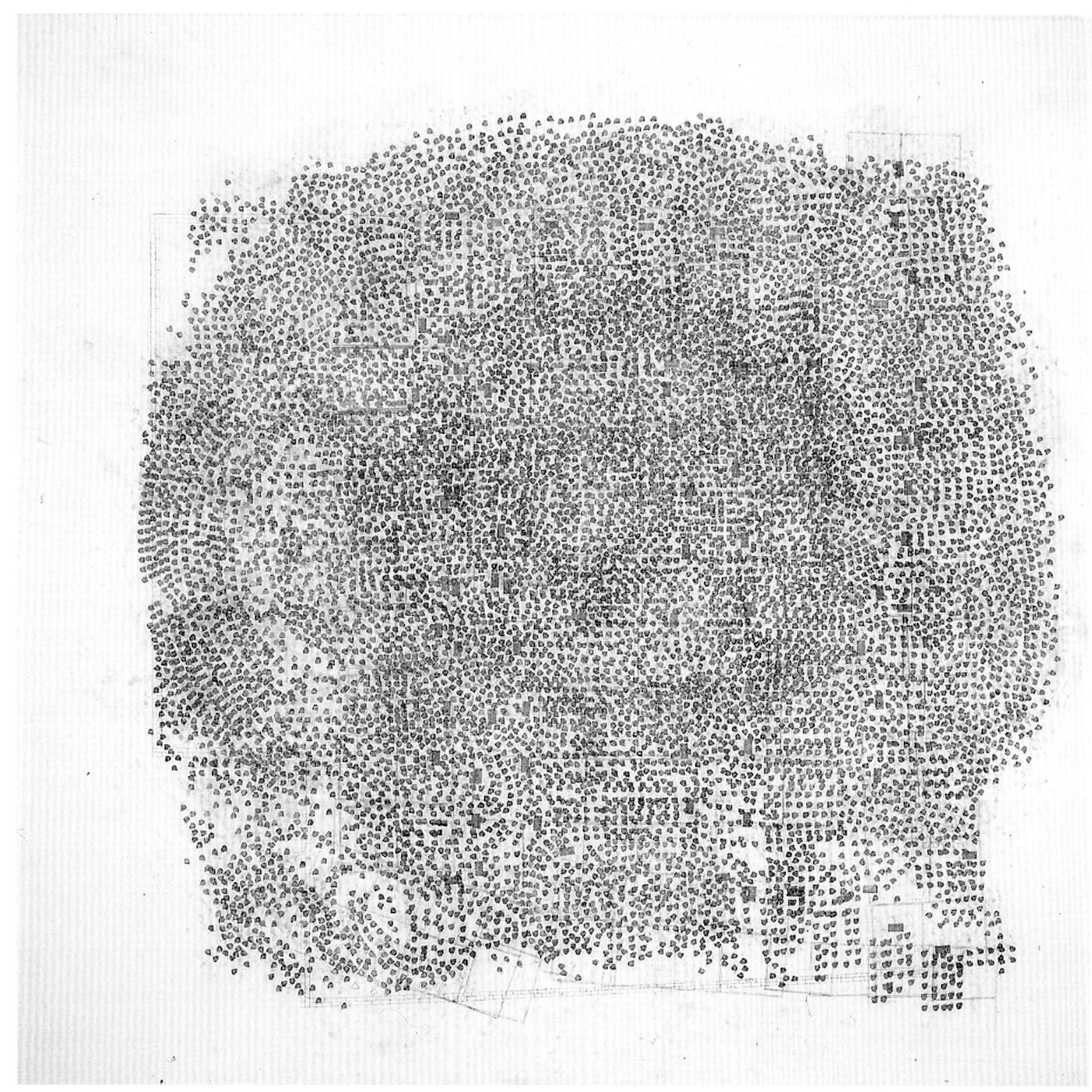

39. Poema Pedagógico II   1996

Acrylic and graphite on canvas
188 × 190.5 cm (74 × 75 in)
Collection Patricia Phelps de Cisneros

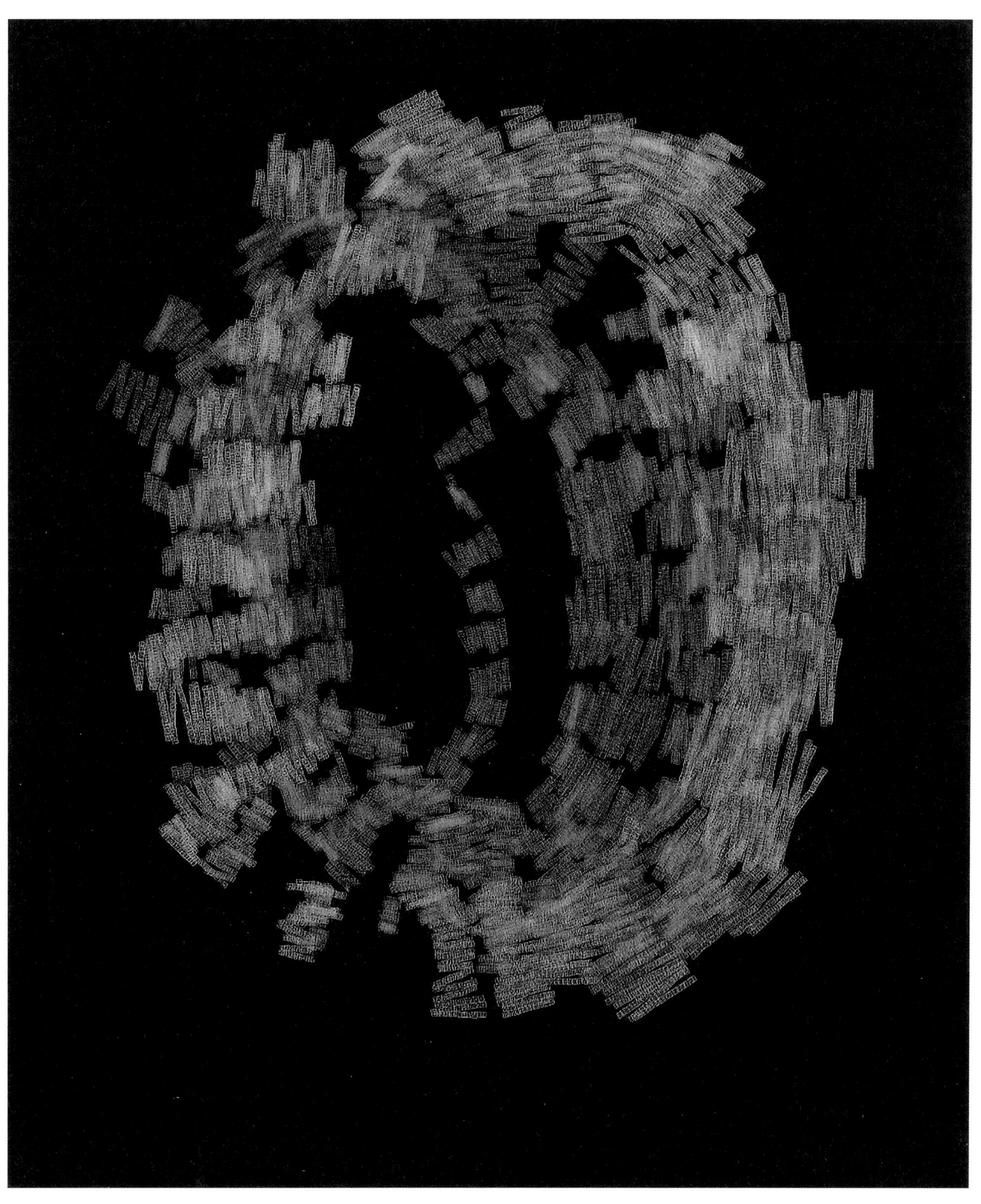

40. Untitled   1996

Acrylic and graphite on canvas
231.1 x 190.5 cm (91 x 75 in)
Private collection, New York

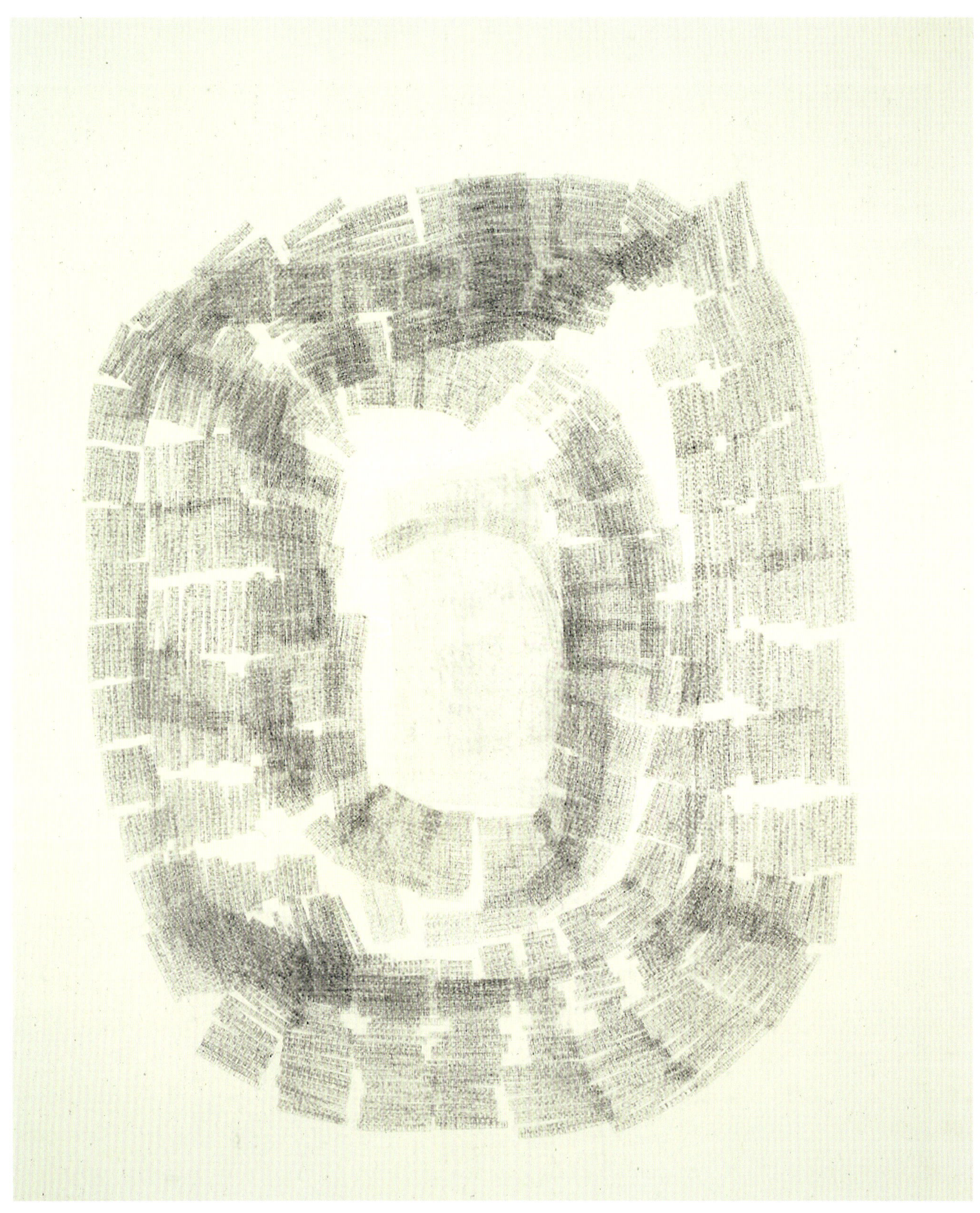

41. Untitled   1996

Acrylic and graphite on canvas
233 × 190 cm (91 ¾ × 74 ¹³⁄₁₆ in)
Pizzuti Collection of Columbus Museum of Art, Ohio

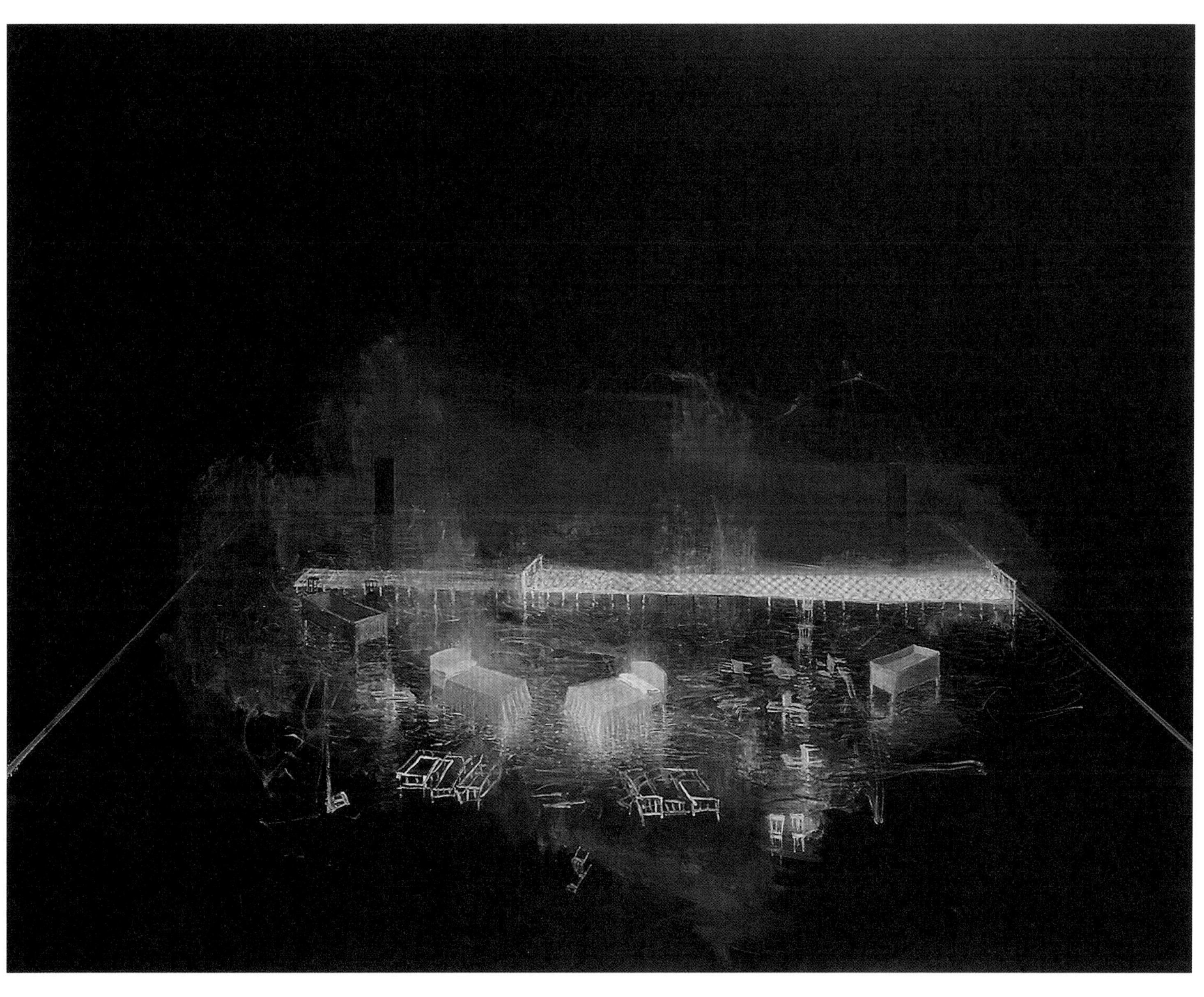

42. Untitled   1996

Oil and acrylic on canvas
190.5 × 233.7 cm (75 × 92 in)
Collection of Marco Brignone, Turin

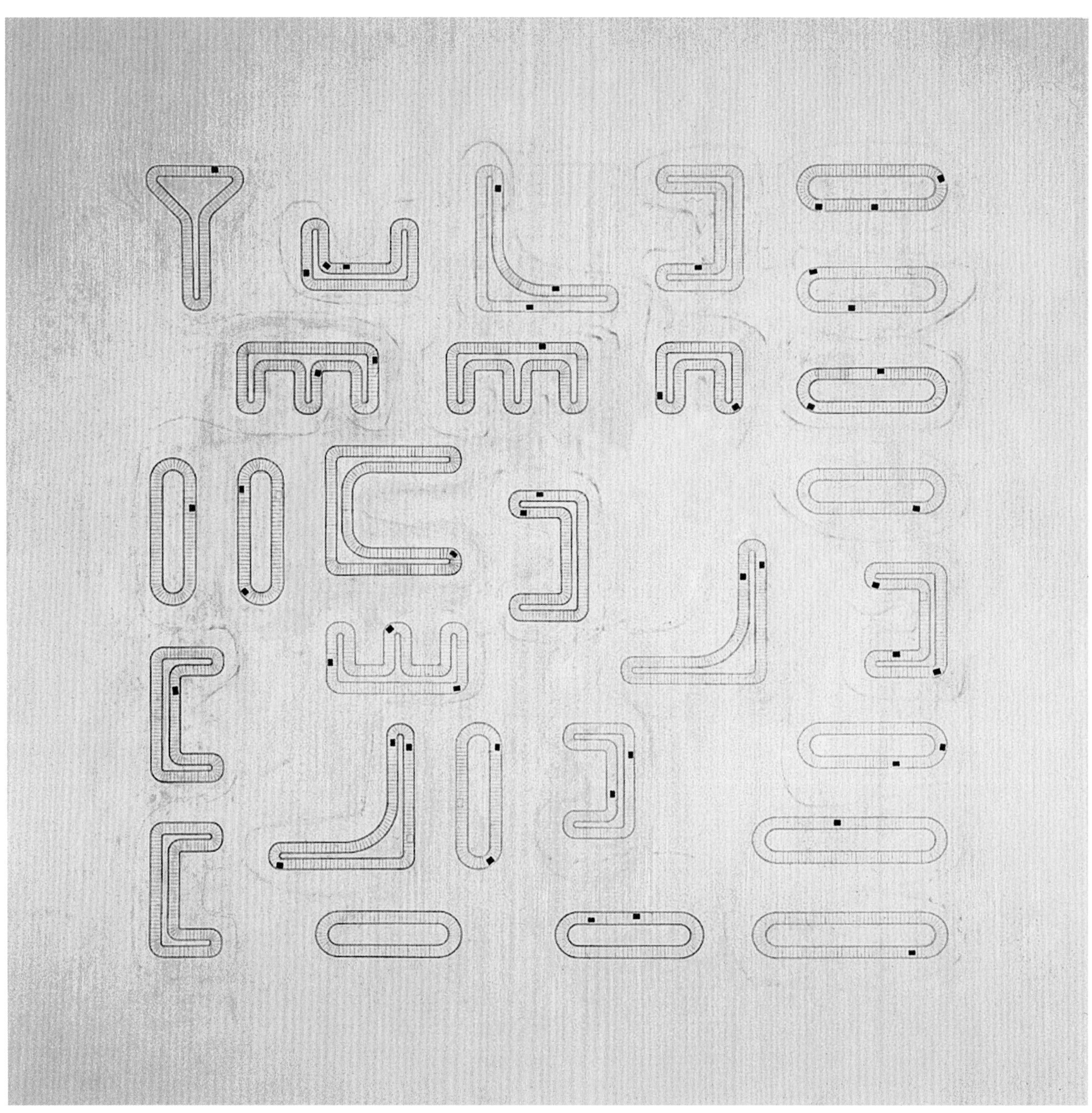

43. Untitled   1998

Oil and pencil on canvas
204.5 x 200.7 cm (80 ½ x 79 in)
Collection of Janet and Peter Boris, New York

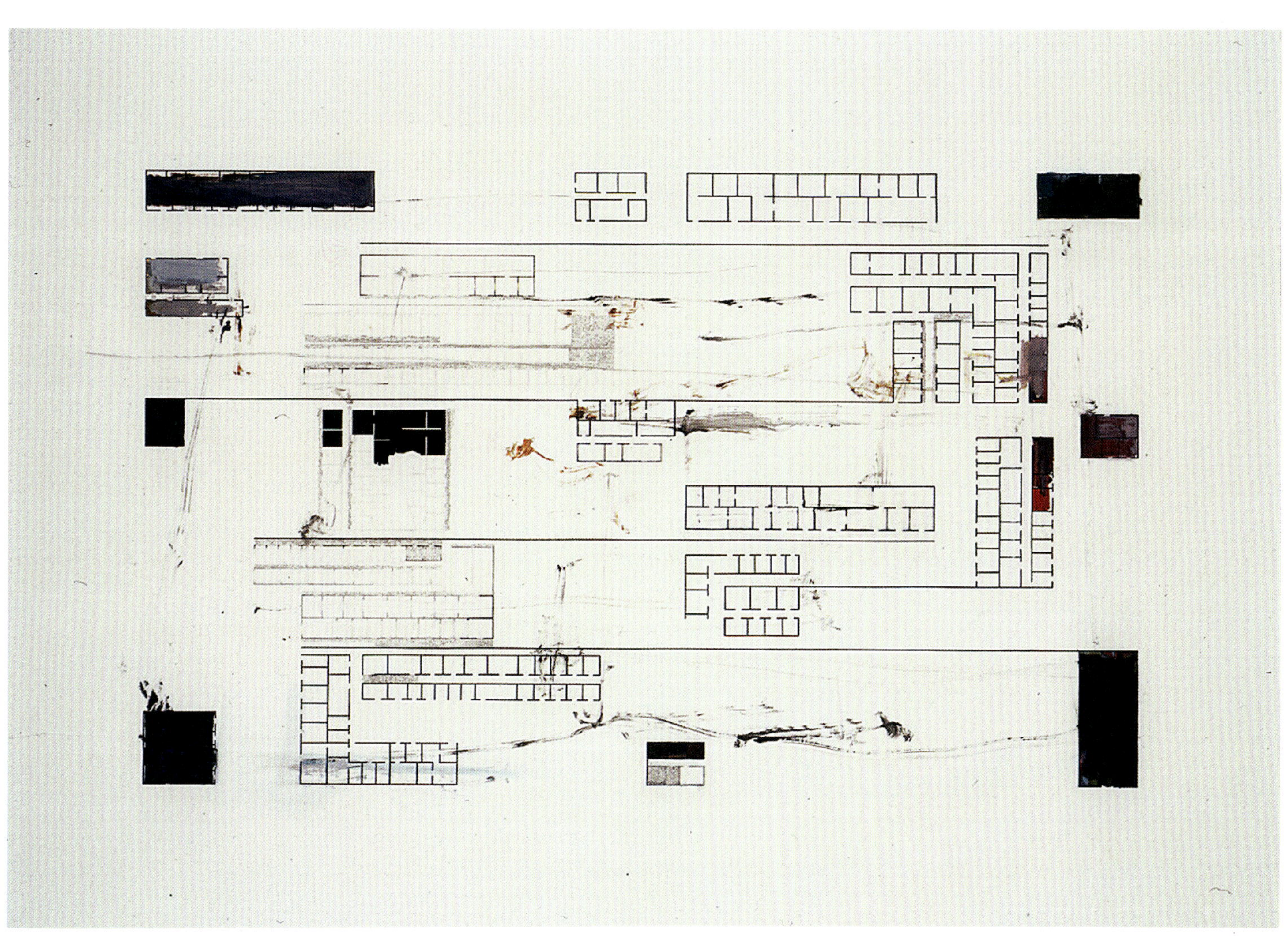

44. Untitled   1998

Oil on canvas
200.7 × 284.5 cm (79 × 112 in)
Mary Lile Collection, Houston, Texas

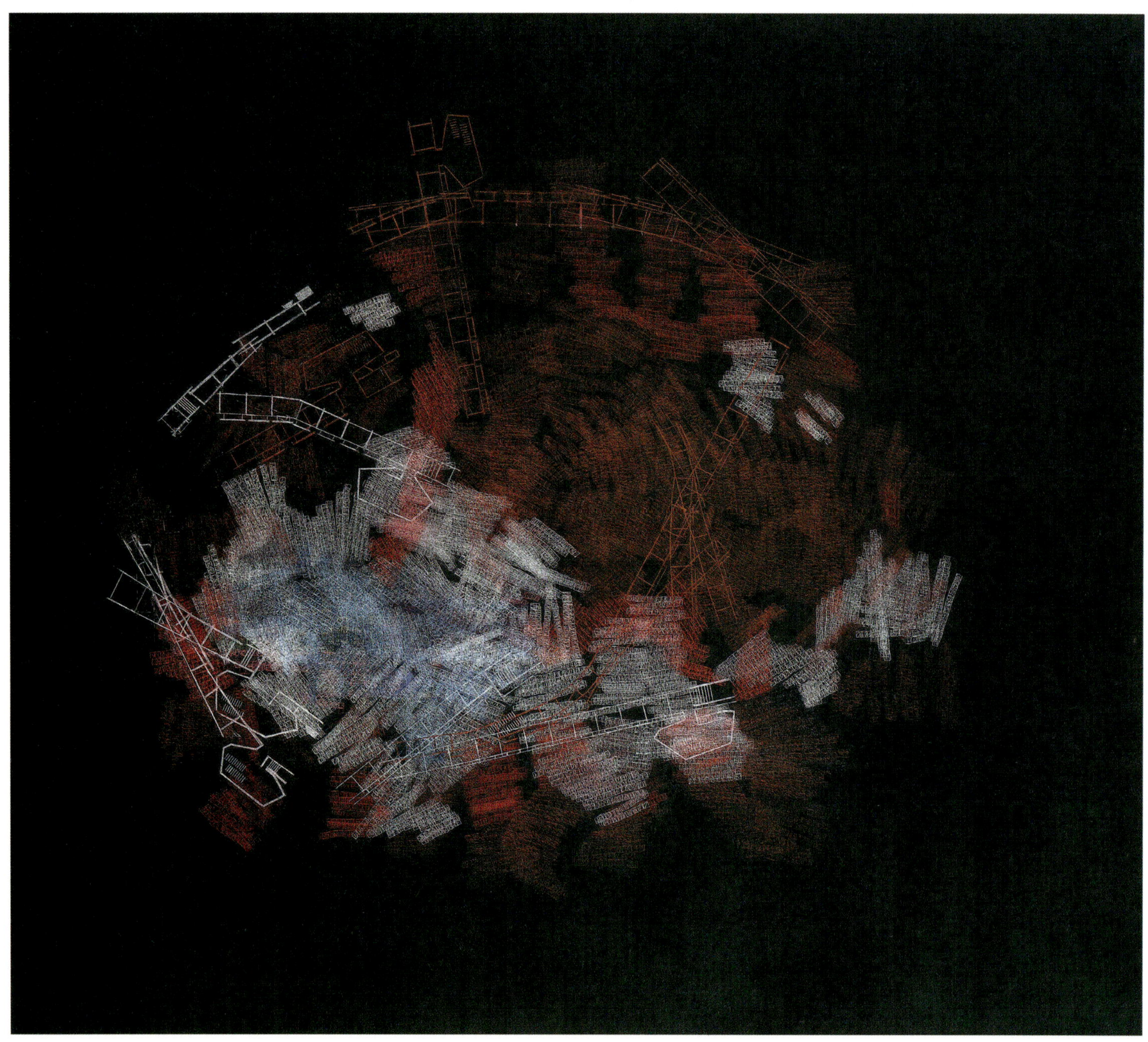

45. Untitled   1997

Oil and colored pencil on canvas
190.5 × 210.8 cm (75 × 83 in)
Collection of Leonard and Nancy Amoroso, Wynnewood,
Pennsylvania

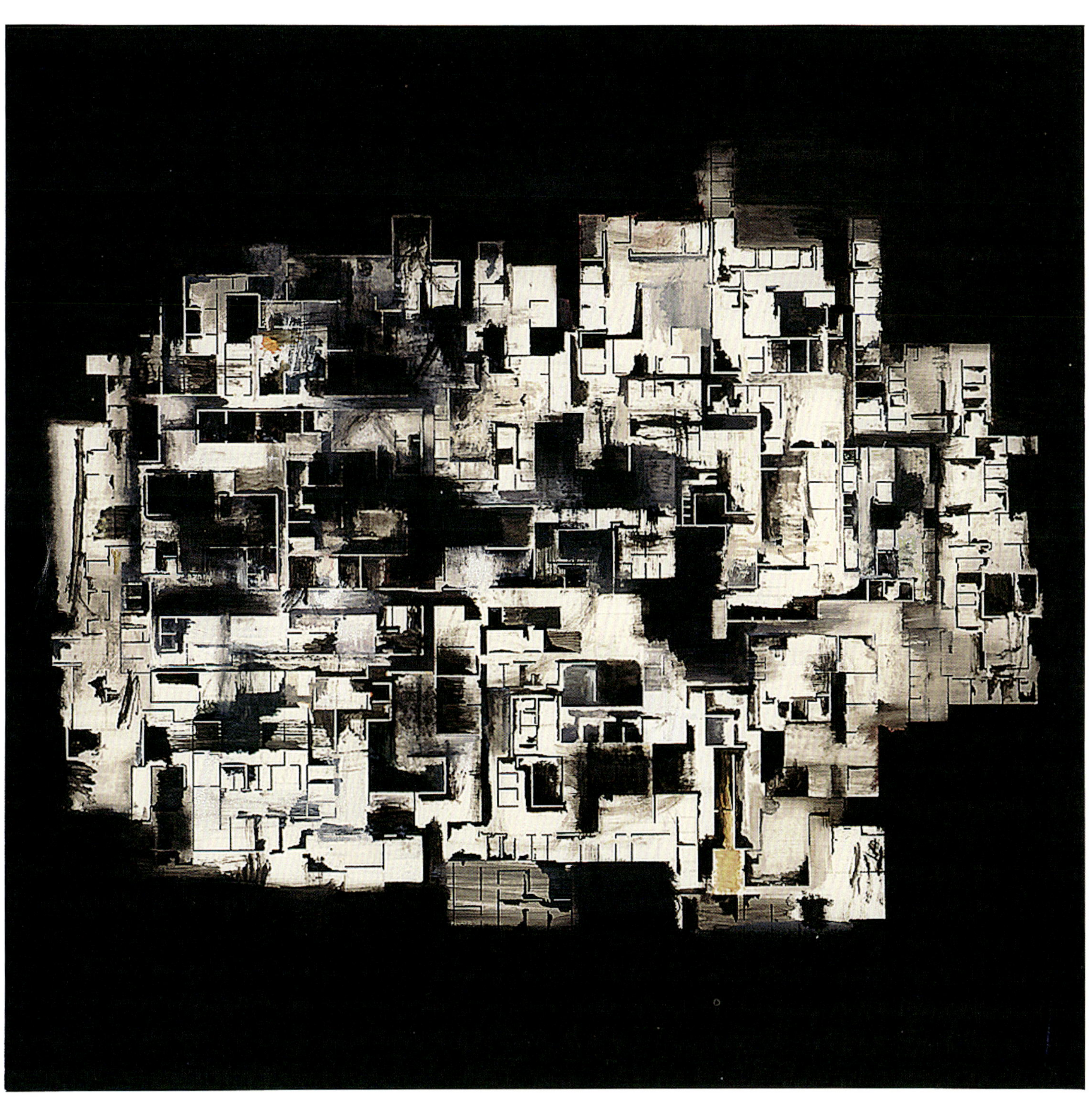

46. Untitled   1998

Oil on linen
188 × 190.5 cm (74 × 75 in)
Collection of Adriana Cisneros de Griffin

linked certain types of institutions and the buildings that housed them to the exercise of power, so does Kuitca invite his viewers to contemplate how our understanding of the world and our actions within it are guided by the architecture that surrounds us.

In a 1994 correspondence with Lynne Cooke, Kuitca discussed how Foucault's ideas regarding the panopticon informed his own work, which, as he says, implies 'a gaze that sees all'. In many of his paintings, Kuitca writes to Cooke, he constructs 'a panoptic viewer even without using a panoptic plan. The same thing happens in the stage paintings and in the house plans. Everything is exposed to the viewer's eyes.'[48]

Foucault believed that the period he was living in would be 'above all the epoch of space'. For him this space was heterogeneous, made up of relationships between different kinds of spaces, which he called 'heterotopias'. Among the examples he offers of heterotopias are several that figure in Kuitca's paintings: the cemetery, which is 'connected with all the sites of the city, state or society or village'; and the theater, which 'brings onto the rectangle of the stage, one after the other, a whole series of places that are foreign to one another'. (It is striking to note how often Kuitca has taken up architectural forms, including the prison and the hospital, that figure in Foucault's writings.) Foucault believed that heterotopias performed two kinds of roles, either 'to create a space of illusion that exposes every real space, all the sites inside of which human life is partitioned, as still more illusory. . . . Or else, on the contrary, their role is to create a space that is other, another real space, as perfect, as meticulous, as well arranged as ours is messy, ill constructed, and jumbled.'[49] In other words, we need to understand how spaces mirror one another, how they compensate for certain lacks, how they are interdependent.

At the same time that he was contributing to this international, interdisciplinary discourse on architecture, Kuitca was, like any other artist, like any other individual, also experiencing architectural space in a specific place, in a specific period. Not to acknowledge the artist's national and local reality would be to perpetuate a suspect universality, just as to focus only on those specifics would be to perpetuate an equally problematic marginalization.

As an inhabitant of Buenos Aires in the 1990s, Kuitca was exposed to a particularly horrific event. On 18 July 1994, a truck bomb exploded in front of the Asociación Mutual Israelita Argentina (AMIA), the community center for Buenos Aires's large Jewish population. Totally collapsing the five-story building, the explosion killed 85 people and wounded some 300 others. Coming just over two years after the 1992 bombing of the Israeli Embassy, which killed 29 people and left over 200 wounded, the AMIA bombing was a traumatic event for many Porteños, especially the city's Jews. It may be no more than a coincidence that the architectural plans in Kuitca's paintings began to 'come apart' after *The Tablada Suite*, that is, in the years immediately following these bombings, but it is a coincidence that, once you become aware of this, affects how you look at the work. Although he was raised in a non-observant family, Kuitca was, like anyone from a Jewish family in Buenos Aires, very much aware of

47. Afghanistan   1990

Mixed media on canvas
170 × 300 × 12 cm (67 × 118 × 4 ¾ in)
Daros Latinamerica Collection, Zurich

the AMIA headquarters. In fact, it was crucial to the initiation of *The Tablada Suite*. As he recalled in a 1997 commentary on his drawings, 'When I saw the big plan [of Buenos Aires's Jewish cemetery], I thought it could be a piece of mine. Later, I got a copy of it at AMIA.'[50] Although the artist has never commented publicly about the AMIA bombing, on hearing the news he surely must have reflected on the connection between *The Tablada Suite* and the destroyed, corpse-filled building where he had gone to get a copy of the cemetery plan that began the series.[51]

It is one of the challenges of Kuitca's work, and also one of its many pleasures, that he rarely declares the content of his work to us, his viewers. This reticence allows us to dwell on his paintings without any quick and easy resolution. A painting that was explicitly about the AIMA bombing – and no doubt such works exist, though not by Kuitca – might confront us more immediately with the violence of the event, but it might not have the open-ended quality, the freedom viewers have to decide for themselves what the painting is about, that is so abundant in Kuitca's work. The artist's preference, except on rare occasions, of any declared content also reminds us that works of art are always overdetermined, they always have more than one cause.

History often seems to catch up with Kuitca's work as events change the meaning of certain paintings. The artist is keenly aware of this phenomenon. In 1990 he painted a topographical map of Afghanistan, a country that 11 years later, after the 9/11 attacks and the U.S. invasion, would take on a different significance (fig.47). Painted onto a shiny plastic material like the kind used for upholstering cheap furniture and punctuated, like the Bed Paintings, with upholstery buttons, this painting is unusual in its geographical explicitness: letters spelling out 'Afghanistan' spread across the painting (Kuitca generally left out such identifying features). The events of 11 September also had an effect on a pair of paintings he made of airport baggage conveyor belts: *Terminal* (2000) and *Trauerspiel* (fig.48).

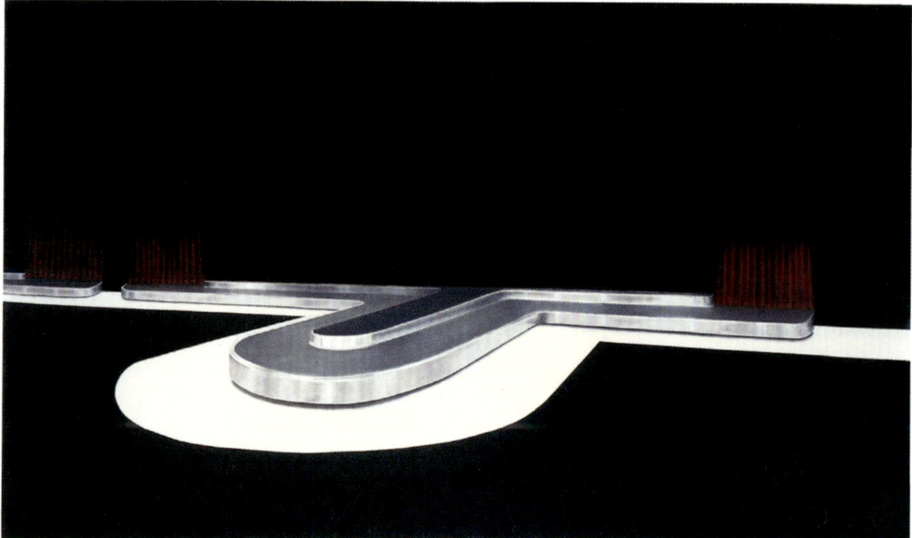

48. Trauerspiel   2000

Oil on canvas
195.6 × 324.5 cm (77 × 127 ¾ in)
Museo Nacional Centro de Arte Reina Sofía, Madrid

As the artist explained to Lynne Cooke, the Conveyor Belt Paintings grew out of the *Neufert Suite* series of paintings in which diagrams of functional objects (rendered with white paint) are removed from their original context and distributed around a monochrome blue field. In one painting, workout machines have been removed from the diagram of a gym; in another, a peep-show booth and video cubicles have been taken from the plan of an adult video store (fig.49, probably not from Neufert, which does not acknowledge the existence of things like porn shops). The series also includes gaming tables from a casino and altars, a confessional booth and prayer benches from a church. (A related series, the *Nocturnes*, features similar motifs, but painted in black on dark blue fields, figs 50 and 51.) One of the paintings depicts conveyor belts from a baggage claim area in an airport. It was this motif that Kuitca decided to render in a quasi-realist style.

In both *Terminal* and *Trauerspiel*, a curving belt reaches out toward the viewer from a dark background. In *Terminal* the effect is more dramatic thanks to extreme foreshortening and a white floor surrounding the peninsular carousel. The dark background is punctuated by a small white square from which luggage might emerge. In *Trauerspiel*, the title of which references Walter Benjamin's book on Baroque German drama, *Ursprung des deutschen Trauerspiels (The Origin of German Tragic Drama)*, the curved part of the belt is not as long, and it is flanked by two openings that are covered not with the expected rubber flaps but with red theater curtains.

Terminal and *Trauerspiel* may be the most extreme departures in Kuitca's entire oeuvre. Although he has over the years shifted between diagrammatic and figurative imagery, between flat representations and illusionistic pictures, there is nothing else in his work that approaches the realist style of the Conveyor Belt Paintings. Kuitca explains to Cooke that *Terminal* began with the idea to change the scale of his painting

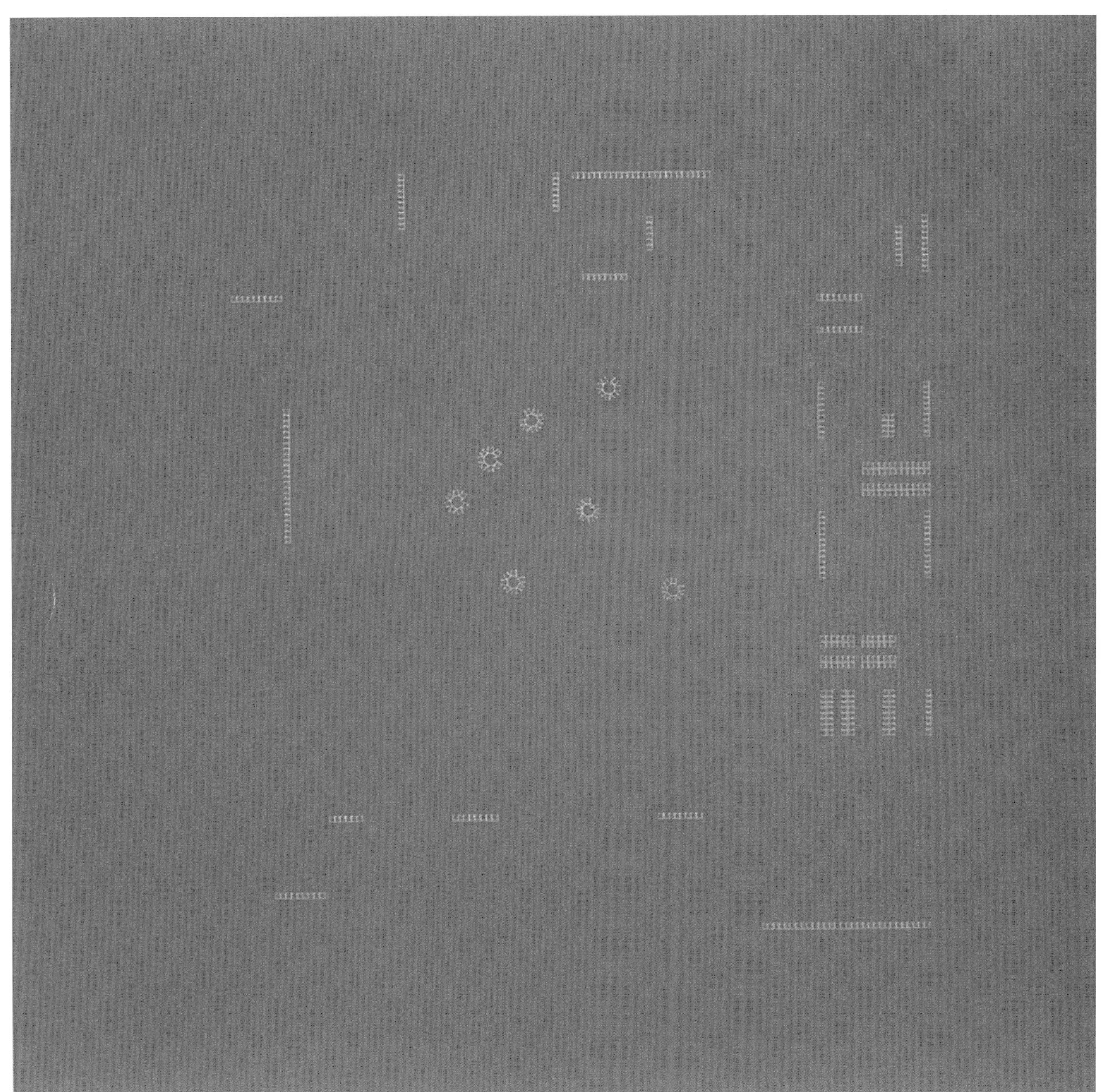

49. Neufert Suite (Peep Show and Video Booths)   1999

Oil and colored pencil on linen
195.6 × 195.6 cm (77 × 77 in)
Foundation Cartier pour l'art contemporain, Paris

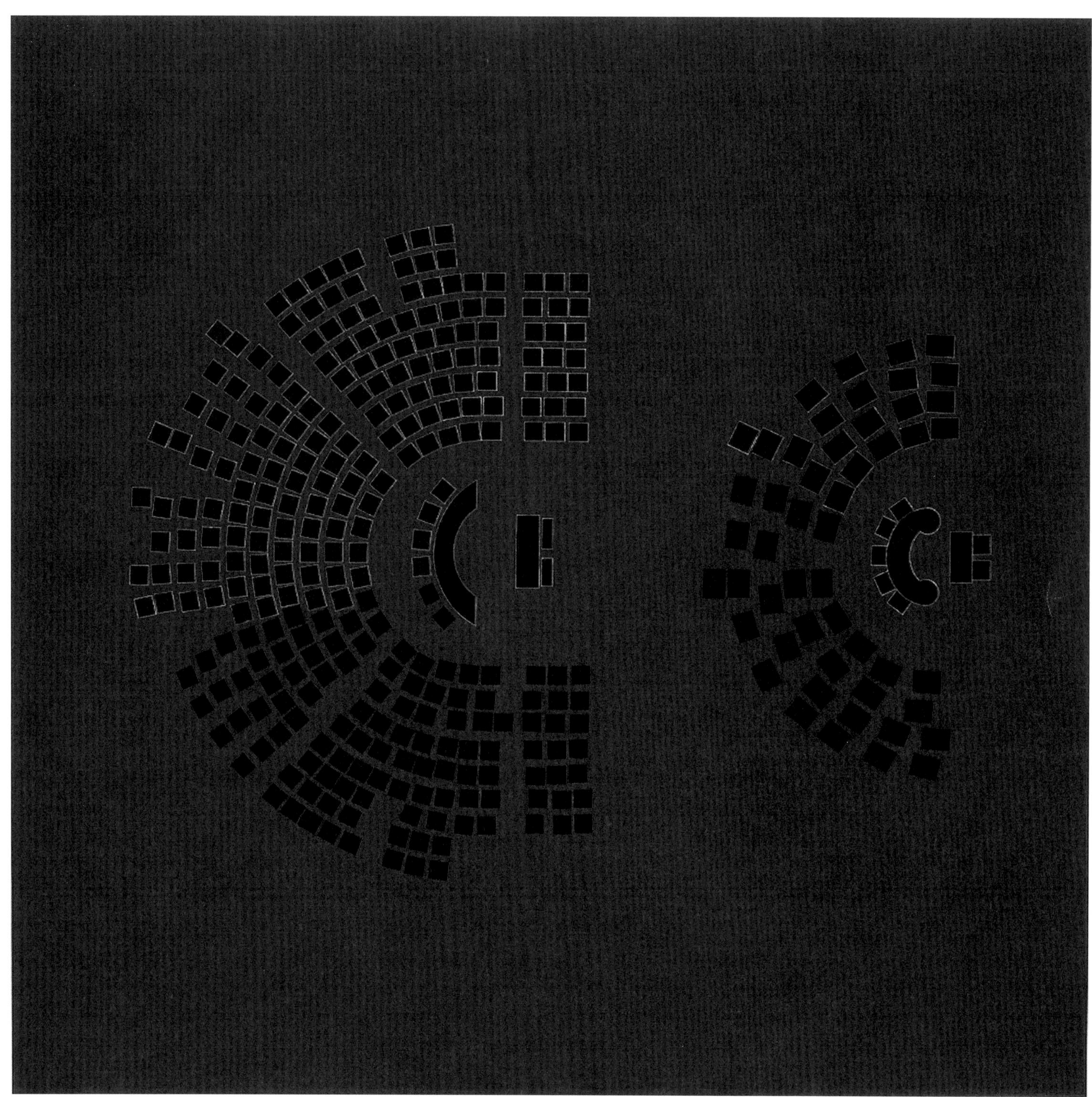

50. Nocturnes (Congressional Seats)   1999–2002

Oil and colored pencil on linen
196.6 × 195.6 cm (77.4 × 77 in)
Collection of the artist

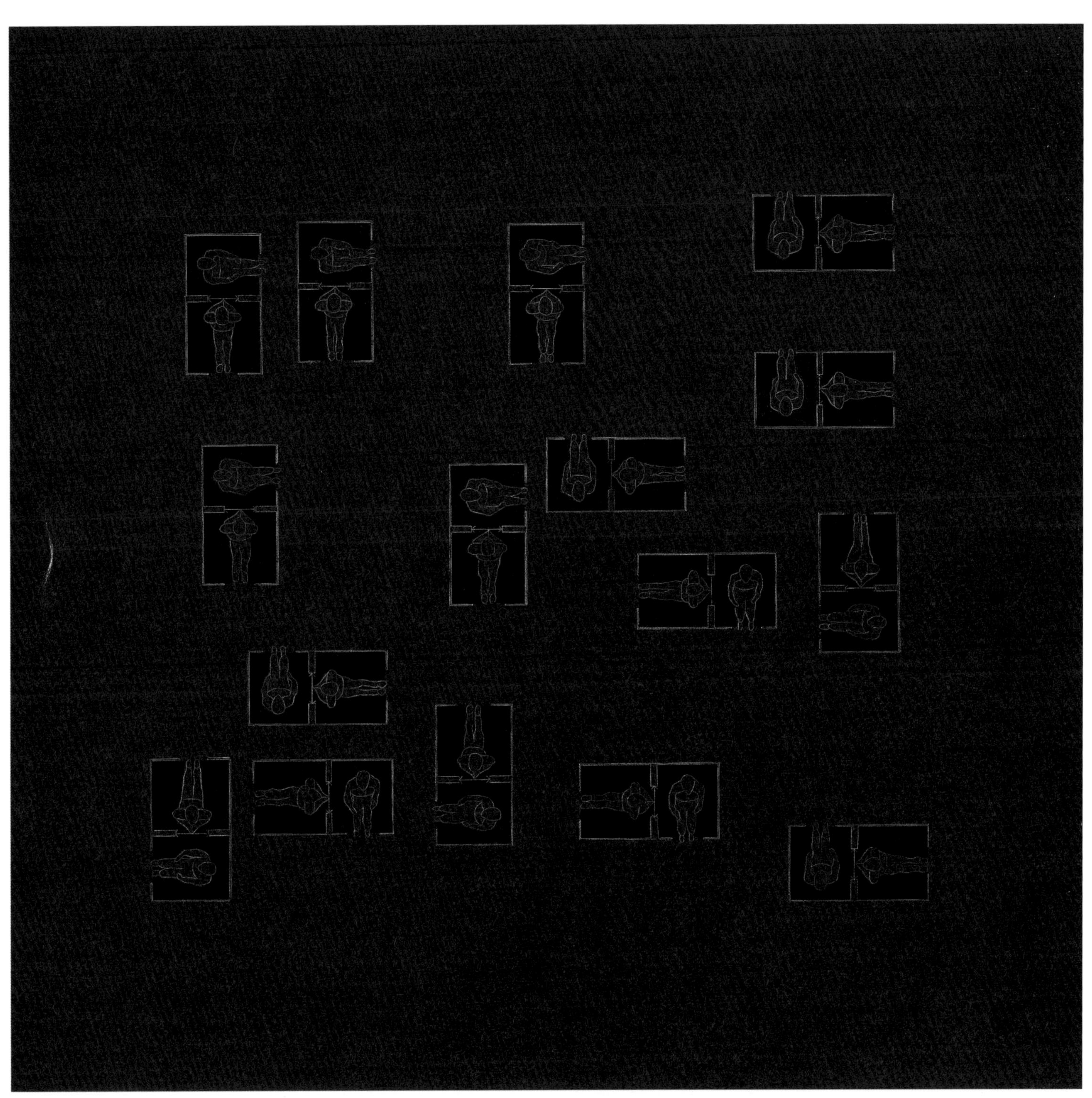

51. Nocturnes (Confessional Booths)   2002

Oil and colored pencil on linen
195.6 × 194.3 cm (76 ¾ × 76 ¼ in)
The Ella Fontanals-Cisneros Collection, Miami

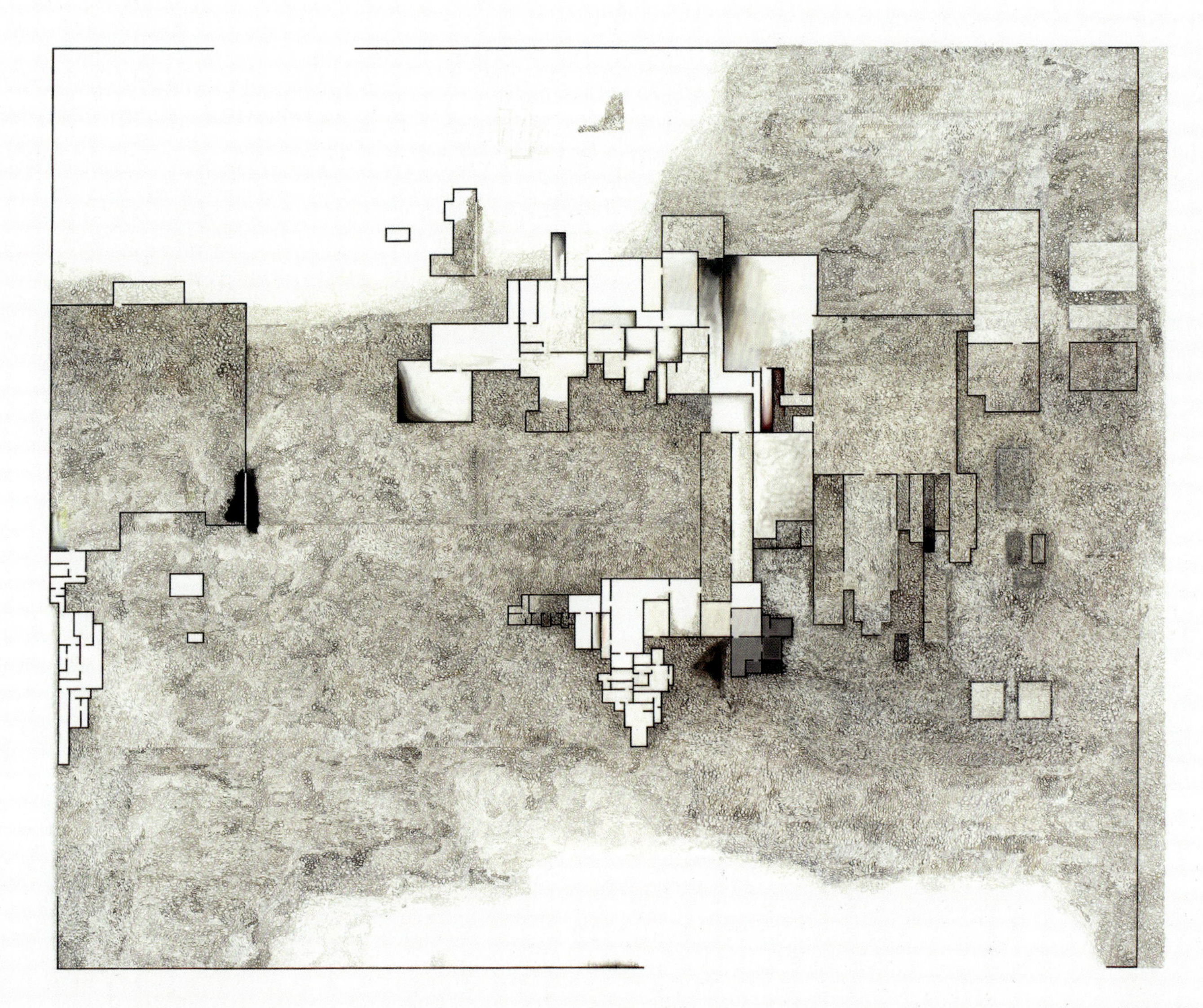

52. Global Order   2001

Acrylic and oil on canvas
200 × 232 cm (78 ¾ × 91 ⁵⁄₁₆ in)
Daros Latinamerica Collection, Zurich

rather than its style. The painting is, however, less consistent than it first appears. While the metal elements are painted with the illusion of light and volume all the other parts (floor, back wall) have been painted flatly.

Kuitca's solo exhibition, which included *Terminal* and *Trauerspiel*, opened on 15 September 2001 at Hauser & Wirth in Zurich. In the immediate aftermath of the September 11 attacks, air travel suddenly went from being a fairly routine experience marred only by occasional anxiety to an ordeal rife with fear and a keen awareness of the world as a dangerous place. It can be difficult now, nearly 20 years on, when those 'security measures currently in place' (as the recorded announcements in U.S. airports continually remind travelers) have long-since become permanent, to recall the shock of that abrupt transition. The baggage carousel that Kuitca had appropriated as some kind of existential metaphor became, especially in the moment when it was first shown just days after 9/11, a memento mori (for the victims whose luggage would never arrive) and a warning (that terror lurks behind the mundane scenes of everyday life). This dramatic annexation of art by reality may be the reason why Kuitca immediately left this mode of painting behind, never to return to it. *Terminal* and *Trauerspiel* remain anomalies in his work.

Another body of work from the period, *Global Order* (fig.52), explicitly addresses geopolitics. Created intermittently over a period of four years (1999–2002), these paintings initially look like a return to the House Plan Paintings that Kuitca had laid aside at the beginning of the 1990s. The first difference one notices is that instead of focusing on the one-bedroom apartment, the *Global Order* paintings feature multiple apartment plans that have been joined together to create floating groups. These conglomerations of structures seem arbitrary or formalist (like a Mondrian that has been broken up and reassembled in a haphazard manner) until one further ponders the title. In a flash, the premise of the series becomes clear: seen as an ensemble the joined-together architectural plans resemble the shapes and positions of various continents, which means that these works are really an extension of the Map Paintings, not the House Plans, or, perhaps, a hybrid of the two. As so often with Kuitca, the boundaries between different bodies of work are porous.

Within the geographical premise that runs through the *Global Order* series there is a striking variety of visual approaches. In one painting the spaces between the architectonic landmasses are filled with thousands of densely packed oval shapes as if the world's oceans were a pebbly beach or a field of bubbles. In another stark black-lines-on-white-ground example, the stiff plans look like they were rendered with an Etch A Sketch. Other works take a more painterly approach. One of the reasons it requires time to see these paintings as maps is that the relative scale of individual countries does not correspond to standard cartography. Instead, the artist relied on a variety of statistical maps to determine the size of the nation-plans. As he told Graciela Speranza in 2007, 'At the beginning I used statistical maps that dealt with big issues like hunger, population density, income per capita, abortions, and so forth, but afterwards, I used other maps with much more peculiar statistics, like the number of beauty queens per country or of plastic surgeons.'[52] In the same interview, Kuitca explained how around the time of the *Global Order* paintings he 'felt more relaxed about political readings' of his work. 'Some misunderstandings were very firmly established and I didn't feel any need to clear them up', he added, alluding, presumably, to how some of his earlier paintings had been misread as being about the Dirty War or the Holocaust.[53] Once he was willing to accept such misreadings of his work, there was no reason not to make an explicitly political painting. The impulse to begin the *Global Order* series was what became known as Argentina's Great Depression. Precipitated by financial crises in Russia and Brazil, the downturn, which lasted from 1998 to 2002, was, as Kuitca explained to Lynne Cooke, 'one of the worst of the many economic crises we have had'. In fact, the Argentine economy shrank by 28 per cent, and 50 per cent of the population was reduced to poverty. There were bank runs, debt defaults, and recurring riots, one of which drove the nation's president to flee from his official residence in a helicopter and led to the collapse of the government. Pressure from international lenders such as the World Bank complicated the situation. Writing to Cooke in the midst of the crisis, Kuitca observed that 'the word "globalization" seems to explain this phenomenon while, at the same time, losing all meaning'.

There is an unfinished quality to many of the *Global Order* paintings. In a 2019 conversation, Kuitca remarked to me that if the phone rang while he was working on one of these paintings he could never get back to it afterwards. He likens the work to an Arnold Schoenberg (1874–1951) piece that ends so abruptly one critic said it seems like the composer just ran out of paper. From the outset of his career with *Nadie olvida nada* to his most recent work, *The Family Idiot*, Kuitca has often been willing to accept what look like unfinished or very casually executed areas on his canvases. It is perhaps this unfinished quality that leads Kuitca to make drawings only after he finishes a painting, rather than making preparatory sketches. His sense of the painting as an always incomplete project also informs the *Diarios* (see fig.64), which begin as failed paintings and, like the proverbial Schoenberg composition, are brought to arbitrary conclusions. One suspects that Kuitca might agree with Chinese art historian Chang Yen-Yuan, who wrote:

> In painting, one should avoid worrying about accomplishing a work that is too diligent and too finished in the depiction of forms and the notation of colors or one that makes too great a display of one's technique, thus depriving it of mystery and aura. That is why one should not fear the incomplete, but quite to the contrary, one should deplore that which is too complete. From the moment one knows that a thing is complete, what need is there to complete it? For the incomplete does not necessarily mean the unfulfilled.[54]

The artist seems to have been in the mood to try new things in 2000. For a painting titled *Planta con juego de pelotas* (fig.53), he bounced a graphite-covered tennis ball

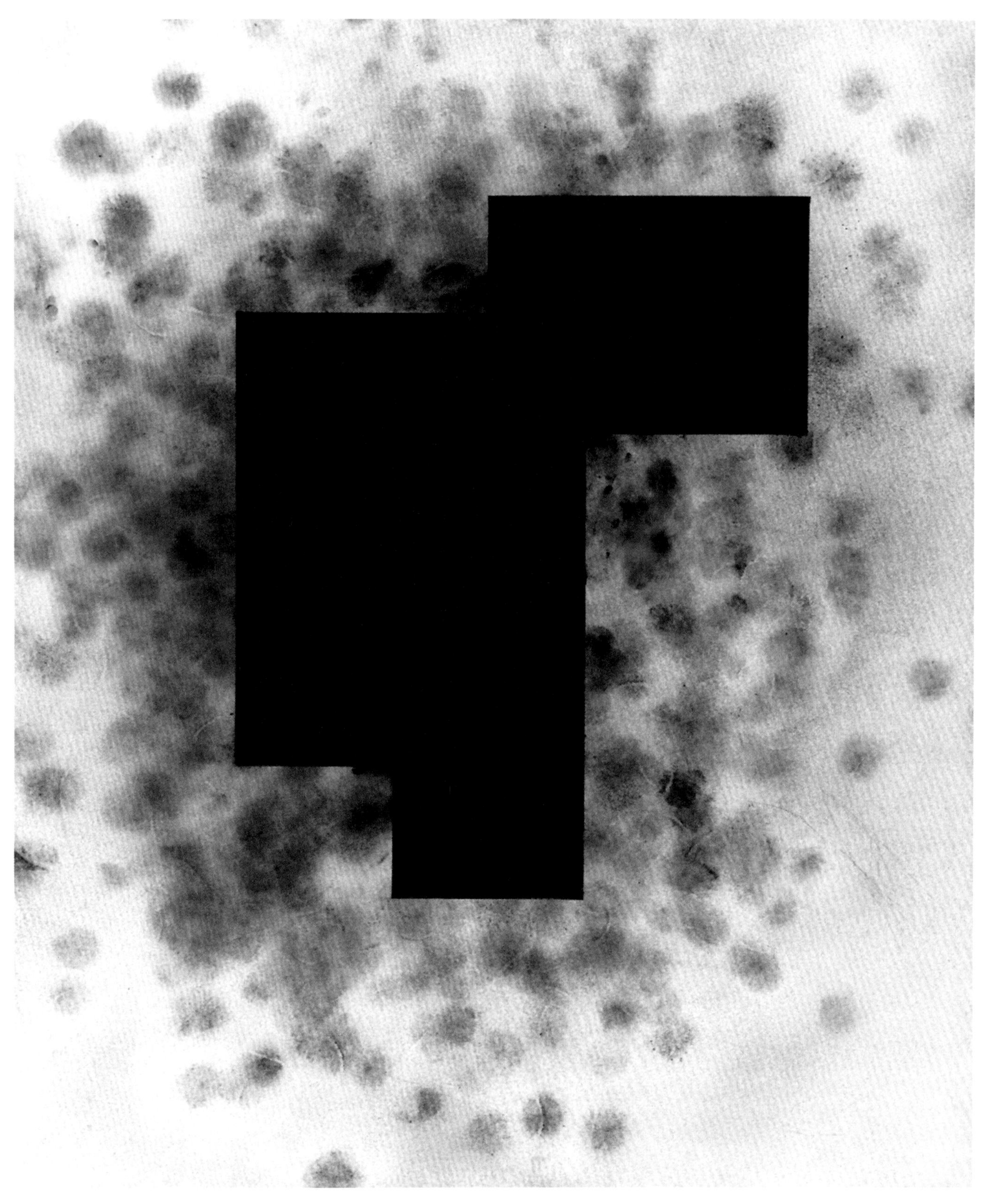

53. Planta con juego de pelotas   2000

Mixed media on linen
94.9 × 78.4 cm (37 ⅜ × 30 ⅞ in)
Ames Collection, New York

against a canvas on which he had painted an all-black apartment plan.[55] This one-off painting may be related to a trio of paintings from 1994 in which Kuitca used a similarly indexical method of mark-making, each titled *Naked Tango (After Warhol)* (fig.54). Inspired, as the title tells us, by Andy Warhol's *Dance Diagram (Tango)* from his 1962 series of paintings based on images from a dance-instruction manual, these canvases bear the imprint of Kuitca's paint-soaked bare feet executing a brief sequence of tango steps. In contrast to the neat lines in Warhol's painting, Kuitca's footprints, after the first imprint, are smeared and of little instructional use. The impression is of someone dancing with more passion and vitality than precision and skill.

Perhaps as much an homage to Yves Klein (1928–62) as to Warhol (1928–87), *Naked Tango* represents a double departure for the artist: it is a performance-action painting, a genre in which he has otherwise shown no interest, and it explicitly evokes Argentine identity, something Kuitca has avoided for most of his career. The tango is, of course, the most clichéd signifier of Argentina, so, we assume, this must be in some way an ironic painting, a knowing quotation. As he has pointed out more than once in relation to this painting, he does not dance the tango, and does not know how to.[56]

Yet the tango figures in one of Kuitca's transformative moments when in 1980 he watched a performance in Wuppertal of Pina Bausch's *Bandoneón*. Named after the classic tango instrument, *Bandoneón* was Bausch's response to the tango music she had heard in Argentina. While *Bandoneón* and the melancholy, tragic mood of the tango had a visible effect on Kuitca's mid-1980s stage paintings, which often looked like they were set in some rundown tango hall, there was nothing obviously Argentinean in his work of the following ten years. Perhaps by 2000 Kuitca was no longer worried about being marginalized as a Latin-American artist; he could make a 'tango painting' without fear of being typecast.

Kuitca returned to Warhol again in 1998 for a series of 63 watercolors based on Warhol's silkscreen paintings *Skulls* (1976), *Diamond Dust Shoes* (1980), *Turquoise Marilyn* (1962), *Disaster* (1963) and *Cow Wallpaper* (1966). In each image, Kuitca eliminated the ostensible subject matter, leaving only the background color rendered in small scale with watercolor (fig.55). (This might be a good place to note that despite his frequent reliance on found imagery – maps, architectural plans – Kuitca has rarely used silkscreening or other photomechanical techniques to transfer imagery onto his canvases. Instead nearly all the maps and house plans have been painted by hand, often by the artist's assistants, with the guidance of a projected image.) As Douglas Dreishpoon perceptively observed about these Warhol erasures, 'The deletion of one perceptual level enables another to dominate. In place of representation is abstraction, with traces of the figure persisting in some as ghosts. Identity, even when inscribed at the bottom of the sheet, is leeched from the image.'[57]

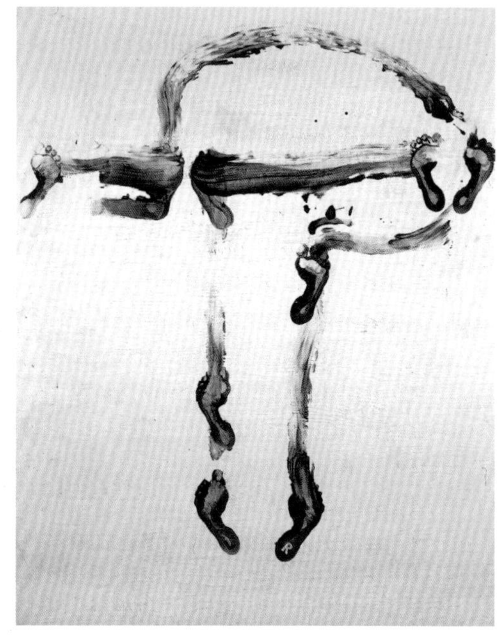

54. Naked Tango (After Warhol) 1994

Acrylic on canvas
195.5 × 148 cm (76 ⅞ × 58 ⅜ in)
Private collection, Buenos Aires

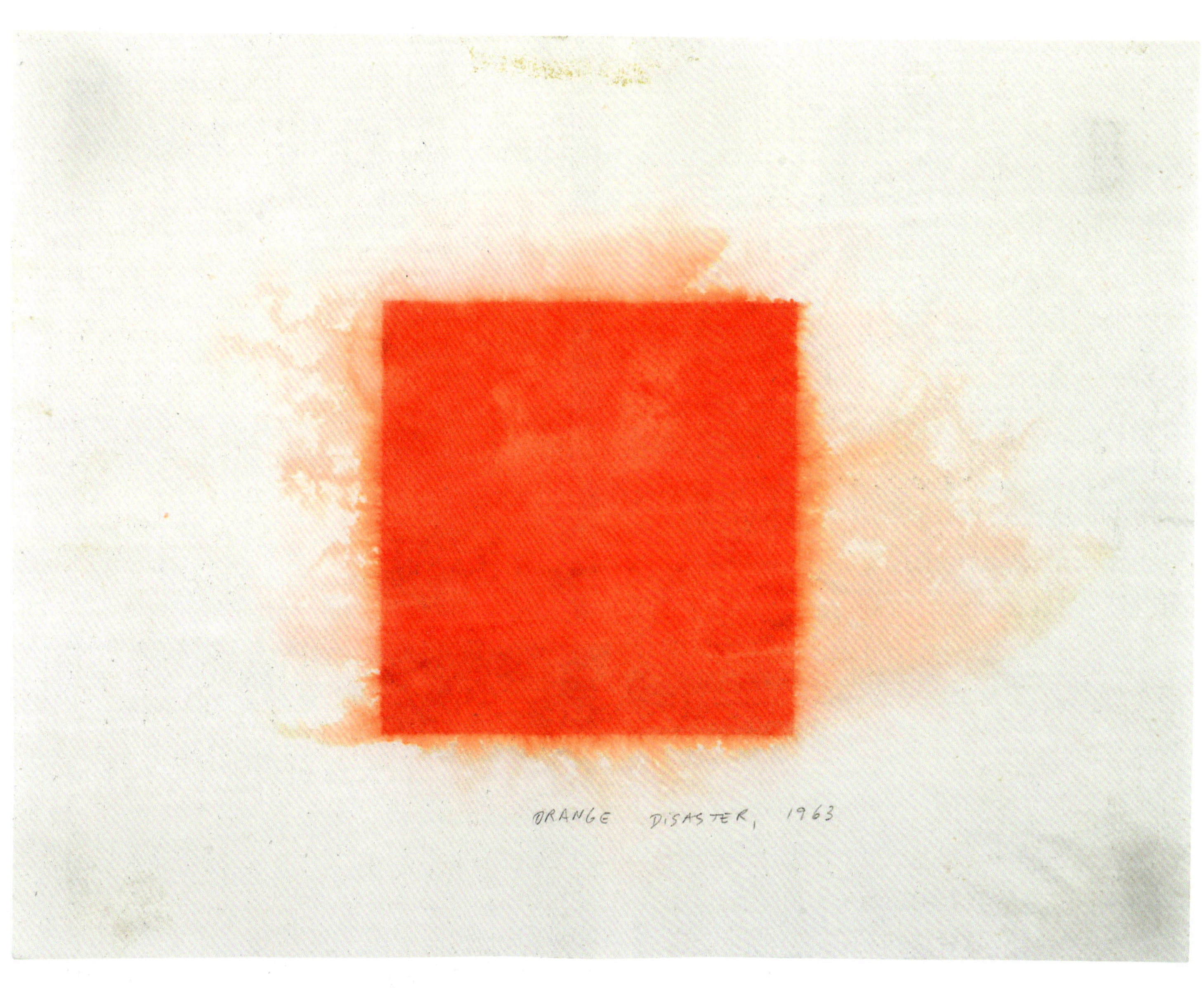

55. Untitled (The Warhol Series) (detail)   2006

Oil on canvas
63 parts, each: 21.6 × 27.9 cm (8 ½ × 11 in)
Museum Voorlinden, Wassenaar, The Netherlands

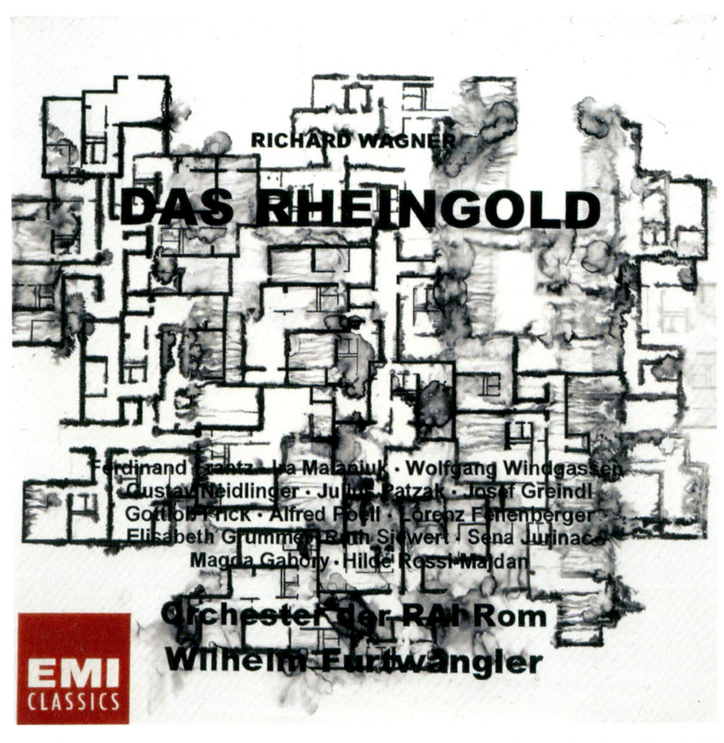

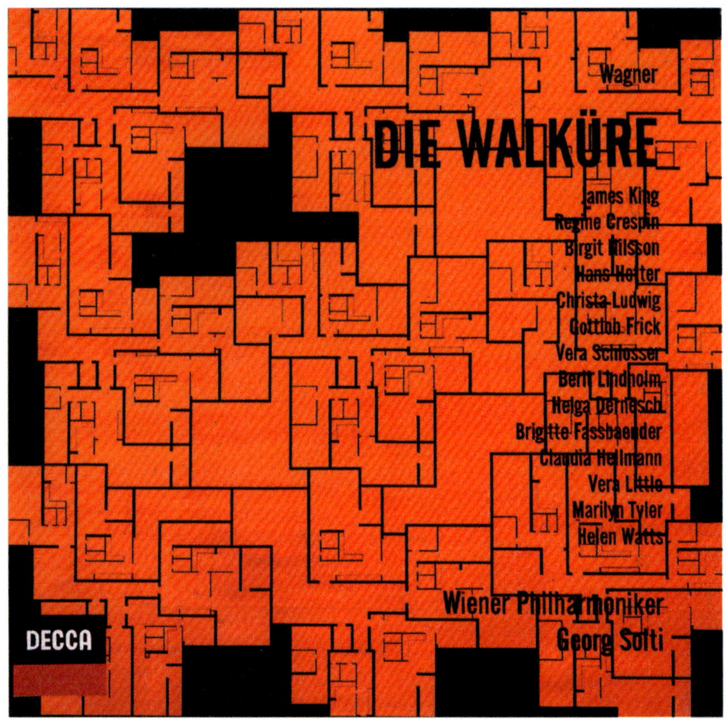

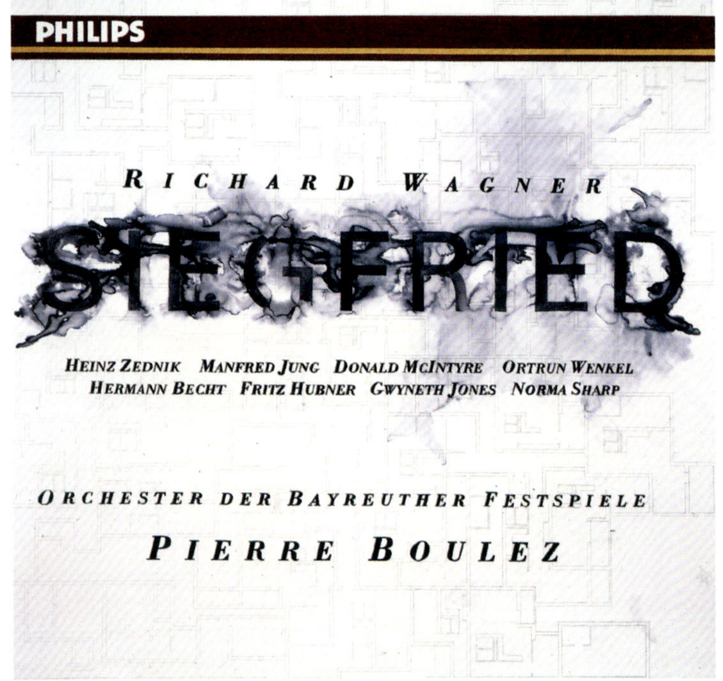

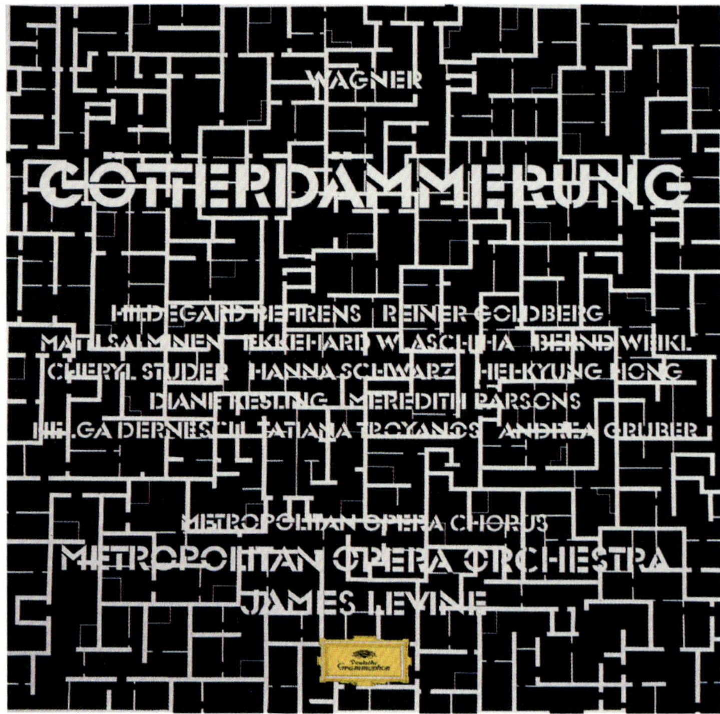

56. The Ring   2001–02

Mixed media on canvas
4 panels, overall 200 × 800 cm (78 ¾ × 314 ¹⁵⁄₁₆ in)
Private collection

During the first half of the 2000s, Kuitca mostly set aside painting in favor of
collage and works on paper. He also stepped away from his studio to create sets
for two ambitious Buenos Aires theater productions. In 2002, he designed sets for
a production of Federico García Lorca's *La casa de Bernarda Alba* (The House of
Bernarda Alba) at the Teatro San Martin (the domestic setting of this claustrophobic
family tragedy clearly resonates with Kuitca's House Plan paintings). The following
year he did the same for a production of Wagner's *Der fliegende Holländer* (The Flying
Dutchman) at the Teatro Colón, the theater where he had first seen Pina Bausch's
company 23 years earlier. He also dreamed of staging *Krapp's Last Tape* by Samuel
Beckett using a large luggage conveyor belt to mirror the operation of the tape
recorder that is central to the play. While the Beckett project never materialized,
Kuitca did incorporate a working luggage conveyor belt into his designs for *The Flying
Dutchman* – to some controversy.

   The last painting he made before his self-imposed hiatus was a large four-panel
work (fig.56) inspired by Wagner's *Ring Cycle*. For each of the four operas in the cycle,
Kuitca began with the CD cover of a recording from a different moment and place:
Das Rheingold conducted by Wilhelm Furtwängler in the late 1940s, Georg Solti's
Die Walkure from 1965, Pierre Boulez's *Siegfried* from the late 1970s and, taking
up two panels, a more recent *Götterdämmerung* conducted by James Levine. As the
recordings being referenced take us through the postwar period, so do the extreme
visual alterations Kuitca has made to them shift, from the Cubist patterns for *Das
Rheingold* to a silvery geometric labyrinth for *Die Walküre*, a schematic blueprint design
for *Siegfried* and a warped and partially erased architectural plan that has faded into a
Robert Rymanesque white for *Götterdämmerung*. The recording labels for each opera
are also different: EMI, Decca, Philips and Deutsche Grammophon.

   To prepare himself for this epic painting – it is nearly 2m (6 ½ foot) tall and more
than 8m (26 ¼ foot) wide – the artist immersed himself in studying the history of
Wagner's operas and their various recordings. This level of research was not typical of
Kuitca. As he later explained to Graciela Speranza, when using imagery from Diderot's
Encyclopédie or from Ernst Neufert's reference book he 'didn't need to be a specialist
in Diderot or Neufert', but with *The Ring* it was necessary to be better prepared as
he entered 'that terrain that has been so much argued about and is so populated'.[58]
Ultimately this degree of preparation brought him to a difficult place as a painter. In
retrospect he saw that the manner in which he had approached and executed *The Ring*
not only ran counter to how he had worked in the past, but was also opposed to his very

idea of painting. That kind of rational attitude, that kind of programmatic framework, he came to understand, 'denies the artist's intuitive movement and invites him to justify the origin of every square inch of the work.'[59] As he finished the enormous work he began to feel that it was not possible for him to go on painting, at least not in this way. *The Ring* may have been made with oil and canvas, but it was not painting as he understood it. And so he turned away from the medium, at least for a while.

Kuitca's works on paper *c.*2003 could more accurately be called 'works *with* paper'. To make them he used basic ink-jet technology to print architectural imagery onto photographic paper, which he then subjected to varying degrees of heat and moisture, often using everyday domestic devices such as a hair dryer or a teakettle. He was fascinated by how the images dissolved in unexpected ways. Dissolution was also key to the collages, which were made at a much larger scale than the ink-jet works. Sometimes using a paper shredder, Kuitca shattered the orderly arrangement of theater seating charts. The scene is chaotic. As one critic accurately noted, in most of the theater collages 'the overall impression is one of extreme violence, as though a bomb has exploded inside the theater'.[60]

The dissolved image is a recurrent feature of Kuitca's work at this time, most dramatically in the *L'Encyclopédie* paintings where he subjects floor plans of architectural monuments (drawn from the pages of D'Alembert and Diderot's epochal reference work) to extensive blurring and smearing (figs 59 and 61). It is also a feature of *Dissolving Dot (after Lichtenstein)*, a 2001 adaption of Roy Lichtenstein's 1966 painting *Alka Seltzer*.[61]

Along with its multilayered visual punning – as Kuitca remarked, his painting belongs to 'a chain of dissolutions in which Lichtenstein dilutes his own Ben-Day dot and I dilute Lichtenstein' – *Dissolving Dot* presages a new theme in Kuitca's work that increasingly occupied him as the new decade, and new century, progressed: art history. Apart from *Naked Tango* (see fig.54), Kuitca had generally avoided loading his art with any obvious art-historical references. In this he stands apart from the postmodernist strategies wielded by many of his contemporaries. As Andreas Huyssen succinctly put it, Kuitca 'is a modernist after modernism, without being a postmodernist, an artist who relies on painting as a mode of knowing the world through structured aesthetic form.'[62] In 2006, however, Kuitca began what would turn out to be a series of paintings – titled, in Spanish and French, *Desenlace (Dénouement)* – in which specific references to past art were not only obvious but also central to the meaning of the work.

Another distinctive aspect of Kuitca's work in the 2000s was an approach to painting that frequently involved real space in the form of installations and three-dimensional structures. After venturing into three dimensions with the beds in the early 1990s, for the rest of that decade and longer Kuitca had shown little interest in venturing off the wall. It was in 2006 that he made his first public art commission in the form of a cartographic mosaic on Allison Island in Miami Beach. The Teatro

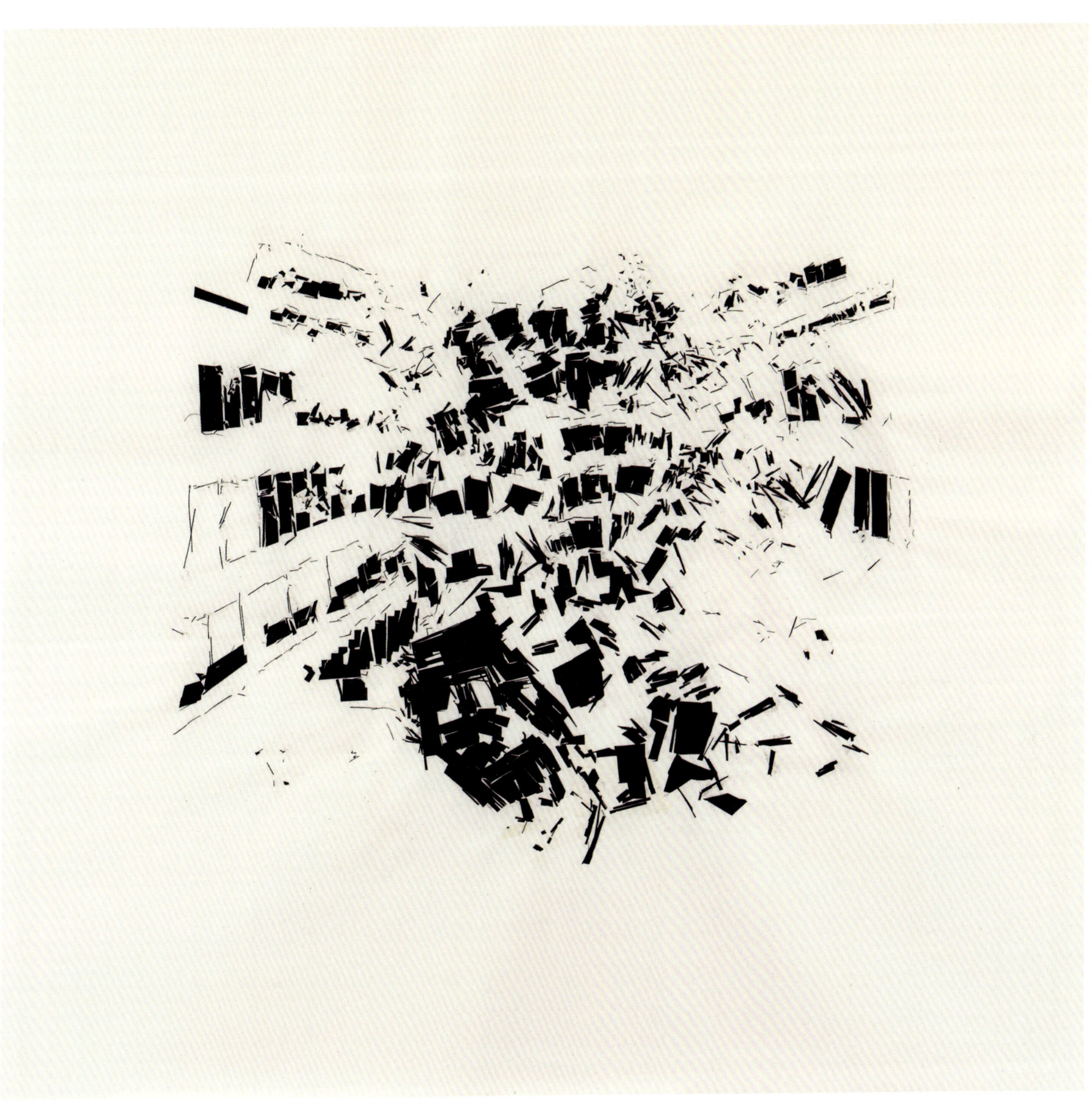

57. Covent Garden VI   2004

Mixed media on paper
148.3 × 149.2 cm (58 ⅜ × 58 ¾ in)
Private collection

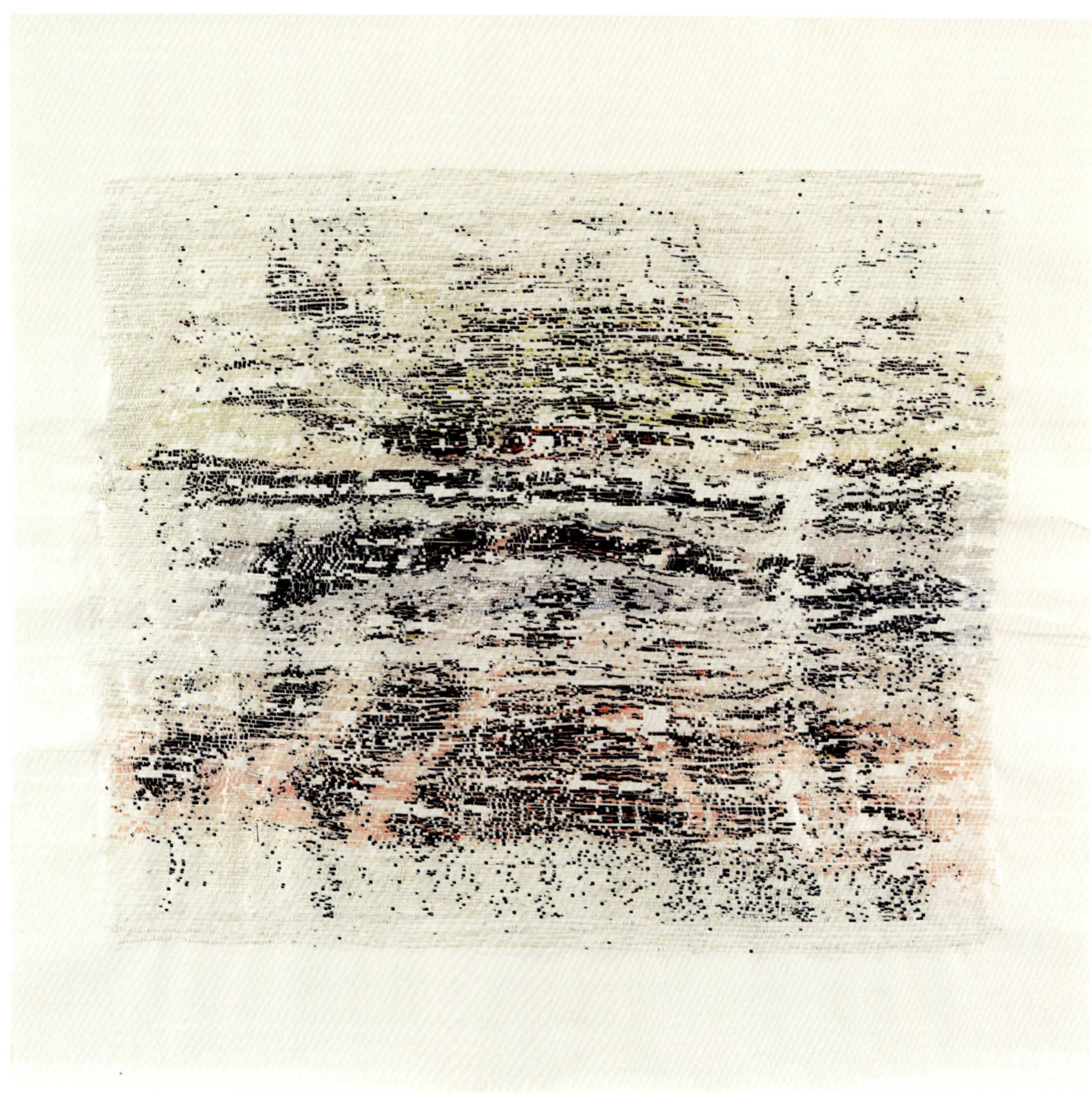

58. Covent Garden VIII 2004

Mixed media on paper
148 × 148 cm (58 ¼ × 58 ¼ in)
Private collection, Courtesy Sperone Westwater, New York

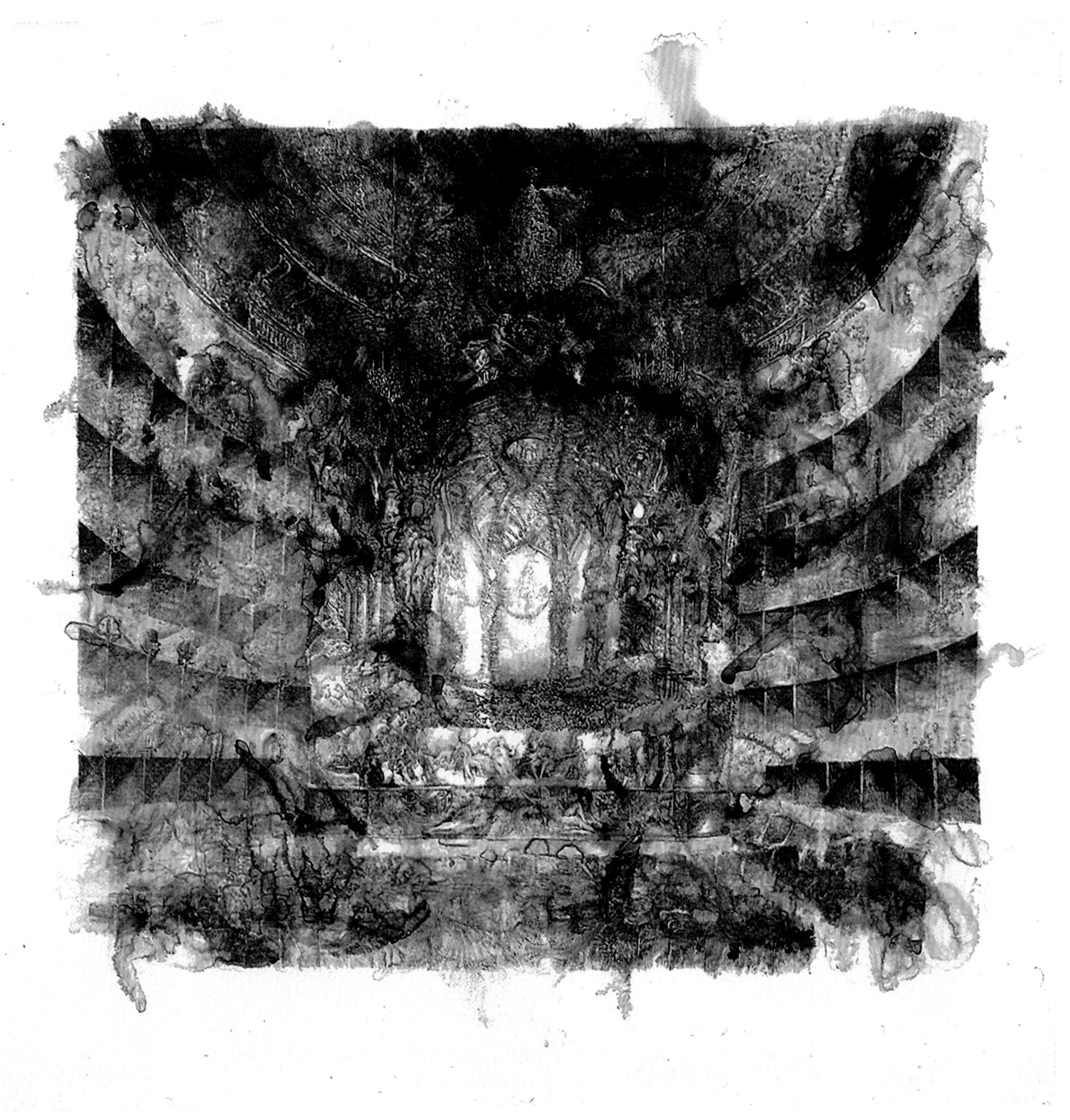

59. Untitled   1998

Mixed media
198.1 × 192.4 cm (78 × 192 ⅜ in)
Private collection

60. Everything   2004

Mixed media on canvas
Overall 305 × 660.4 cm (120 × 260 in)
Walker Art Center, Minneapolis

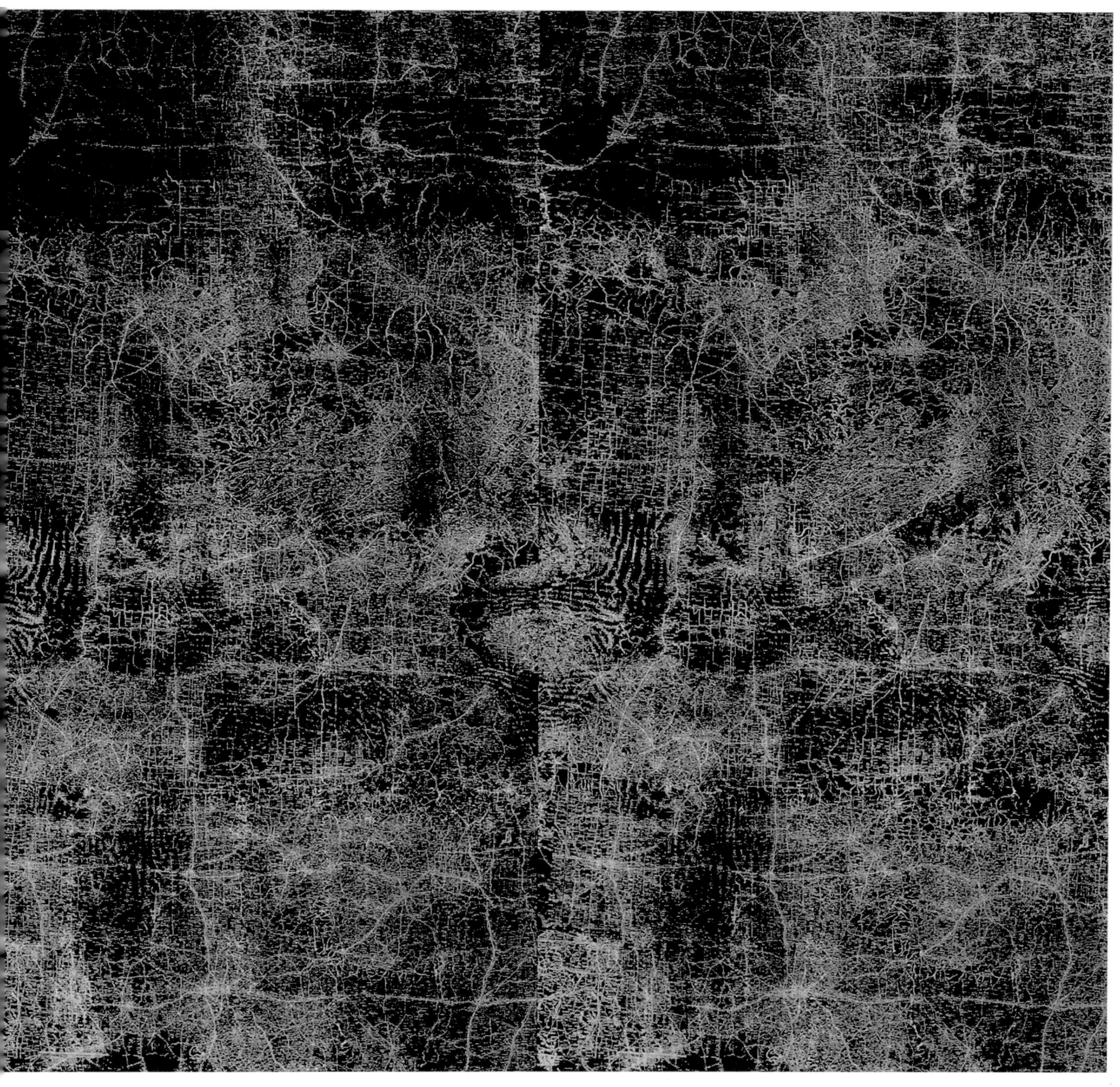

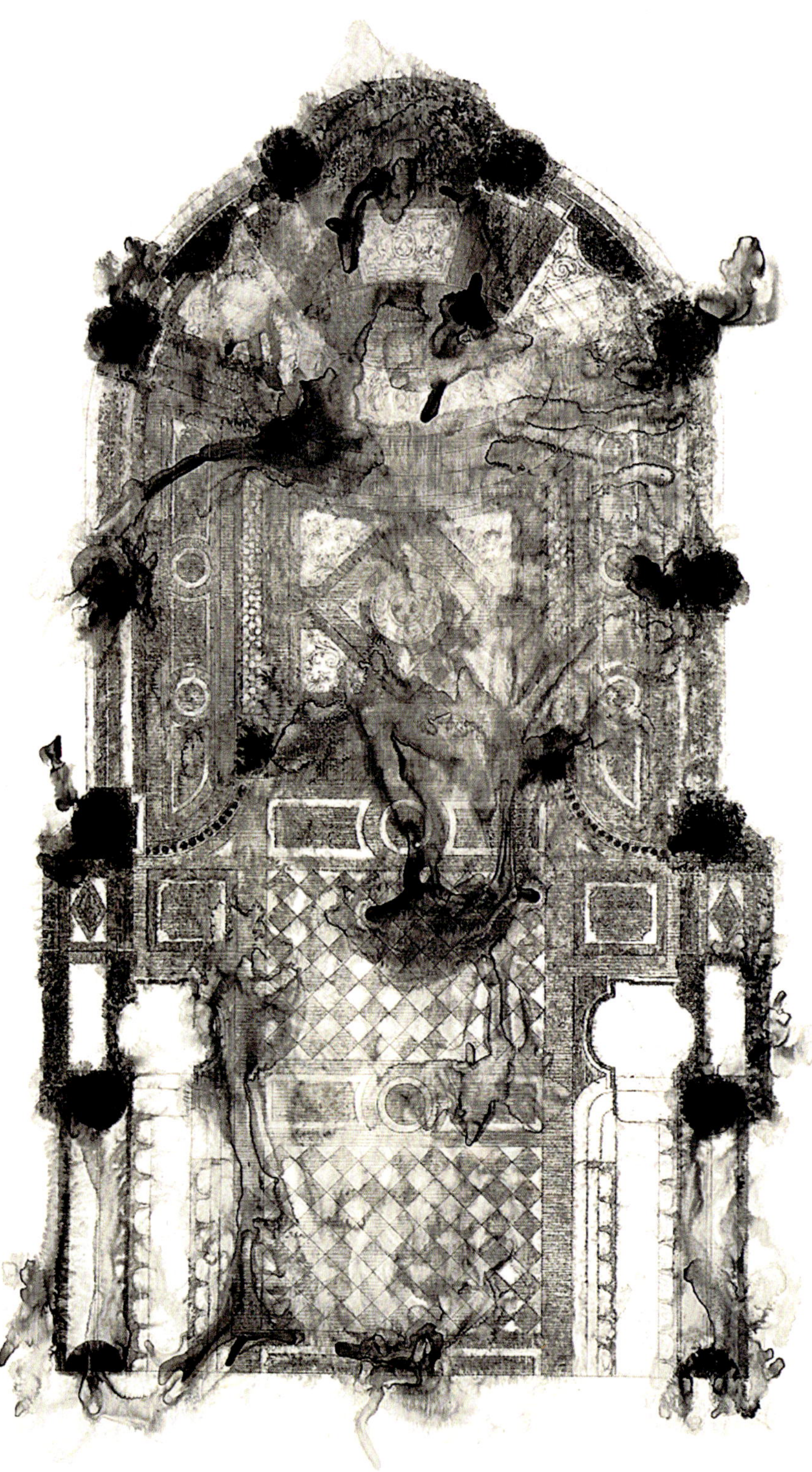

61. L'Encyclopedie (Marble Flooring Plan of
the Sanctuary and Part of the Choir of the
Cathedral of Notre-Dame de Paris)   1999

Mixed media on linen
196.9 × 160 cm (77 ½ × 63 in)
Private collection

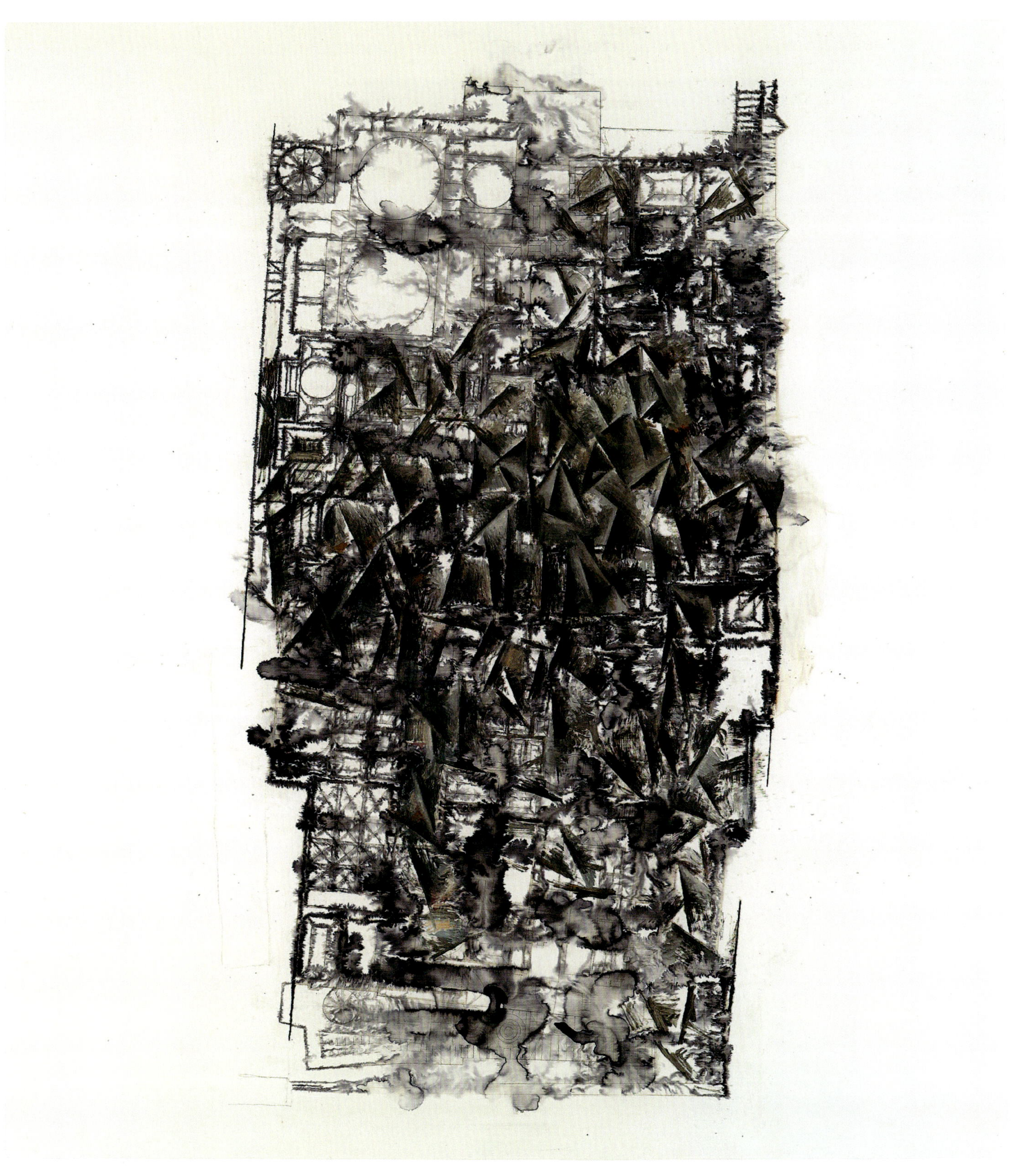

62. Untitled   2009

Ink and oil on canvas
224.5 × 196 cm (88 ⅜ × 77 ⅛ in)
Collection of the artist

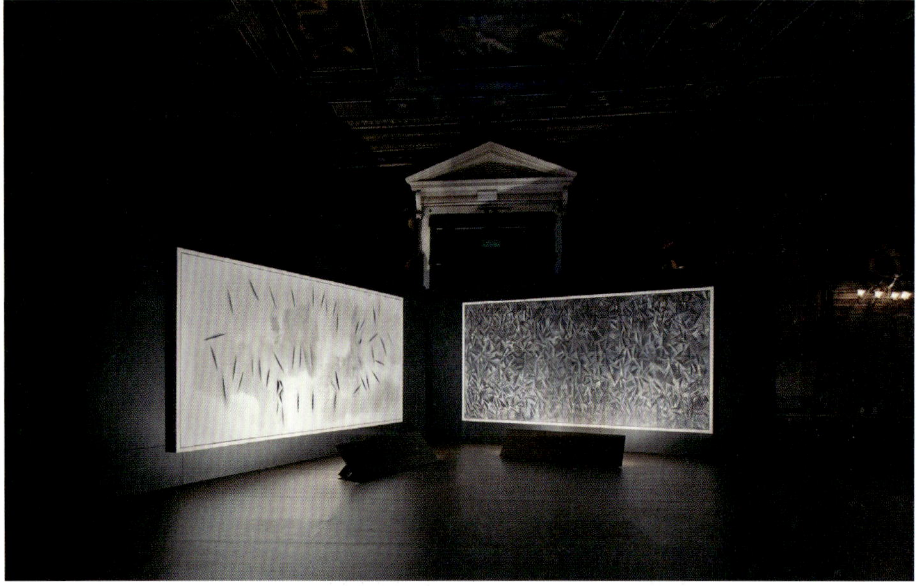

63. Installation view of *Si yo fuera el invierno mismo* (If I were Winter Itself), Argentinean Pavilion, Ateneo Veneto, 52nd International Art Exhibition, Venice Biennale, Italy, 2007

Colón production of *The Flying Dutchman* inspired a 2008–09 work with images printed onto three scrims arranged *en filade*. On a larger scale, in 2009 he designed the stage curtain for the new Winspear Opera House by Foster + Partners in Dallas, Texas. In a conceptually elegant move, the image Kuitca created for the curtain was based on the Winspear's own seating plan so that waiting audiences find themselves gazing upon a representation of the very space they occupy.

Throughout his theater paintings Kuitca jumps from one side of the fourth wall to another, encouraging confusions about performers and spectators, actors and audiences. Attacks on the fourth wall were, of course, a feature of radical theater, film and dance during the 1960s and 1970s, from Peter Handke's *Offending the Audience* (1966) to Luis Buñuel's *The Discreet Charm of the Bourgeoisie* (1972) and the Squat Theater's *Andy Warhol's Last Love* (1978). In some of her dance pieces, such as *Blaubart* (Bluebeard, 1977), Pina Bausch turned the house lights on during performances. By transposing this dynamic into painting, and doing so without including a single human figure, Kuitca invites viewers of his paintings to become more aware of their own position. Just as in those avant-garde works of the 1970s, Kuitca's paintings want us, his viewers, to reflect on our role and our physical place in the aesthetic transaction.

The two new components of Kuitca's work – art-historical reference and three-dimensionality – finally merged in 2007 when he was chosen to represent Argentina at the Venice Biennale. The exhibition that Kuitca created was presented in the Ateneo Veneto, a 17th-century building near La Fenice opera house. The paintings on view – from the *Desenlace* (*Dénouement*) series – were displayed in a period room in which ornate woodwork and wall and ceiling mural paintings made it impossible

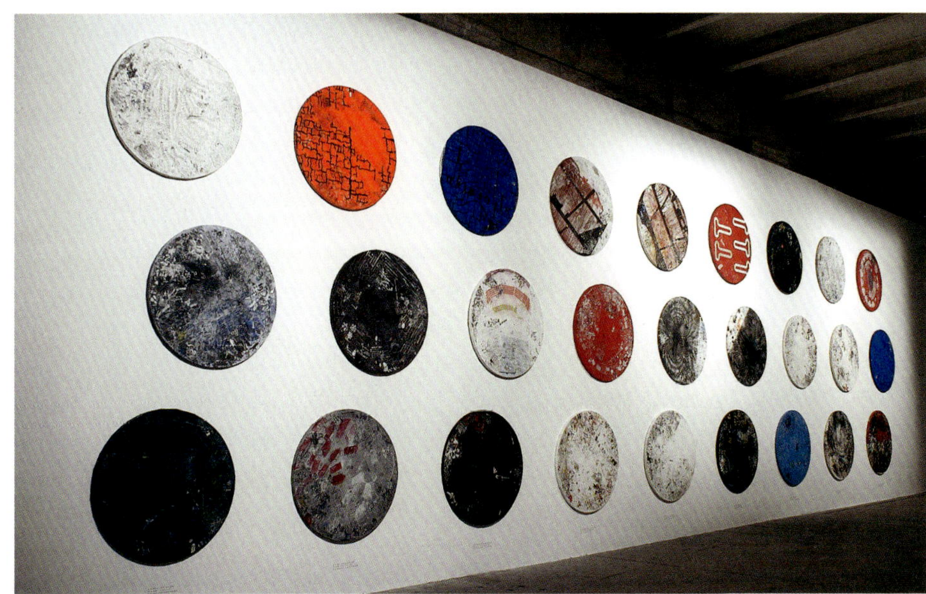

64. Diarios 1994–2004

Installation view of Think with the Sense – Feel with the
Mind, Art in the Present Tense, 52nd International Art
Exhibition, Venice Biennale, Italy, 2007

to hang work directly on the walls. Instead, Kuitca's canvases were presented
on freestanding walls that had been upholstered in black leather and positioned at
oblique angles to the room's permanent walls. The only lighting came from long floor
lights that had the effect of spotlighting the canvases from below, not unlike stage
lights. The effect was highly theatrical.

Without being specific, Kuitca has dropped hints that the *Desenlace* paintings
were born out of a difficult time in his life and that, at least for a moment, they might
have marked the end of his engagement with painting. In order to reflect the acute
loneliness he was feeling, for the Venice exhibition Kuitca resuscitated a title from a
melancholic painting he had made in 1986, *Si yo fuera el invierno mismo* (*If I were Winter
Itself*). Paradoxically, the *Desenlace* works were also the occasion when he experienced
an enthusiastic return to painting after several years of working largely in collage. For
viewers who associate Kuitca with diagrammatic imagery, with what might be called
an 'informational imagination', the *Desenlace* paintings can be confusing. They were
his first fully abstract works, totally devoid of references to the built and mapped
world that had previously been the foundation of Kuitca's art. Instead they use
chiaroscuro effects to suggest the illusion of a folded and crumpled plane. The jagged
shallow space of the *Desenlace* paintings is achieved with what Clement Greenberg
termed 'homeless representation', a mode (employed by Willem de Kooning and
Philip Guston in the 1950s) the critic defined as 'a plastic and descriptive painterliness
that is applied to abstract ends'.[63]

Kuitca was as surprised as anyone by his turn to abstraction, which materialized one
day when he noticed how some downward brushstrokes he had made on a blank canvas
looked like Cubist faceting. Art historian Michael Fitzgerald has noted how while

painting *Desenlace I*, Kuitca 'undertook the task of surreptitiously filling the canvas by walking back and forth along the suspended cloth, laying down marks as he passed.'[64] Instead of being bothered by the Cubist reference, Kuitca relished the resulting temporal ambiguity, the notion that the painting could have been the work of some obscure Latin-American Cubist. He also was cognizant that 2007 was the centenary of that founding work of Cubism, Picasso's *Les Demoiselles d'Avignon*. While there was no specific citation involved, Kuitca believed that this unexpected throwback to an earlier period came out of 'a sort of emotional, pictorial memory' of Cubist painting.[65] He also detected the belated influence of Alfredo Hlito (1923–93), a pioneering Argentine abstractionist whom Kuitca had gotten to know in the 1980s. The antiquated look of the paintings also has to do with their palettes: *Desenlace I* (fig.65) is dominated by dark grays, *Desenlace II* (fig.66) by a drab off-white and *Desenlace III* (fig.67) again is mostly gray. In an interview, Kuitca has recalled how he 'tried to find that slightly muffled color typical of academic painting' by using a can of turpentine 'that was getting loaded with all this half-grayish, half-brownish, sky blue impasto.'[66]

As the series progressed, Kuitca noticed that the darkest shapes, which resemble the ridges or indentations in bunched-up fabric, suggested illusionistic slashes. When isolated from other elements they looked like cuts in a Lucio Fontana (1899–1968) canvas. In the first three *Desenlace* paintings, Kuitca would stop short of anything that looked like a 'parodistic gesture', but once he noticed the resemblance to Fontana's *tagli* (cuts), he decided to embrace this accidental connection and make paintings (such as *Desenlace IV*) with trompe l'oeil slashes that explicitly cited Fontana (figs 68 and 69). Beyond the surprise of discovering Fontana's *Concetto Spaziale* nestled within the language of Cubism, Kuitca was delighted with the idea of making Fontana, who was born in Argentina but usually considered as an Italian artist, a part of his Venice Biennale show. Kuitca liked the notion that the work representing Argentina would include elements from an artist whose nationality was full of confusion and ambiguity.

As the 'cubistoid' (a term he began to use for the Cubist-like paintings that followed the *Desenlace* series) paintings progressed, Kuitca noticed similarities to his past work: the faceted surfaces looked like the mattresses of *Le Sacre*, and also like topographical maps (figs 71, 72, 73 and 74). He had not intended to revisit his own work, but after the Venice Biennale he began inserting motifs from older paintings into these abstract fields: a road map (fig.75), fragments of architectural plans (figs 76, 78 and 79; in one painting he overlaid an array of Fontana cuts with a tangled line of thorns. In other paintings, however, such as a 2011 group inspired by Wagner operas, the Cubist fields are barely present; although the palette remains gray and subdued, Kuitca seems to be venturing back into figuration. One of the paintings, *Bayreuther Festspiele 2011 (Lohengrin)*, includes the carefully painted head of a swan rising from a clump of Cubist reeds (fig.81). Others feature women's faces.

65. Desenlace I   2006

Oil on canvas
195 × 381 cm (76 ¾ × 150 in)
Daros Latinamerica Collection, Zurich

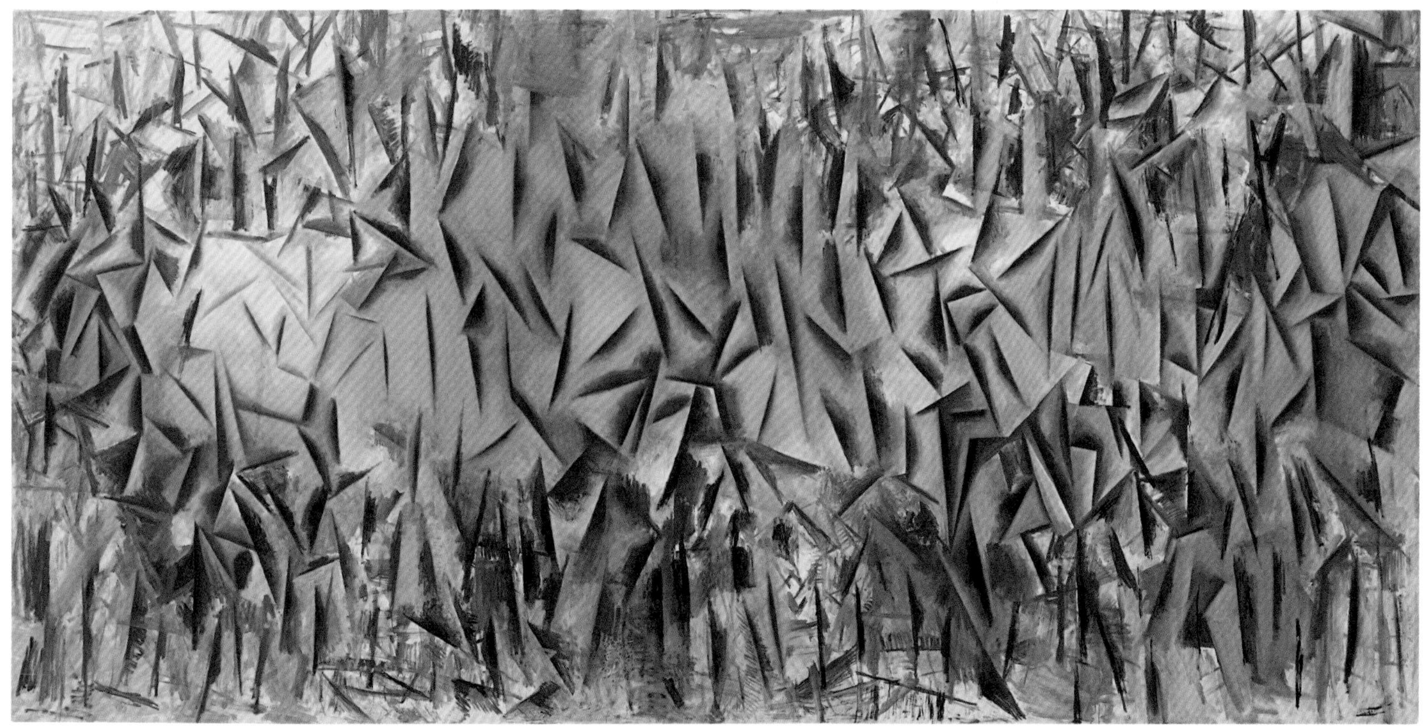

66. Desenlace II   2006

Oil on canvas
195 × 381 cm (76 ¾ × 150 in)
Daros Latinamerica Collection, Zurich

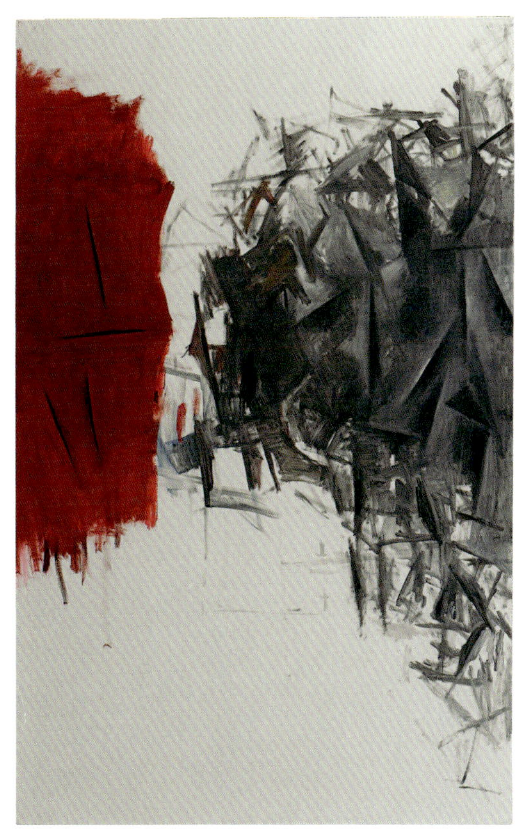 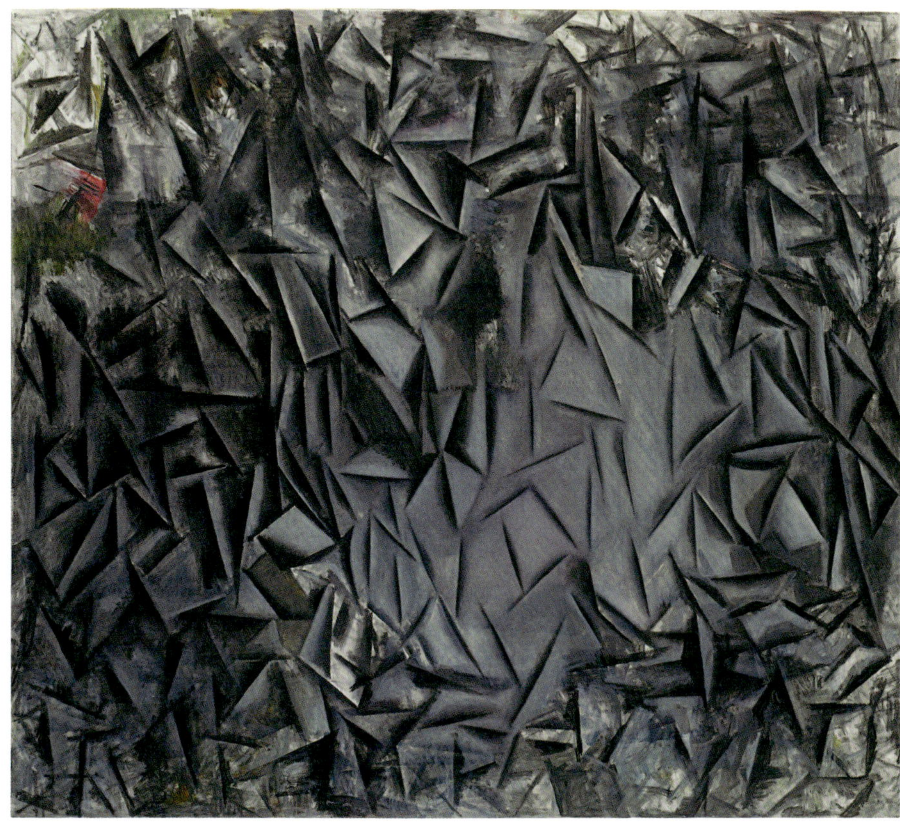

67. Desenlace III   *2007*

Oil on canvas
diptych 195 × 119 and 195 × 214 cm (76 ¾ × 46 ⅞ and 76 ¾
× 84 ¼ in)
Daros Latinamerica Collection, Zurich

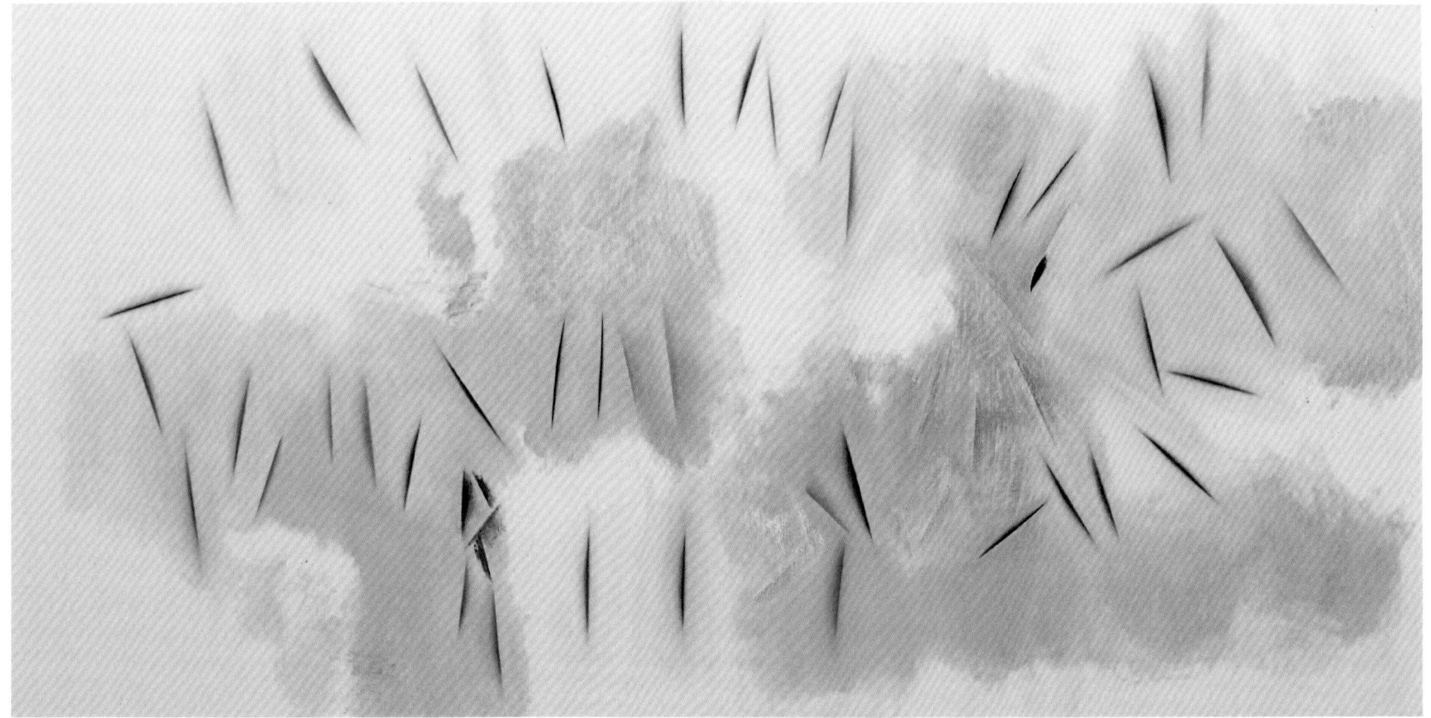

68. Desenlace IV   2007

Oil on canvas
195 × 381 cm (76 ¾ × 150 in)
Daros Latinamerica Collection, Zurich

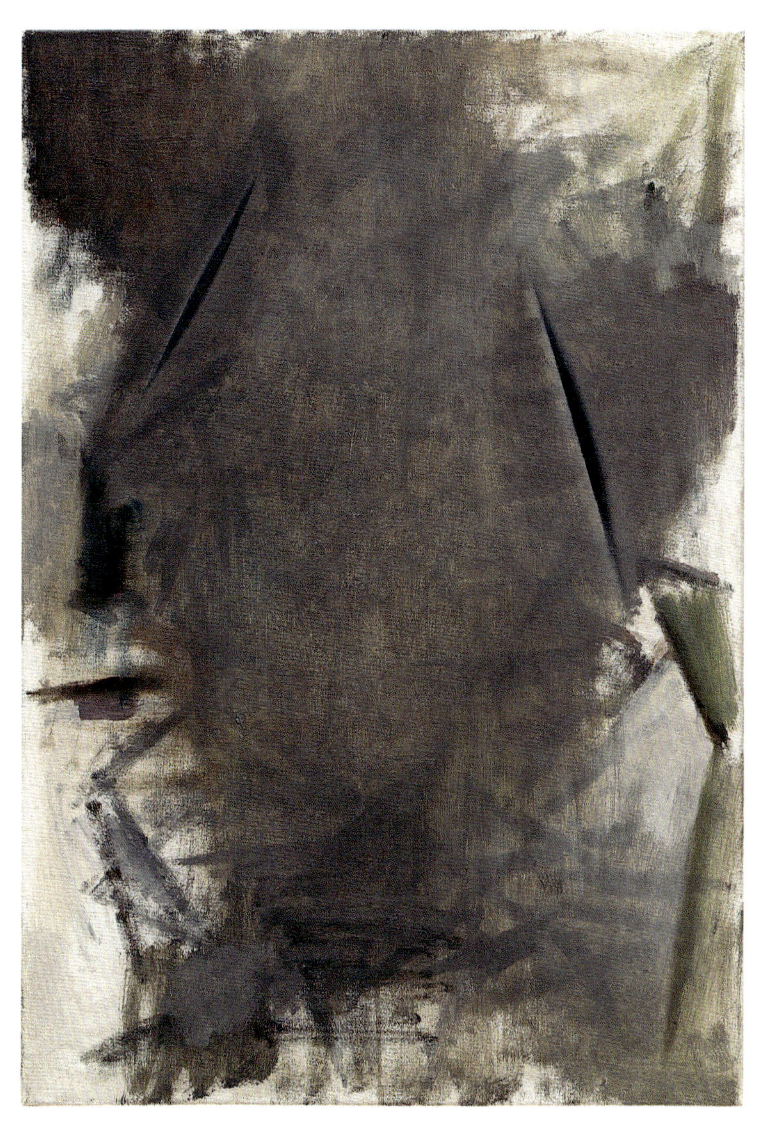

69. Untitled   2008

Oil on canvas
60 × 40 cm (23 ⅝ × 15 ¾ in)
Private collection

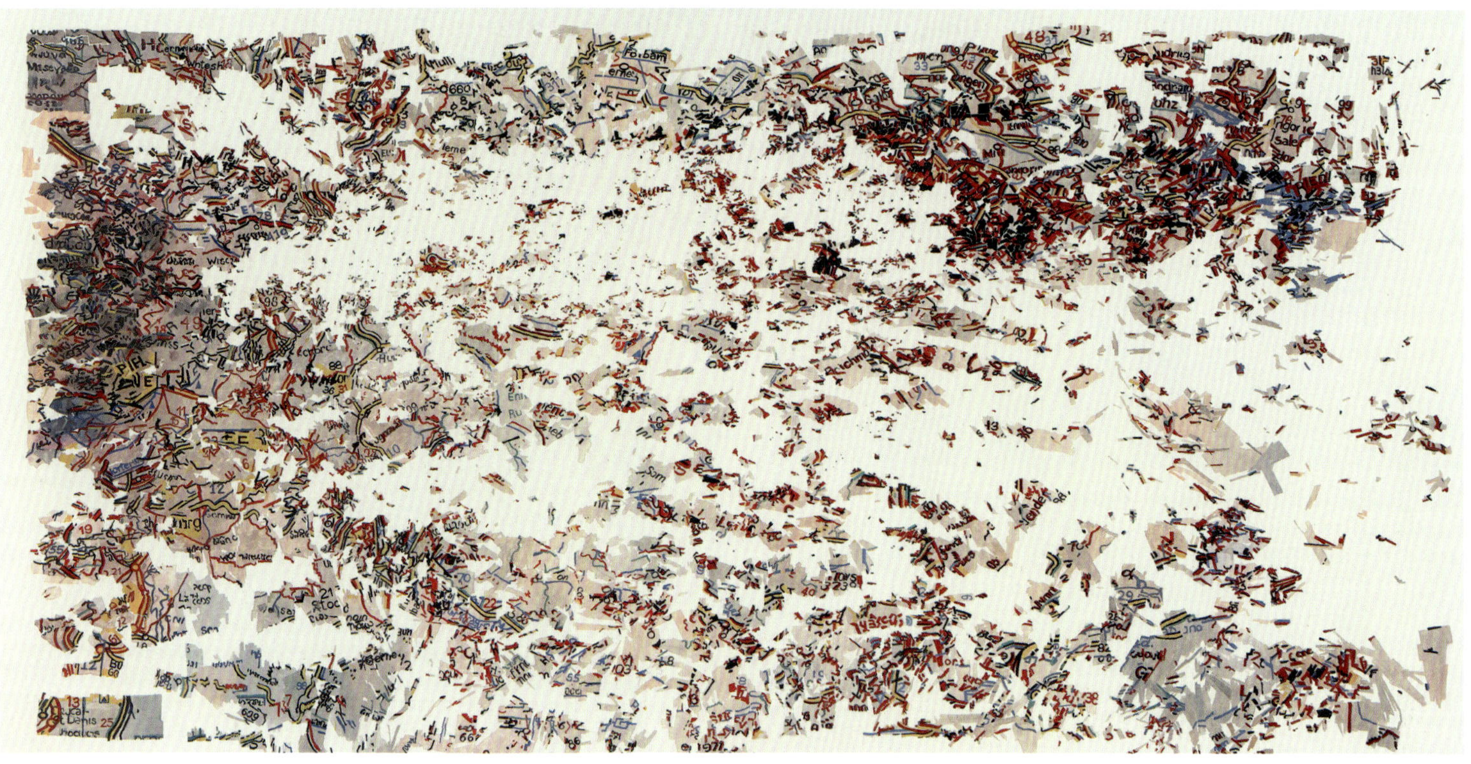

70. Untitled   2007/2008

Oil on canvas
195 × 380 cm (76 ¾ × 149 ⅝ in)
Private collection

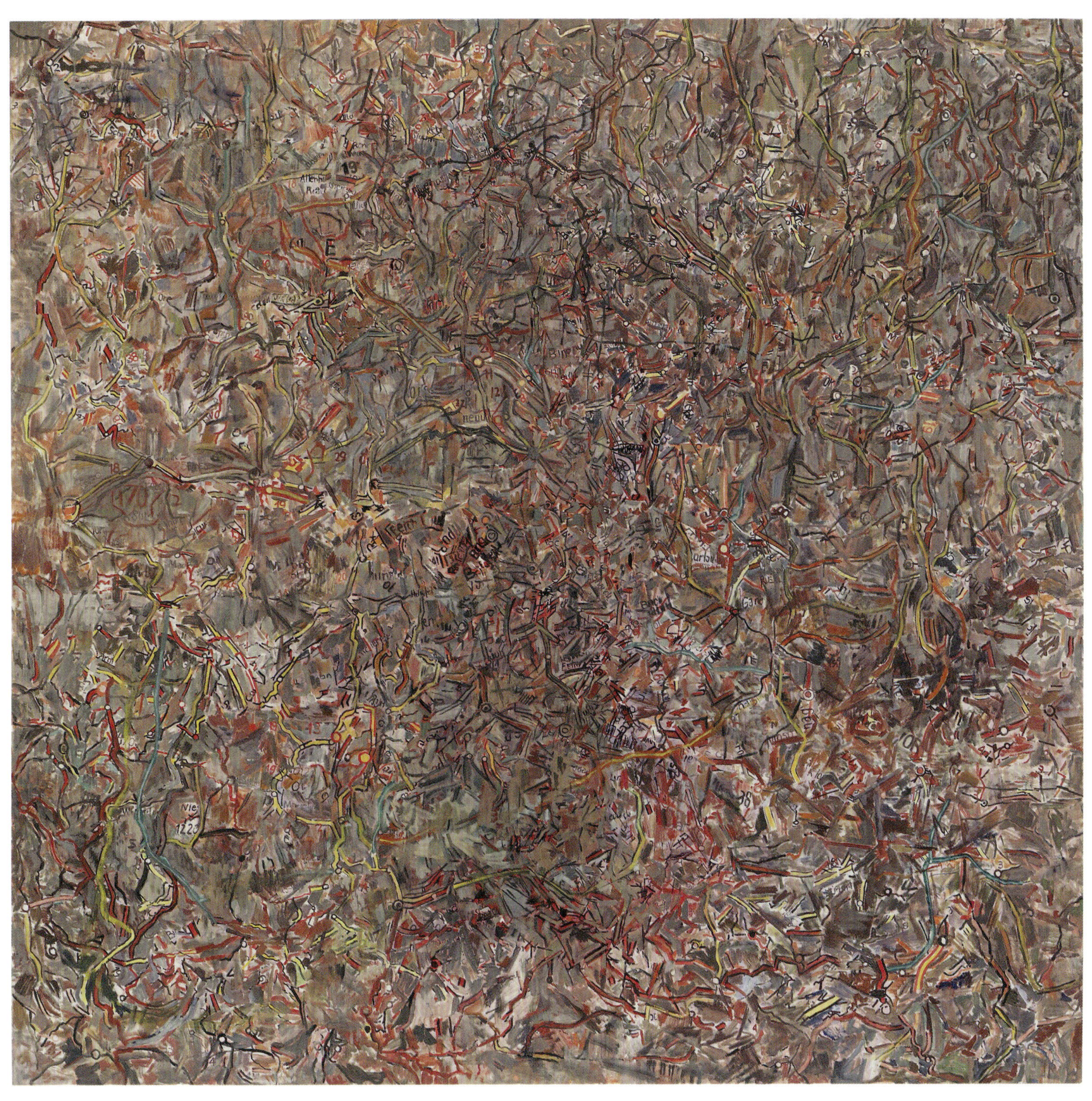

71. Untitled   2010

Oil on linen
181 × 181 cm (71 ¼ × 71 ¼ in)
Collection of Robin and Marc Wolpow

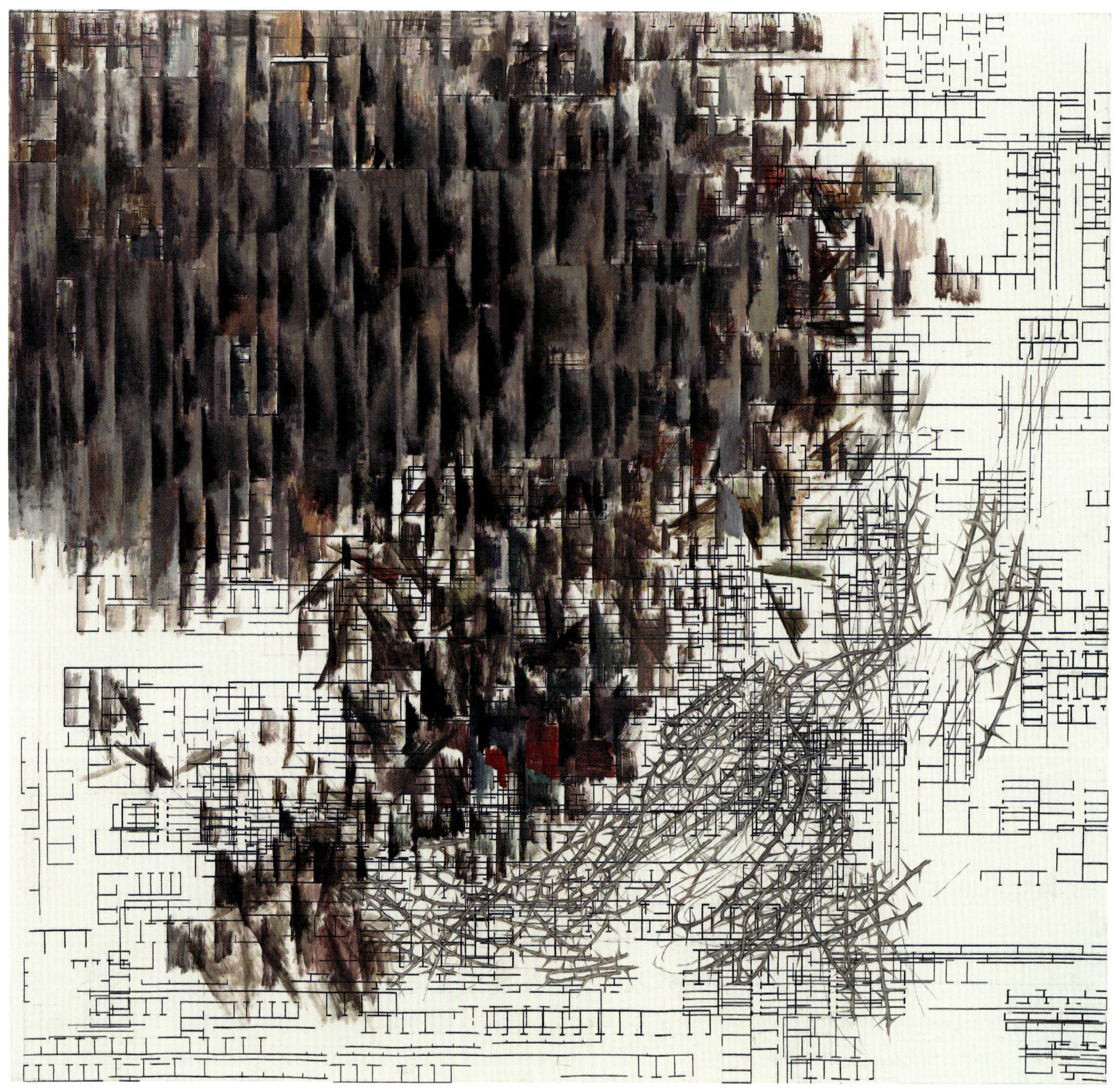

72. Philosophy for Princes III   2009

Oil on linen
157 × 160 cm (61 ⅞ × 63 in)
Private collection

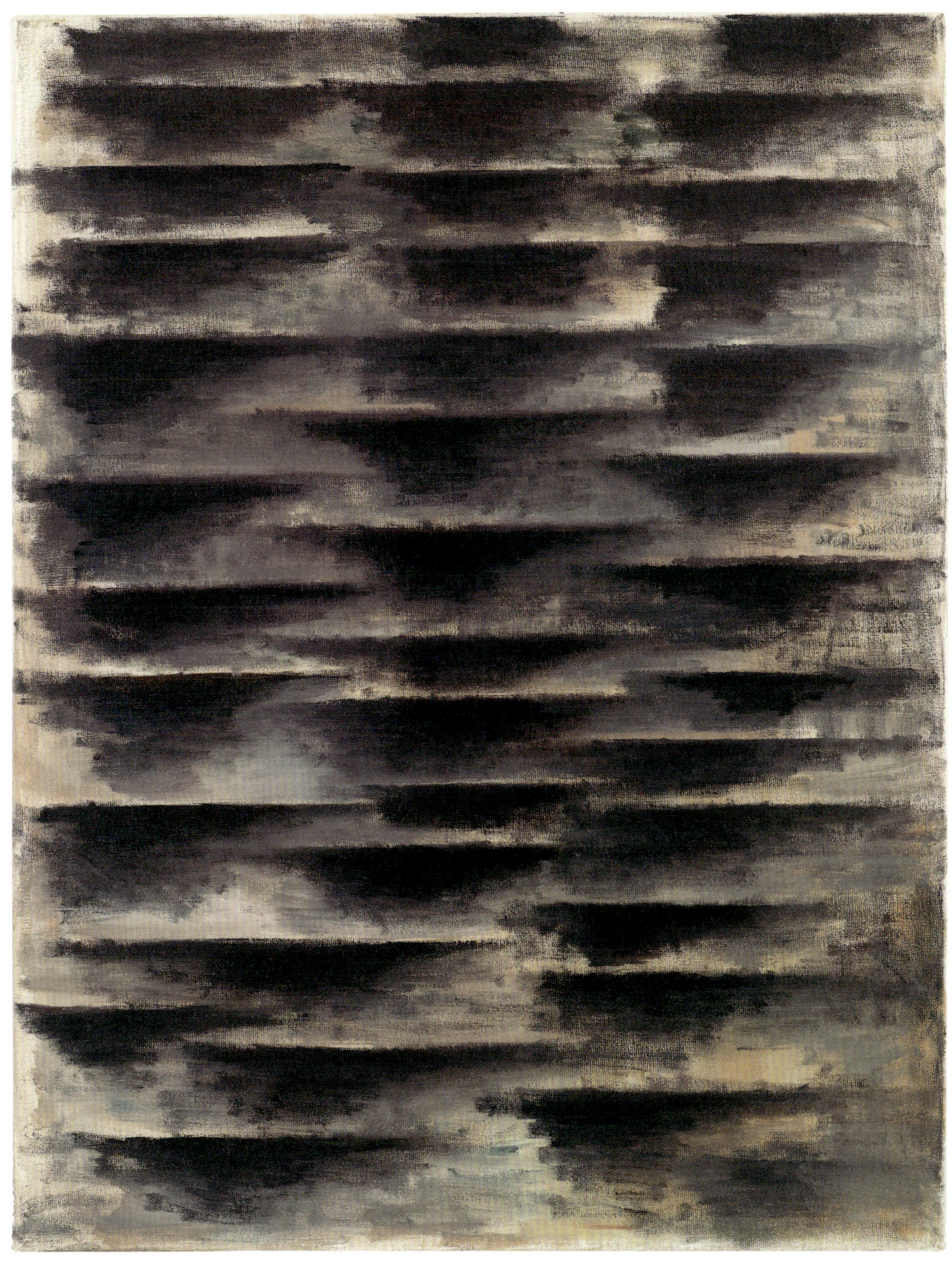

73. Philosophy for Princes I   2009

Oil on linen
60 × 45 cm (23 ¾ × 17 ¾ in)
Collection of Pierre Bourgie, Montreal

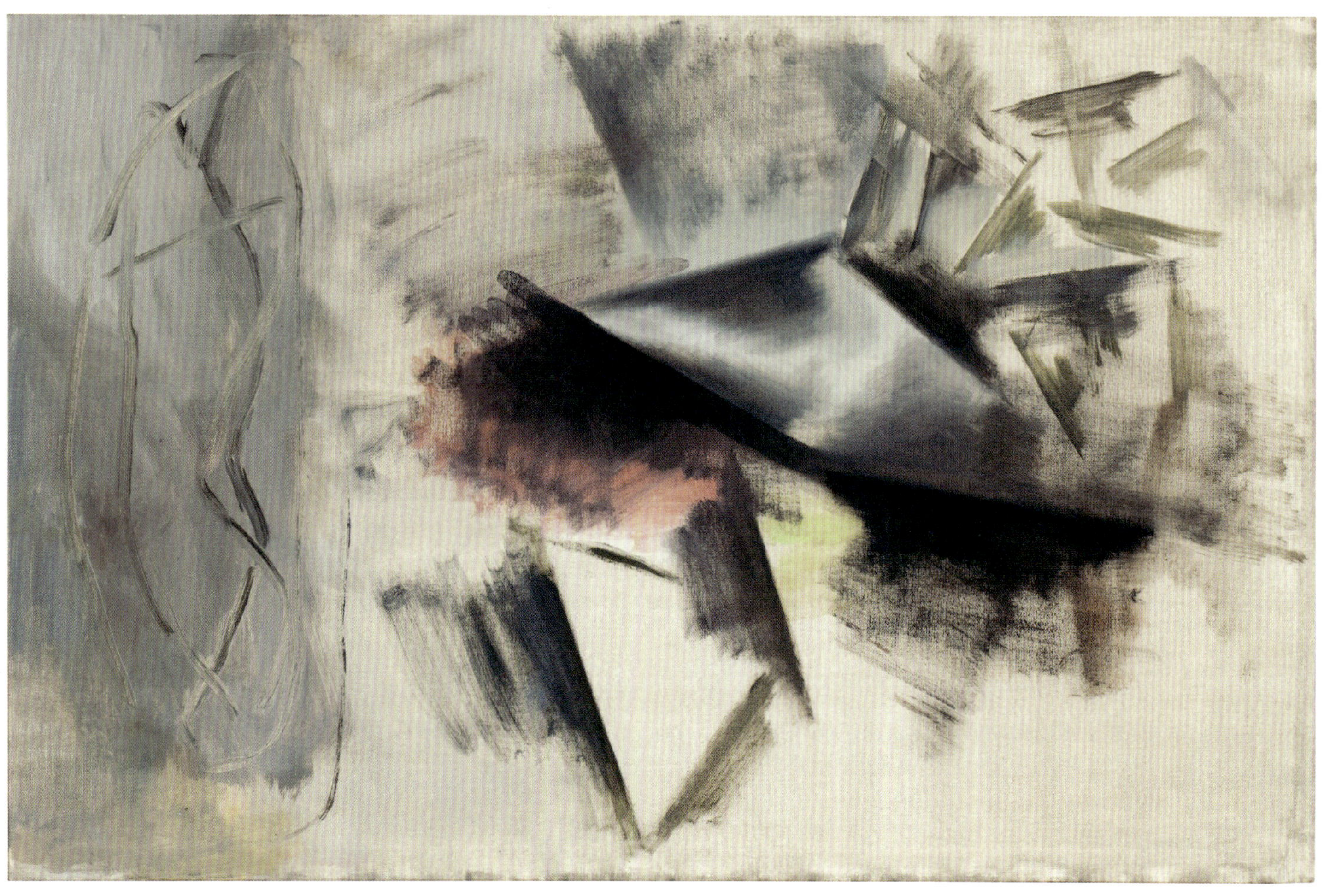

74. Untitled   2010

Oil on canvas
40 × 60 cm (15 ¾ × 23 ⅝ in)
Collection of Jorge Schwartzman, Buenos Aires

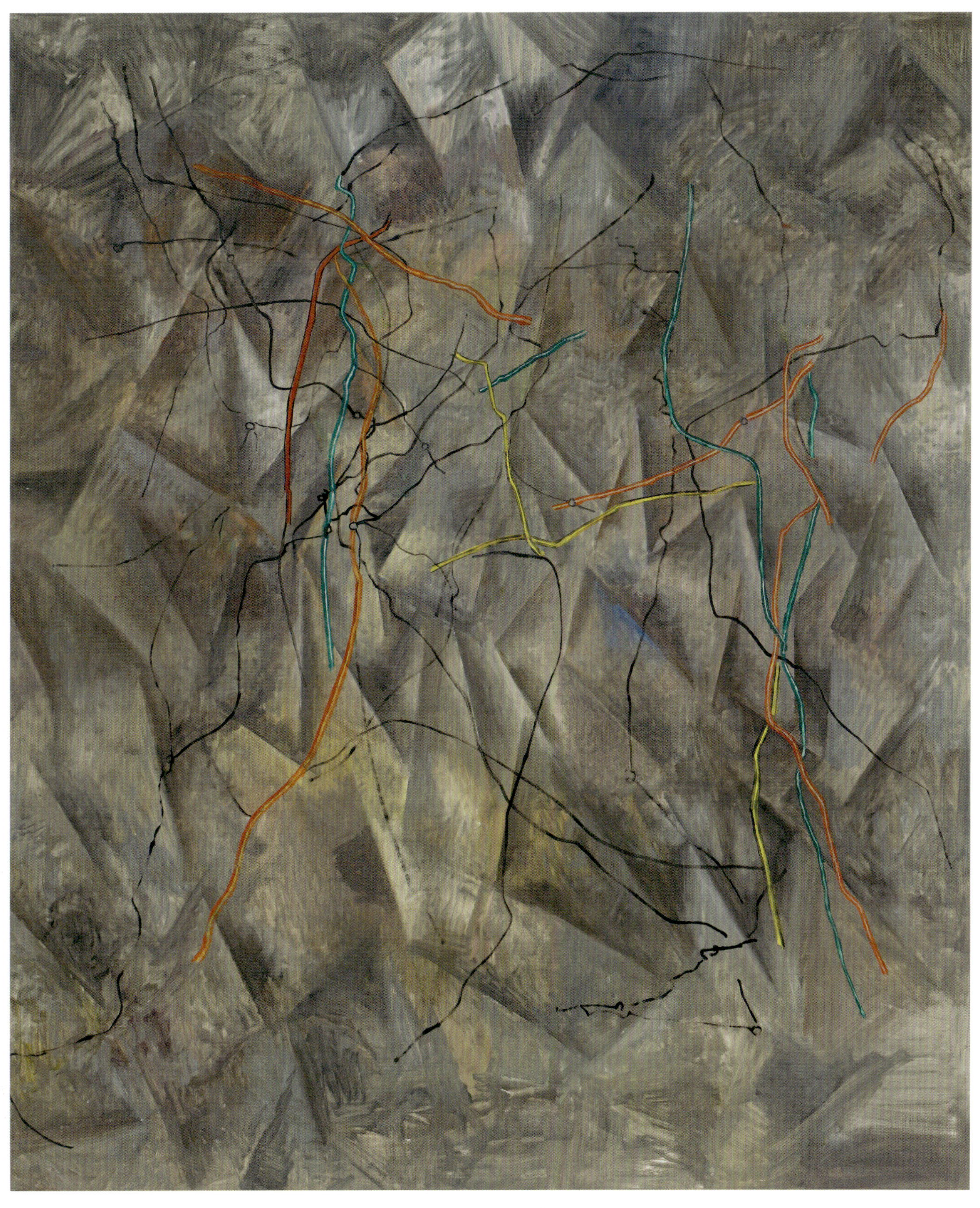

75. Untitled   2010

Oil on canvas
198.5 × 161.3 cm (78 ⅛ × 63 ½ in)
Private collection

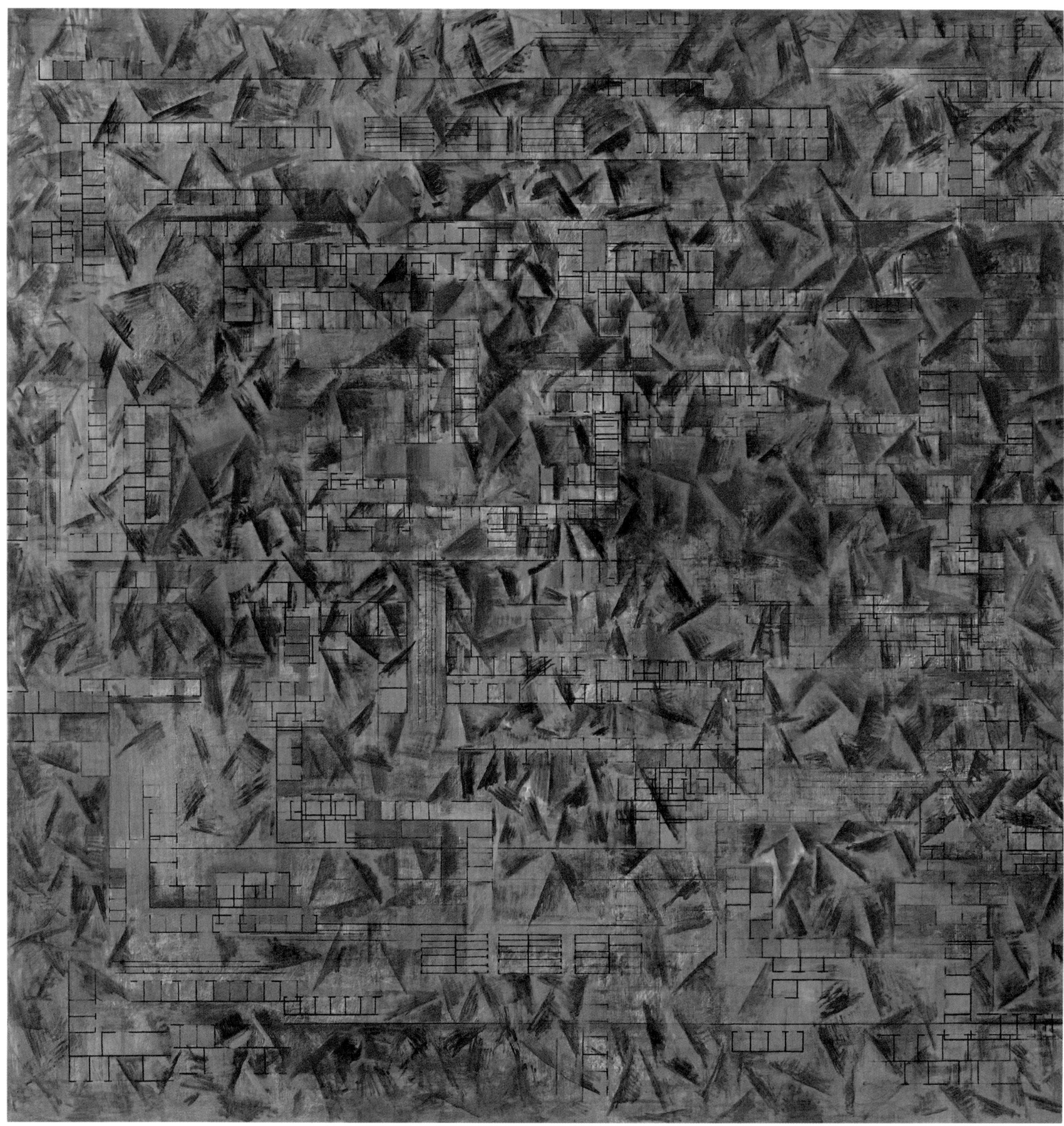

76. Untitled   2007

Oil on canvas
195 × 183 cm (76 ¾ × 72 in)
Private collection

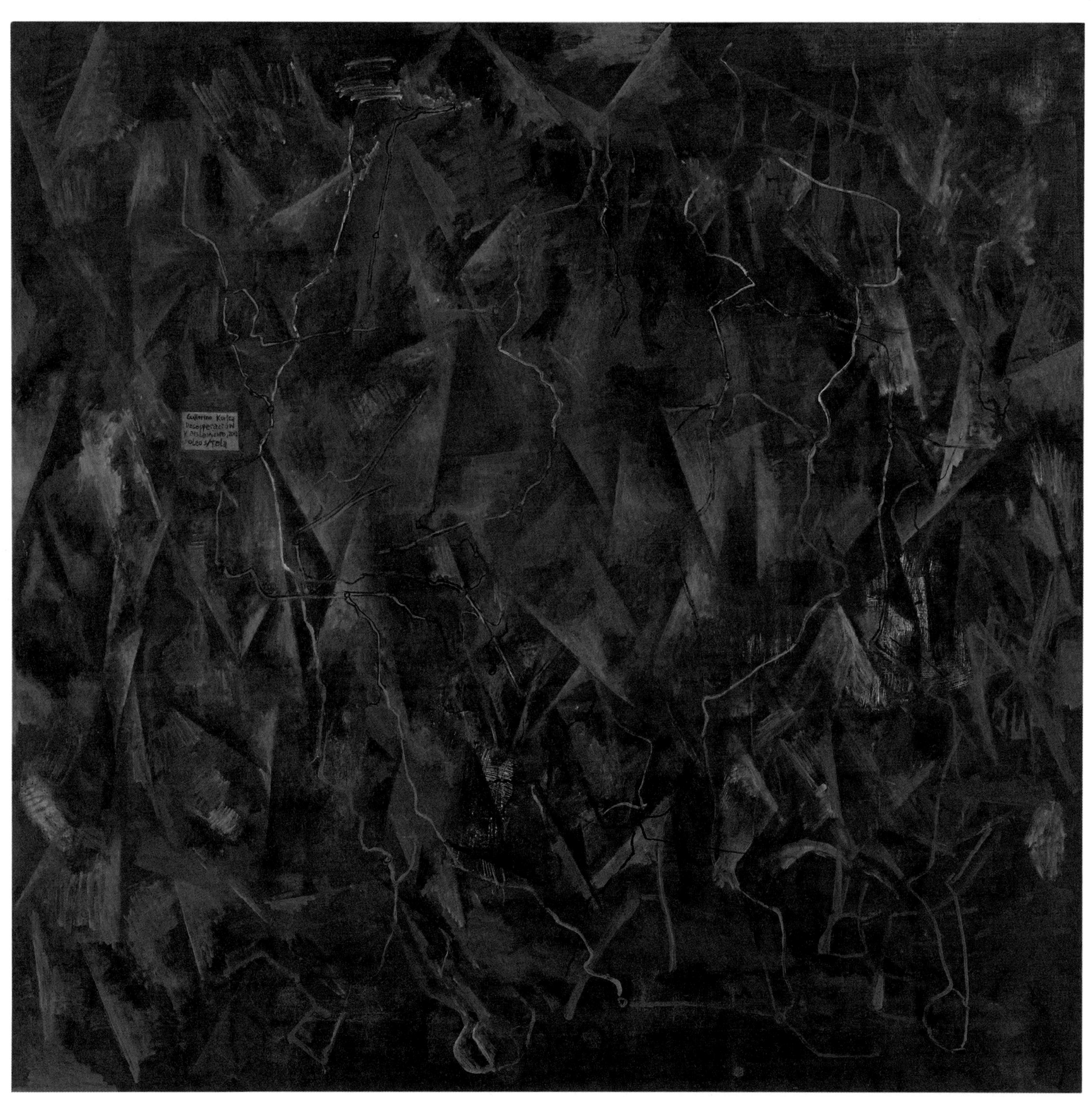

77. Despair and Isolation   2012

Oil on canvas
196 × 194.5 cm (77 ⅛ × 76 ⅝ in)
Mary Lile Collection, Houston, Texas

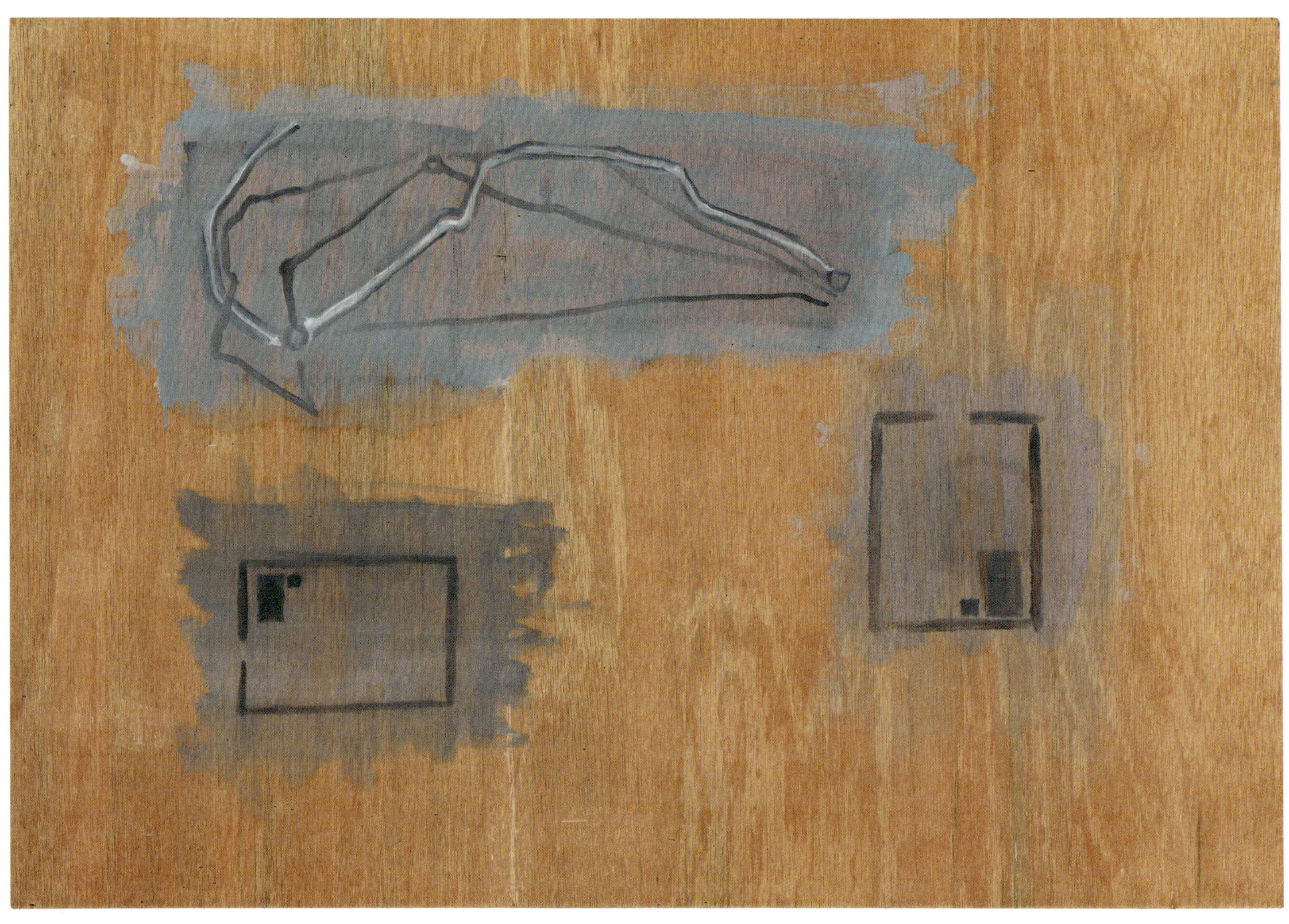

78. Untitled   2011

Oil on plywood
48.5 × 65 cm (19 × 25 ½ in)
Collection of the artist

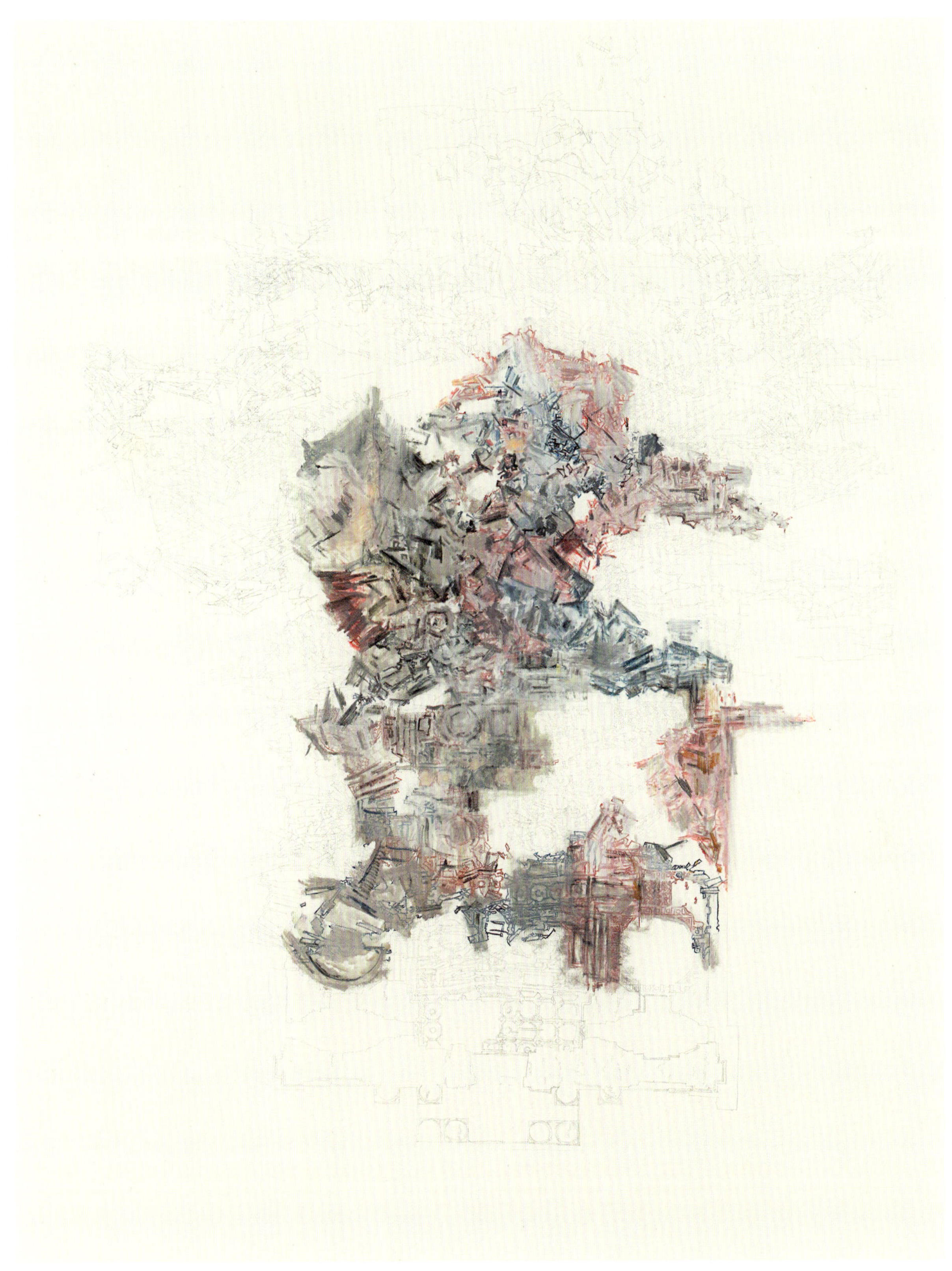

79. Untitled   2012

Graphite and oil on canvas
195.5 × 146.5 cm (77 × 57 ⅝ in)
Collection of the artist

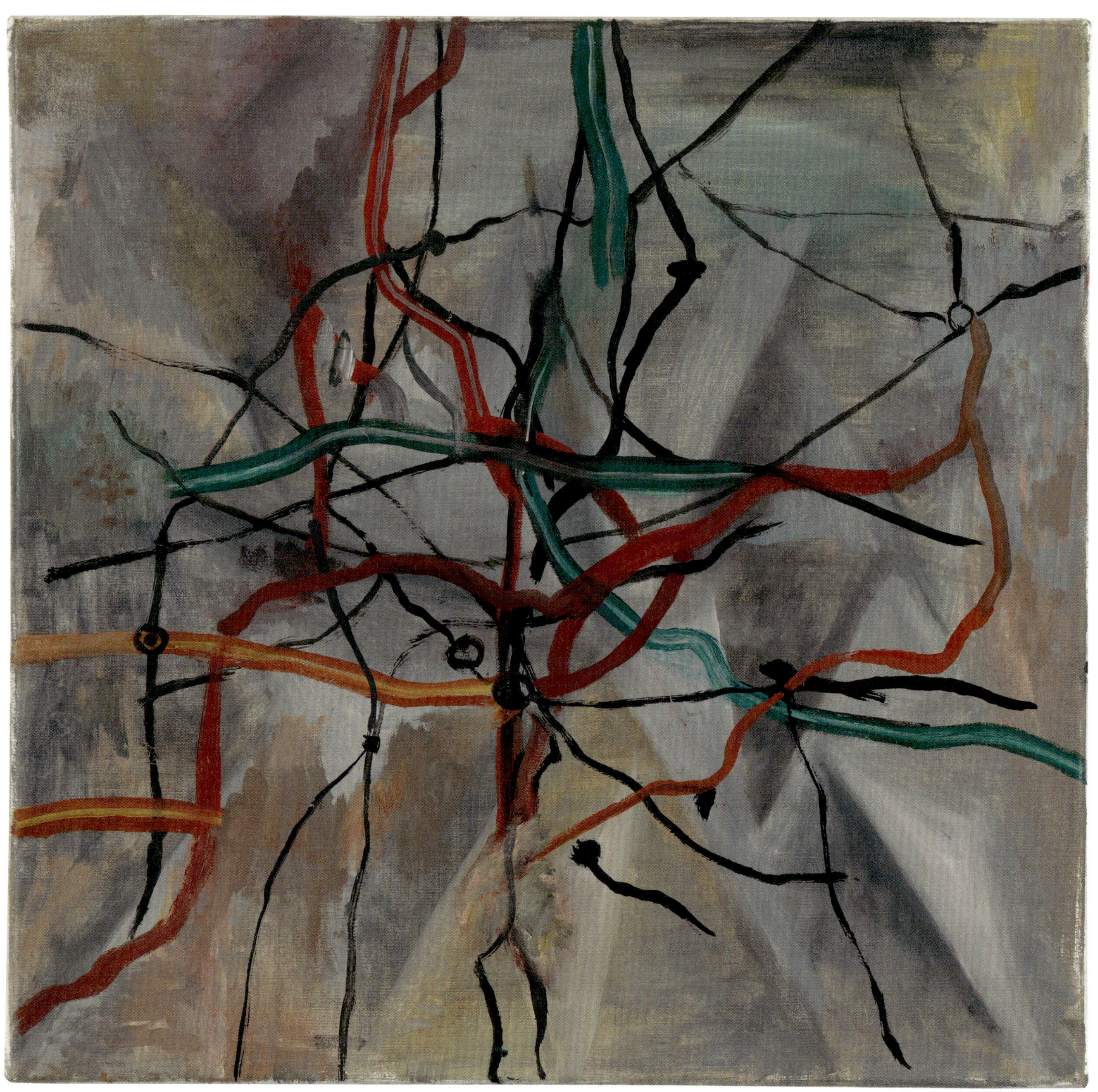

80. Untitled   2010

Oil on canvas
40 × 40 cm (15 ¾ × 15 ¾ in)
Collection of the artist

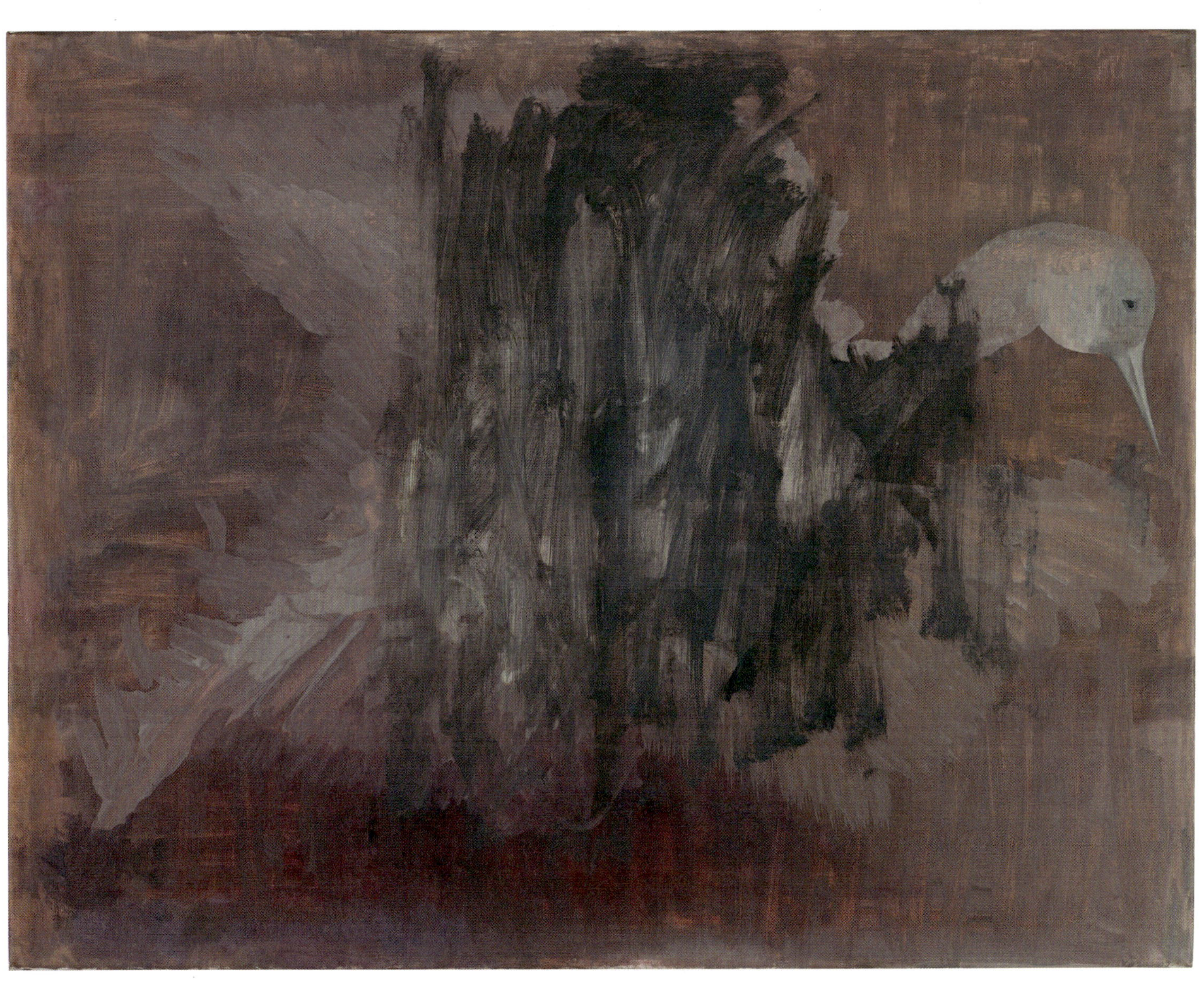

81. Untitled   2011

Oil on canvas
75 × 95 cm (29 ½ × 37 ⅜ in)
Ursula Hauser Collection, Switzerland

82. Double Eclipse   2013

Oil on canvas
283 × 362 cm (111 ⅜ × 142 ½ in)
Collection of the artist

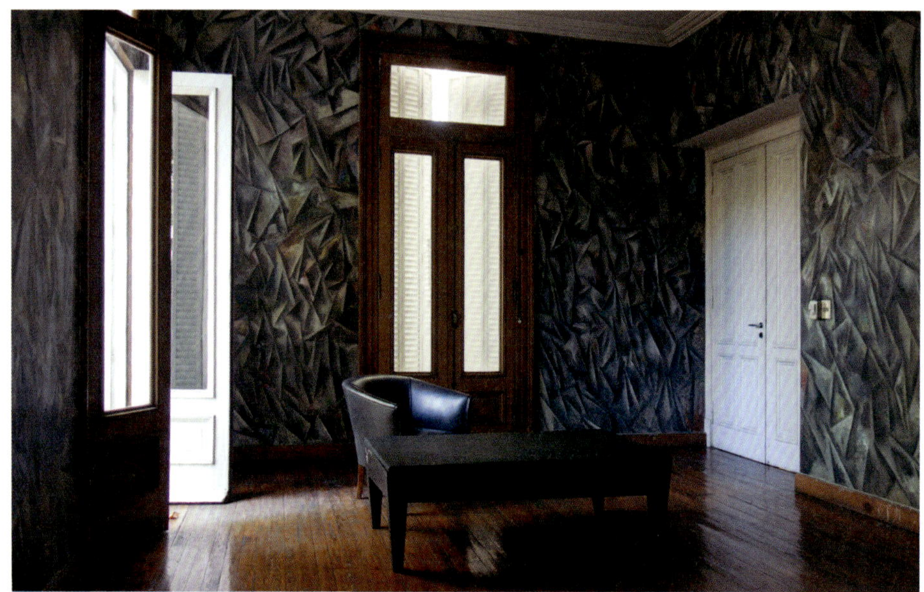

83. Wall paintings in Guillermo Kuitca's studio–home   2013

Oil on wall

Although Kuitca at first thought of the Cubistoid Paintings as the end of the line
– hence the title *Desenlace* (*Dénouement*) – they proved to be full of new possibilities.
In 2013, he decided to paint cubistoid motifs on the walls of a room in his studio–home,
an imposing multistory former boarding house in the elegant Belgrano neighborhood
of Buenos Aires (fig.83). Later that year the owners of Hauser & Wirth Gallery
commissioned him to create a set of murals in a restored farmhouse in the county of
Somerset in southwestern England (fig.85). Over the course of five weeks, Kuitca
covered the walls of a dining room from floor to ceiling with angular motifs that
suggest barren rocky mountains. This was the first time the artist made a totally
immersive painting. When the following year he had a show at Sperone Westwater
in New York, he made a mobile immersive painting by enclosing another cubistoid
painting inside a small freestanding room in the gallery (fig.84). On a much more
ambitious scale, in 2014 he presented *Les Habitants* at the Cartier Foundation in Paris.
Inspired by an exhibition film director David Lynch (b.1946) had done at the Cartier
Foundation in 2007, Kuitca's multi-room installation featured film projections (by
Armenian filmmaker Artavazd Pelechian), a recorded poem by musician Patti Smith
(b.1946), a painting by Vija Celmins (b.1938, one of the contemporary artists Kuitca
most admires), furniture Lynch had designed for his exhibition and, in one intensely
immersive space, a patterned red and black floor and cubistoid murals painted in an
eerie scarlet palette (fig.86). (In 2017, the exhibition, renamed *Les Visitants*, traveled
to the Kirchner Cultural Center in Buenos Aires.)

Kuitca was still working in his Cubistoid style in 2015 when he embarked on
Untitled (*Exodus*), a large painting with an unusual feature: a trompe l'oeil doorway
inserted in the middle of the over-6m (20 foot) long canvas (fig.88). While there is

84. Untitled   2014

Oil on wooden panel
260 × 236 × 306 cm (102 ⅜ × 92 ⅞ × 120 ½ in)

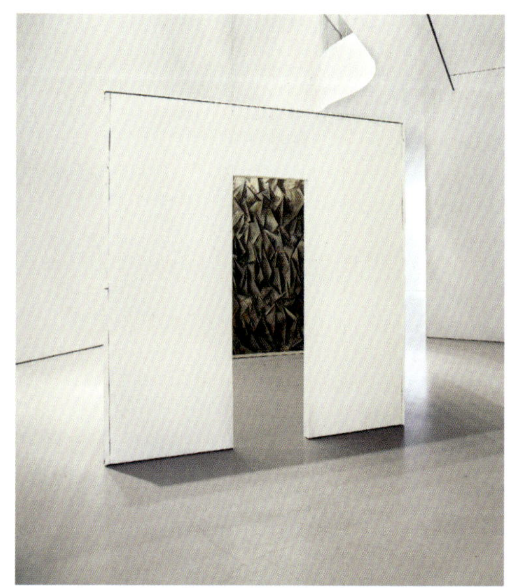

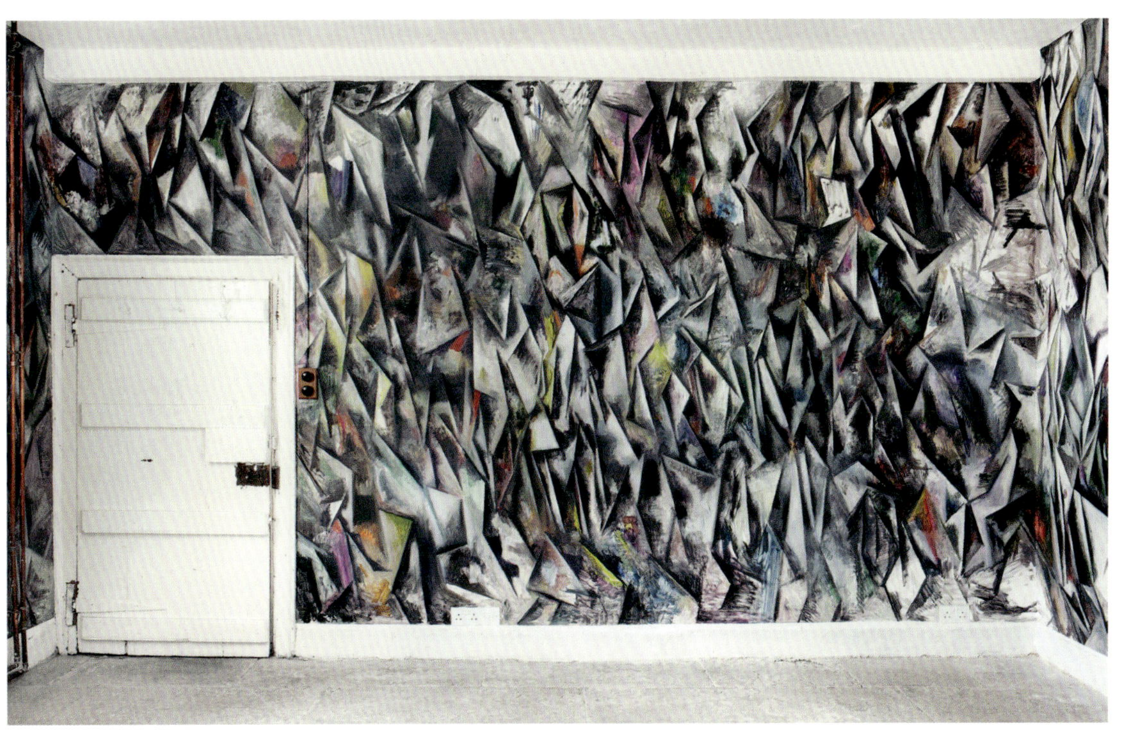

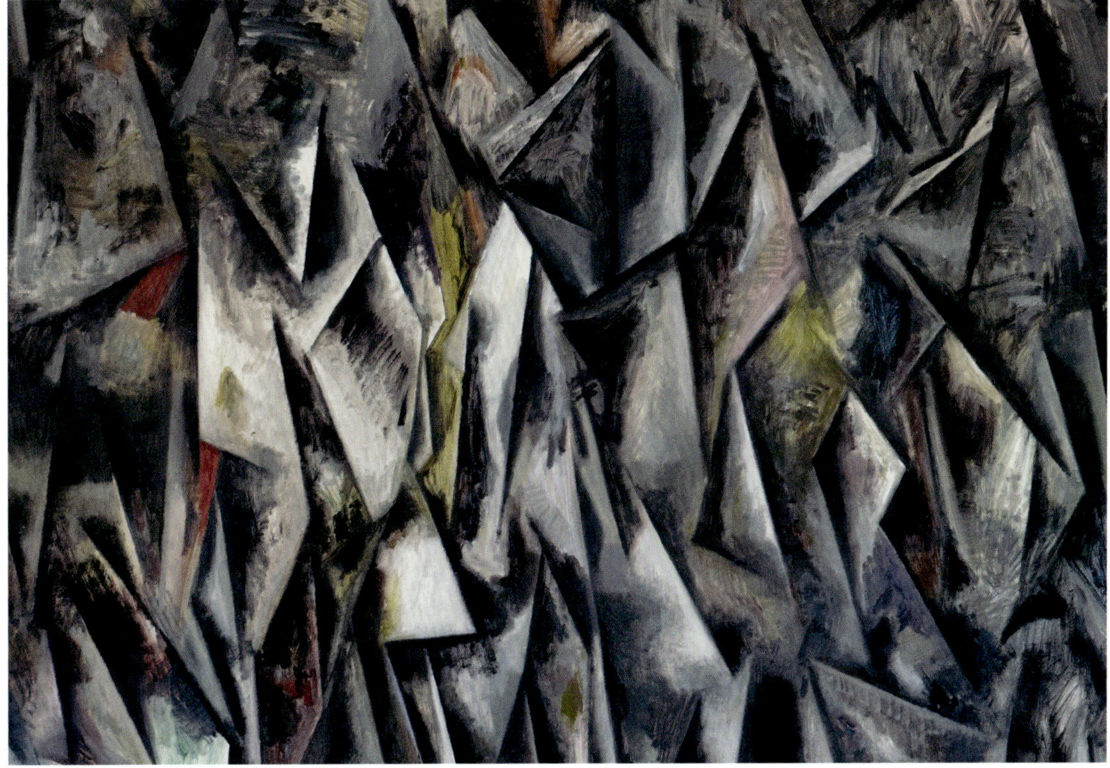

85. Mural in Durslade Farmhouse,
Hauser & Wirth, Somerset   2013

Oil on wall

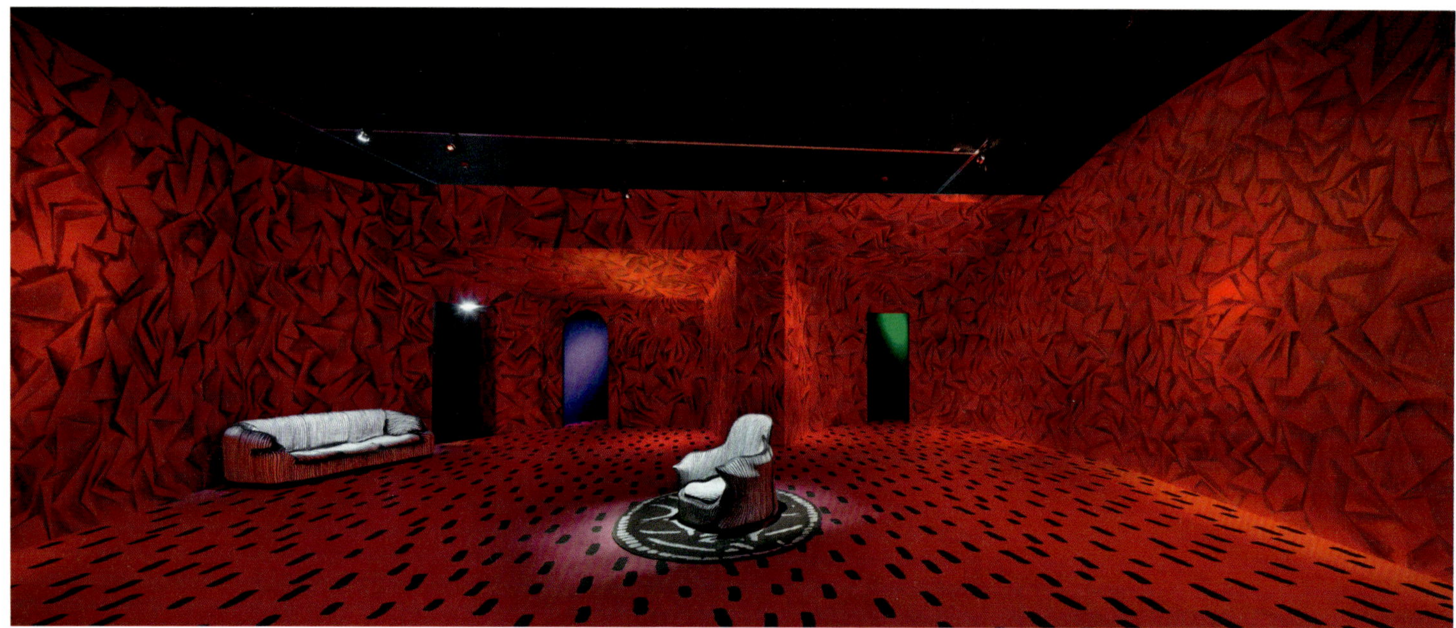

86. Les Habitants, Foundation Cartier Pour l'art contemporain, Paris

an obvious relationship between the doorway depicted in *Untitled (Exodus)* and the actual doorways Kuitca had to accommodate when he was painting murals in his studio and in Somerset, there is also a world of difference between them: the mural doors are contingent features of the world that are not part of the artwork; the painted door is the result of a deliberate choice. What is more, it is a choice that disrupts the rest of the painting by inserting illusionistic space into a non-referential abstraction. The painting's title encapsulates the biblical departure of the Jews from Egypt, but it can apply to any mass leaving. For instance, the flight of large numbers of Argentineans from the terror of the Dirty War has been referred to as an exodus, and so, too, the wave of Eastern European Jews who, like Kuitca's grandparents, migrated to the Americas in the early 20th century. In a 2016 interview with the online art magazine *Artdependence*, Kuitca noted that the Syrian refugee crisis was dominating the news while he was working on *Exodus*. Admitting that he has always felt uncomfortable tying his work to current events, and that he was not consciously making a painting about the refugees then turning up on the shores of Southern Europe, he also confessed that he could not decide 'whether this tragic and painful news is or is not in my painting'.[67]

At same time he was painting *Exodus*, Kuitca completed a 2m² (21 ½ square foot) untitled painting he had begun in 2003 as part of his Wagner series. Through a sequence of photographs it is possible to trace the evolution of the painting. At the start the artist had imposed a labyrinthine architectural plan onto the cover design for a recording of *Der Ring des Nieblungen*. Over the years other elements invaded the composition, gradually obscuring much of the bright yellow ground and the complicated building plan; the letters spelling out the title of the opera also

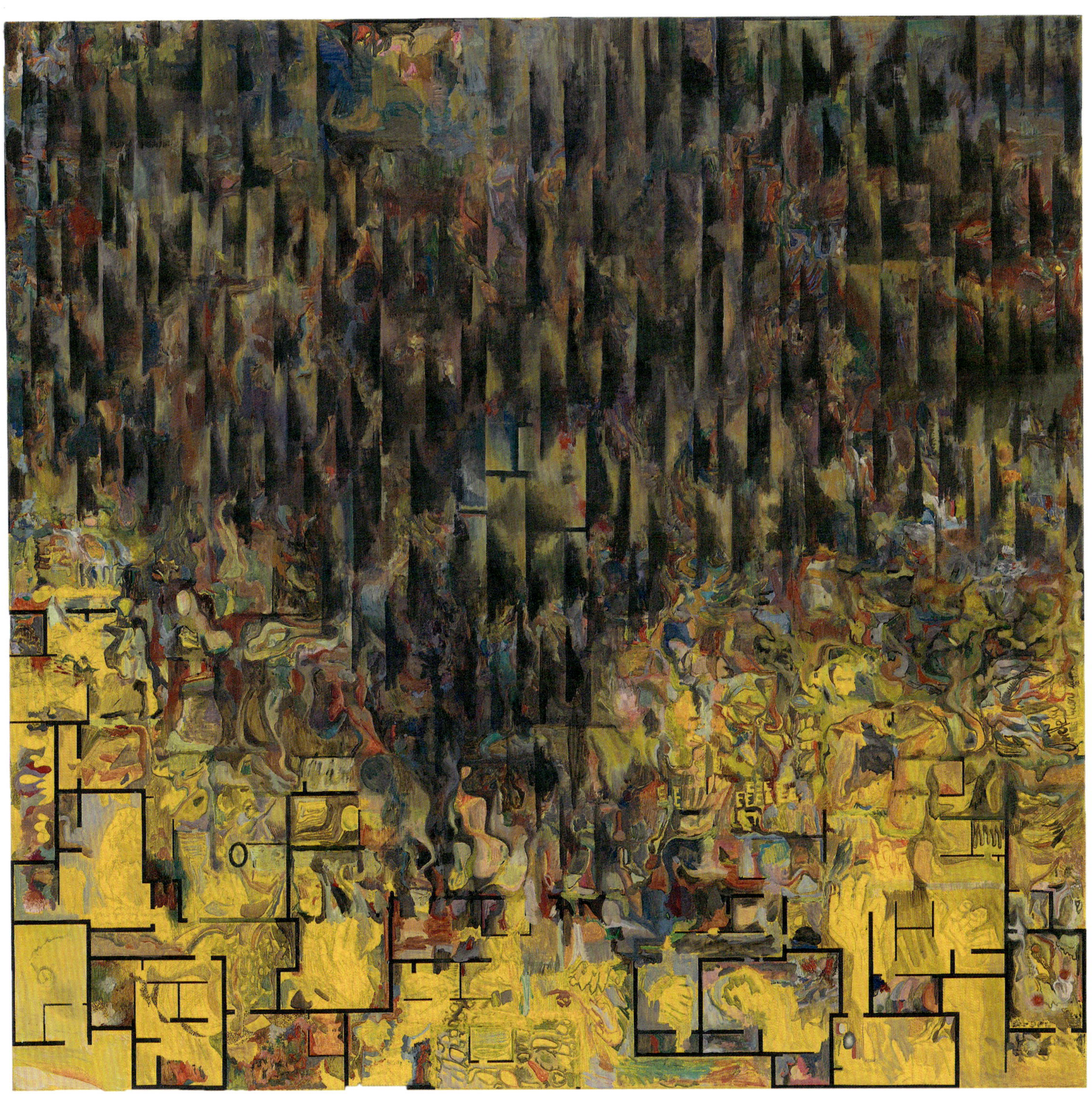

87. Untitled 2003–15

Oil on canvas
196.5 × 196.3 cm (77 ⅜ × 77 ¼ in)
Private collection

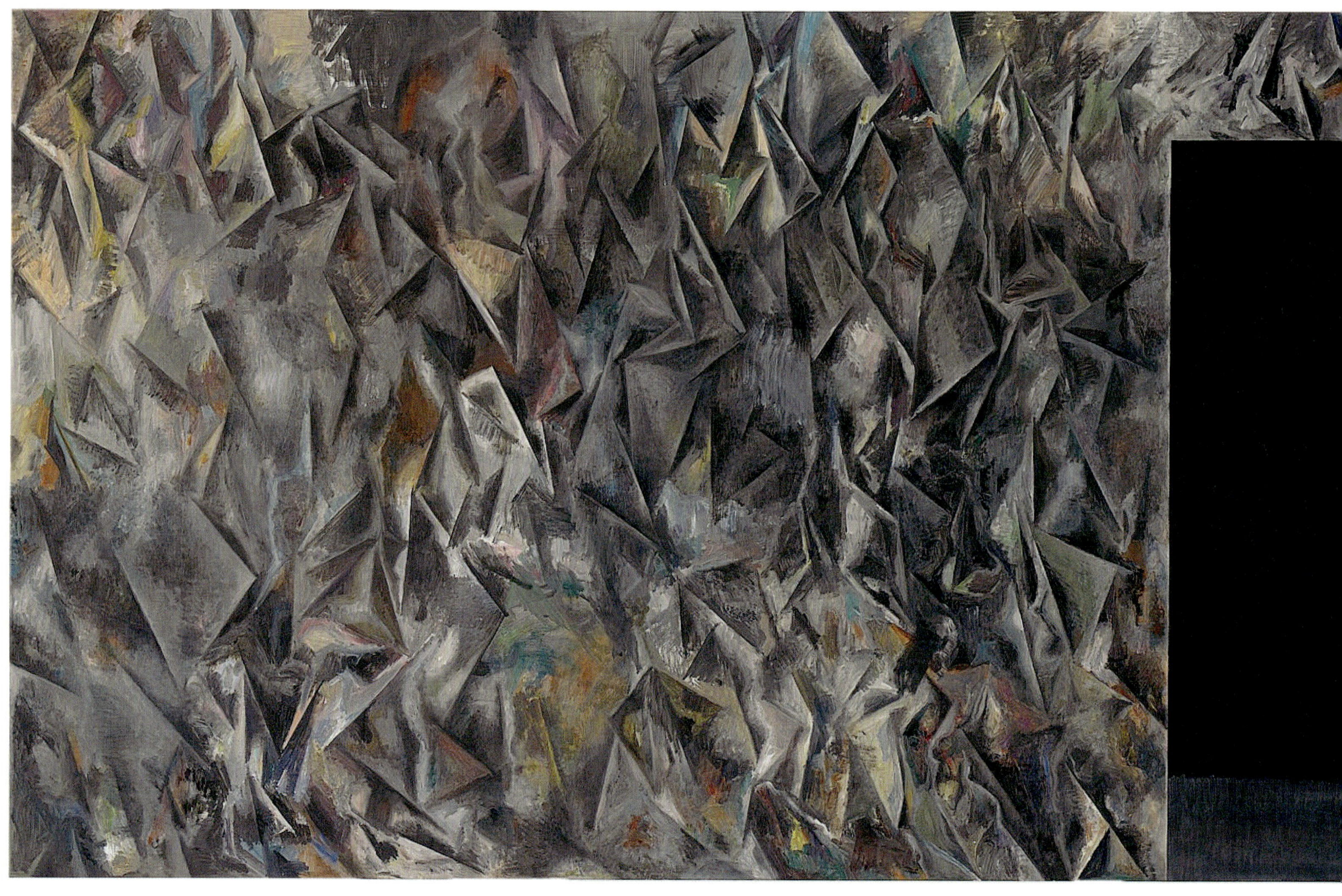

88. Untitled (Exodus)   2015

Oil on canvas
200 × 630 cm (78 ¾ × 248 in)
Private collection

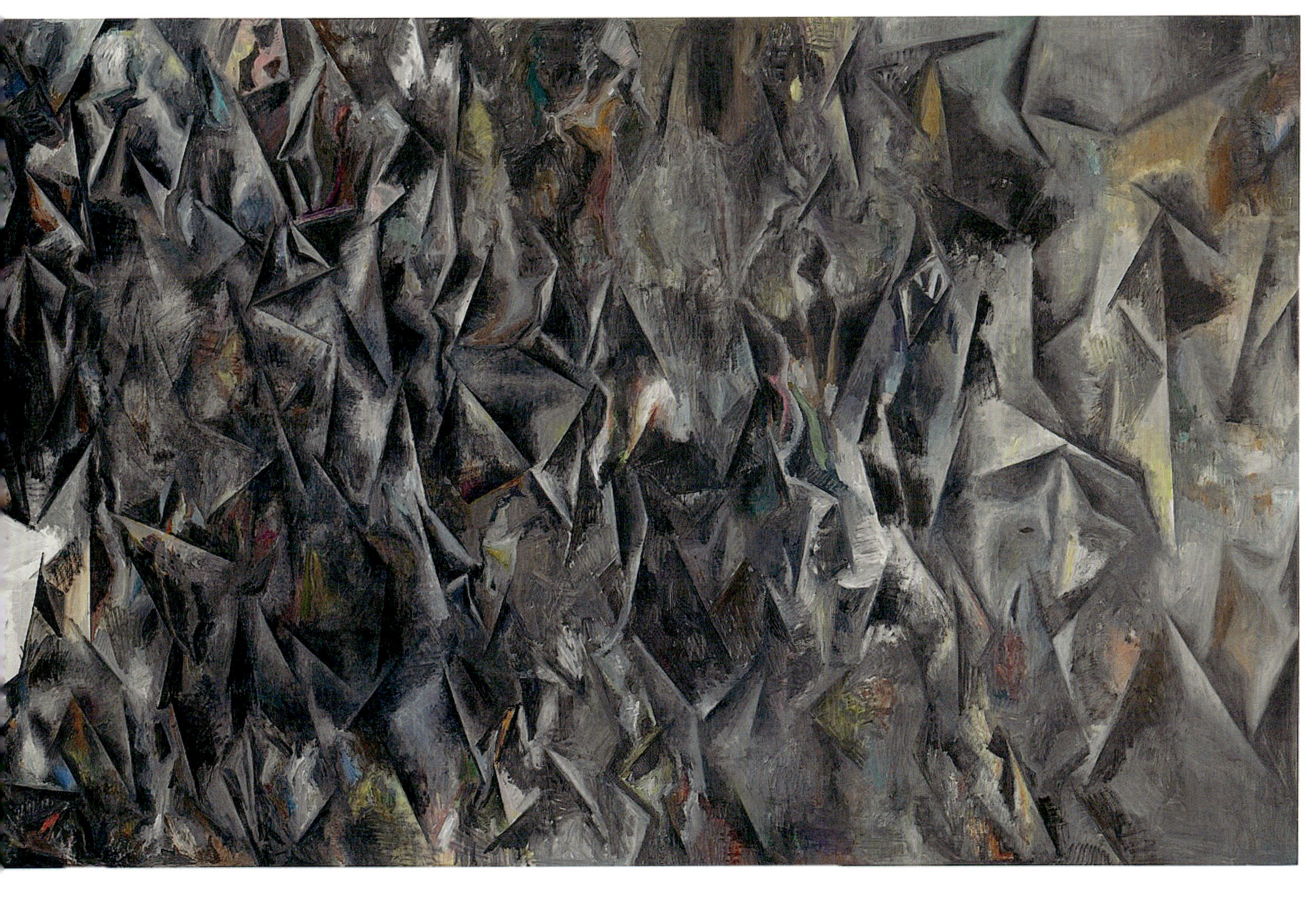

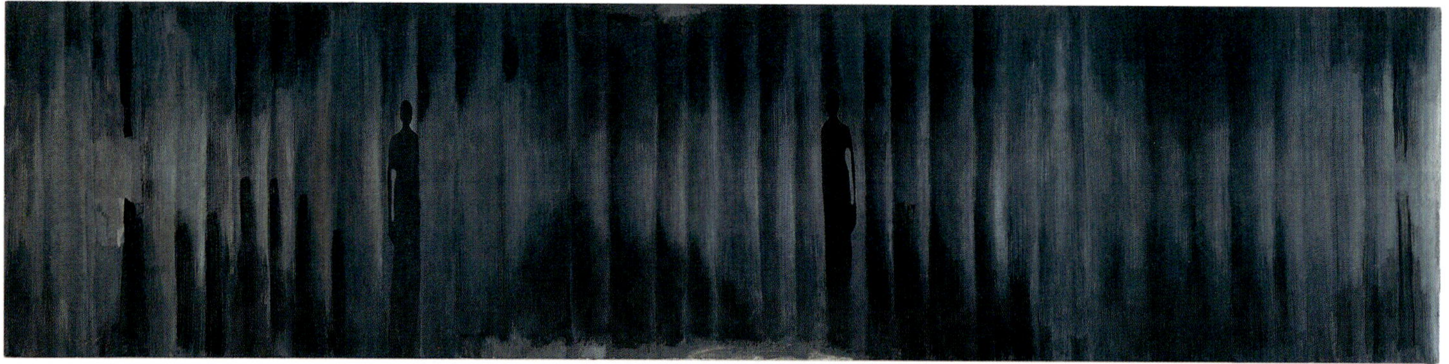

disappeared. The invasive shapes and marks were more painterly than anything
Kuitca had ever made, featuring sinuous biomorphic forms, modeling-like effects,
loose brushwork, and here and there suggestions of human faces. With their hints
of Arshile Gorky (1904–48), De Kooning (1904–97) and Guston (1913–80),
these painterly elements constitute Kuitca's most direct engagement with the
legacy of Abstract Expressionism. Ultimately, however, many of these features were
overwhelmed by a phalanx of vertically oriented planar units that occupy the top
half of the painting like neatly arranged sand dunes. Similar ridge-like motifs can
be seen in another 2015 painting, the somber, claustrophobic *Untitled (yo mujer)* in
which silhouetted figures are wedged into narrow gray spaces (fig.84). The quiet
materialization of these figures, taken with the figures and faces that had been slipping
into certain paintings in the preceding few years (including some figures that harked
back to *Nadie olvida nada*) suggest that figuration, having been largely absent from
Kuitca's work for nearly 30 years, was once again knocking at the door of his studio.

89. Untitled (Yo, mujer) 2015

Oil on wooden panel
50 × 200 cm (19 ¹¹⁄₁₆ × 78 ¾ in)
Private collection, Buenos Aires

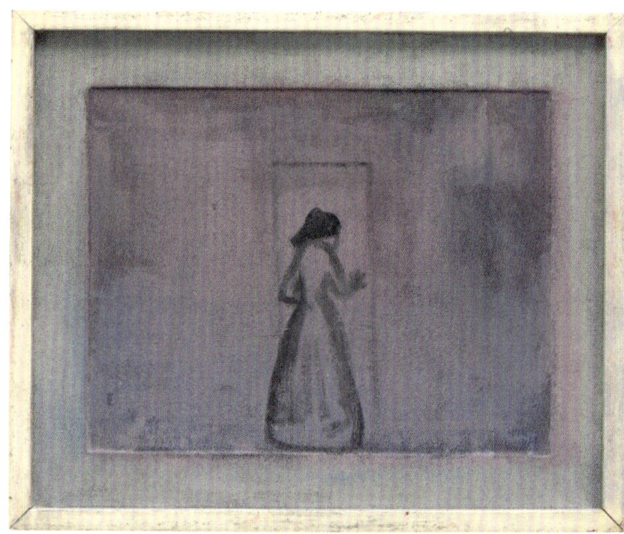

90. Untitled 2014

Oil on canvas mounted on board
in artist's frame
30.6 × 36.8 × 3cm (12 × 14 ½ × 1 ¹⁄s in) (framed)
Collection of the artist

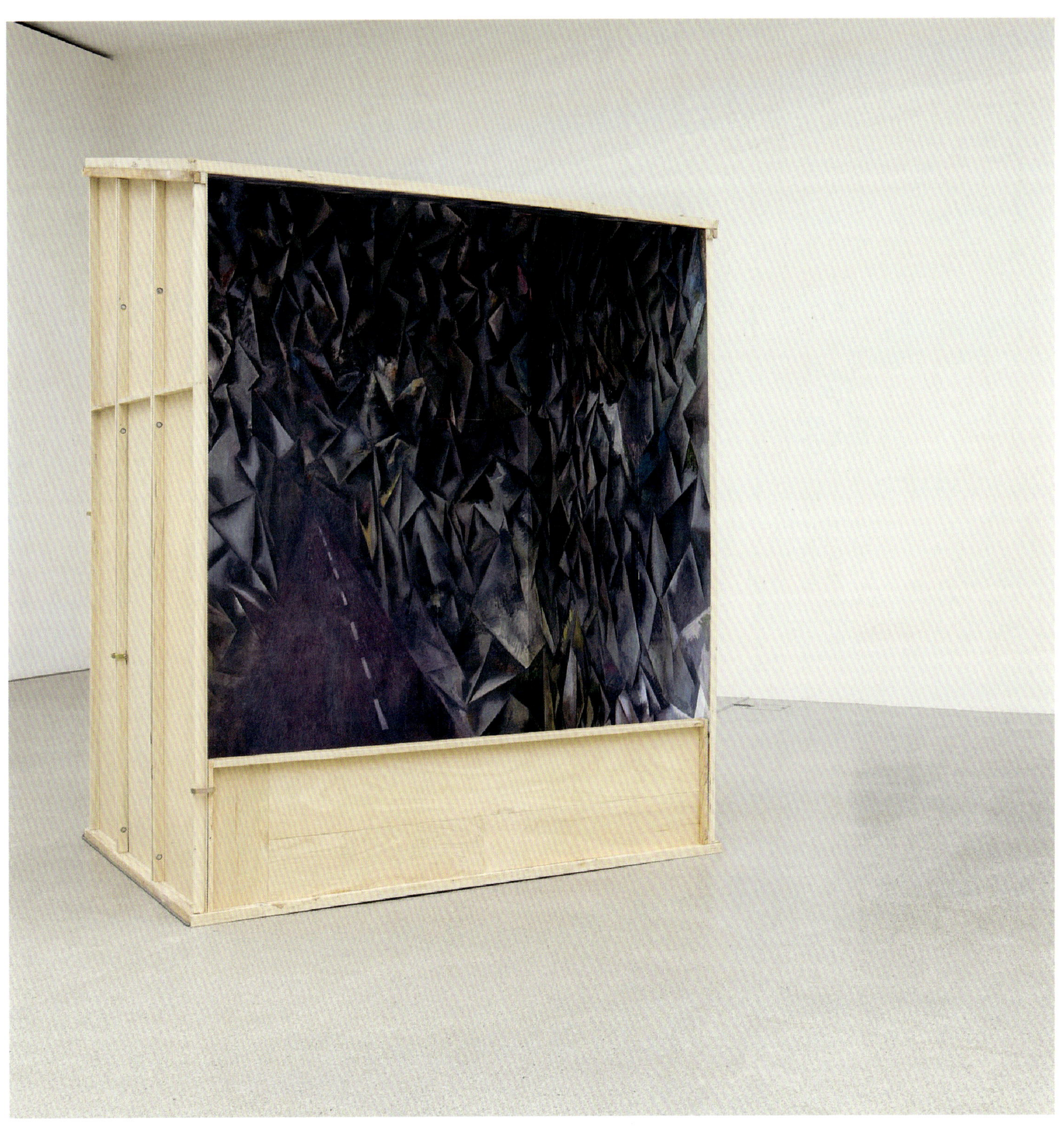

91. Retablo   2016

Oil on wooden panel
330 × 245 × 185 cm (129 ⅞ × 96 ½ × 72 ⅞ in)

91. **The Family Idiot**   2018

Oil on canvas in artist frame
Triptych, 82 × 177.5 cm (32 ¼ × 69 ⅞ in)

7 Space is a Doubt

In the spring of 2019, Kuitca unveiled a new body of work, *The Family Idiot*, at Hauser
& Wirth in Los Angeles. After years of making large-scale paintings and a decade of
experimenting with murals and immersive environments, with these new paintings
Kuitca made a turn toward a more intimate art. The canvases are easel size and each
one is executed in a single consistent style, one that looks back to the artist's theater
painting of the 1980s, before the beds, before the maps, before the house plans. Instead
of the flat, diagram-like iconography that he became known for, and in contrast to the
essentially abstract Cubist style that had been occupying him since 2006, *The Family
Idiot* paintings (the title is borrowed from Jean-Paul Sartre's unfinished multi-volume
study of Gustave Flaubert) depict illusionistic spaces, featureless rooms defined by
towering walls that dwarf the sparse figures and objects within them. Several of the
paintings are made on multiple panels, including two triptychs that are hinged like a
traditional altarpiece so that the paintings can be displayed standing upright on narrow
shelves. Most of the paintings, including the hinged triptychs, have been framed by the
artist with thin lengths of unpainted wood. The simplicity of the frames carries into
the paintings themselves, which use the most basic of devices to suggest space: a few
angled lines, some desultory shading, a minimum of perspective. Also contributing to
the overall feeling of modesty are the deliberately unfinished-looking areas in some of the
paintings, where the primed canvas seems to have been barely touched with a brush.

But things are not as simple as they seem. In one small triptych, painted in a
velvety grisaille, a haloed moon appears to be shining from a corner of a high-ceiling
room. Are we inside or outside? In many of the paintings there are walls that look
like they are made of glass or of mirrors. One diptych depicts an enormously tall
space that seems like the setting for a strange ritual, or a battle between mystics, or a
waiting room in some Kafkaesque bureaucratic headquarters (fig.92). Or maybe it is
a museum atrium that has been set up for a piece of performance art. A few isolated
chairs ring the empty square gray floor. The division between the panels runs down
the center of the room. The two halves are so similar that you think one might be a
mirror image of the other, until you notice that the chairs are not arranged identically
in the two panels. At the far corner the walls stop short, brighter walls suggest the
presence of two additional rooms. Or are these images in mirrors? A couple of small
flat objects leaning against the walls also look like mirrors but the images in them do
not correspond to the space they are in. Could they be paintings instead of mirrors?

It soon becomes clear that these visual conundrums are not there to be resolved.
Painting, Kuitca reminds us, is a medium in which anything is possible, even

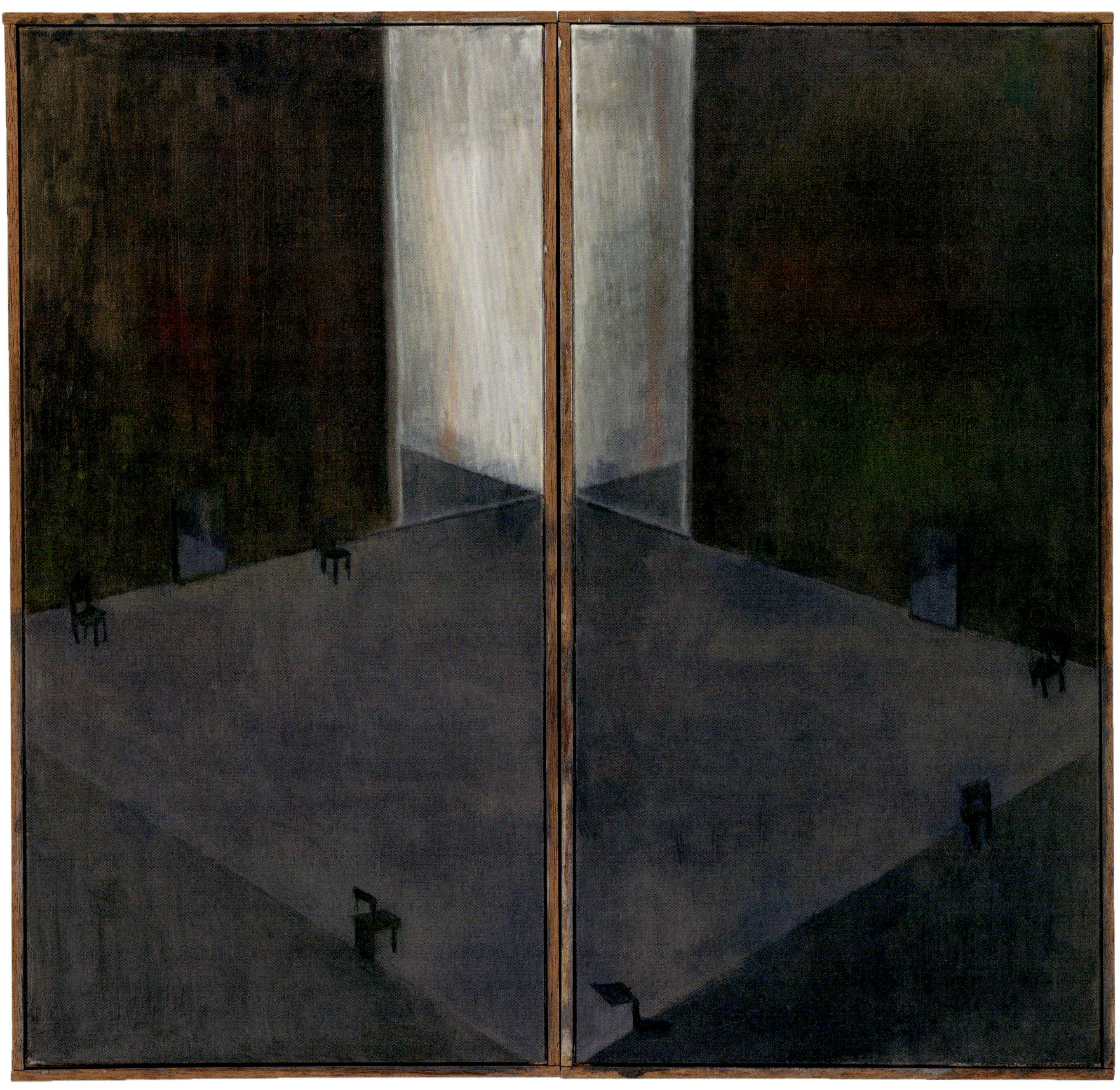

92. The Family Idiot   2019

Oil on canvas in artist frame
diptych, 82 × 84 cm (32 ¼ × 33 ⅛ in)

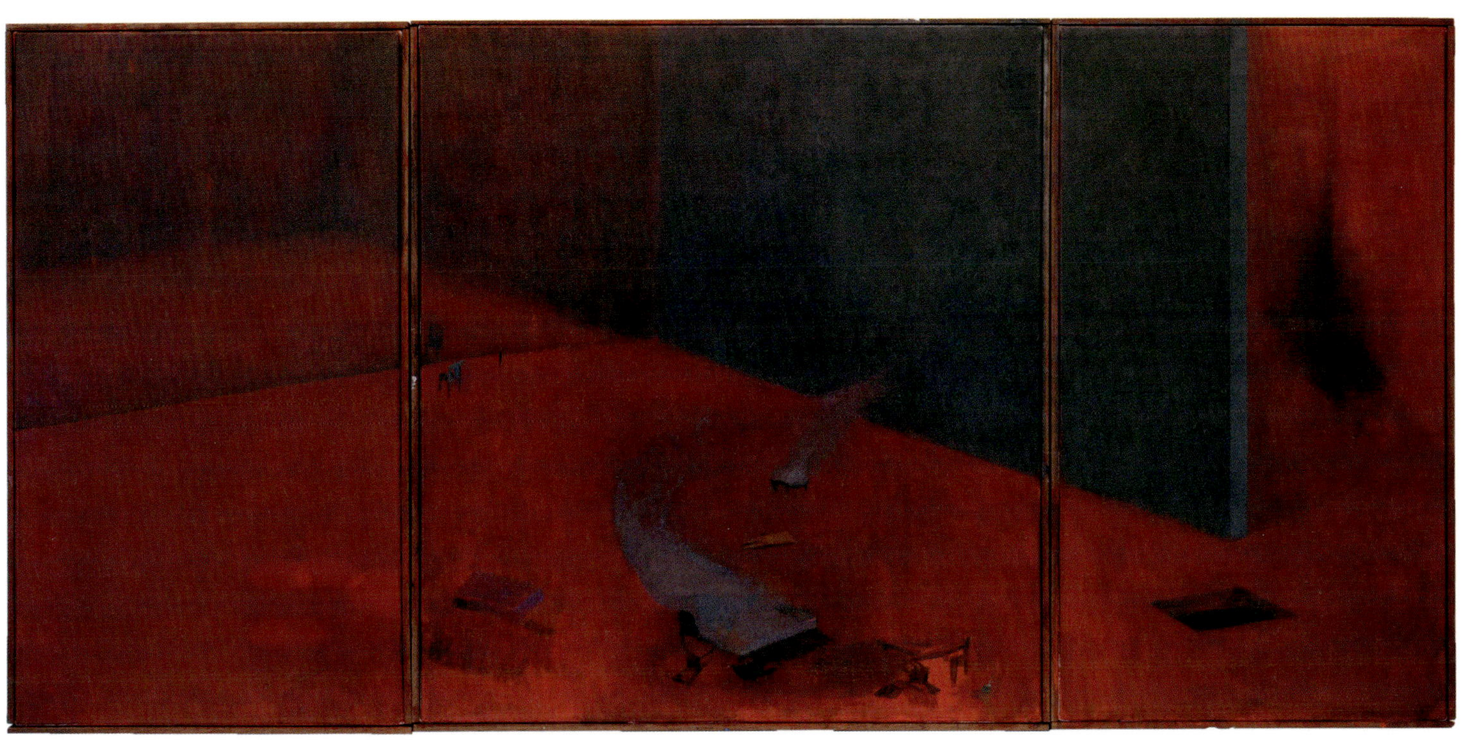

93. The Family Idiot   2019

Oil on canvas in artist frame
triptych, 92.5 × 186 cm (36 ⅜ × 73 ¼ in)

the physically (and mentally) impossible. It is a realm in which explanations are ephemeral, and motivations can be obscure. Not even the artist knows what is happening or why. Take, for instance, a detail in one of *The Family Idiot* triptychs where several burning beds and knocked-over chairs appear in a big red room (fig.93). In the lower right corner of the middle panel is a precisely painted detail that looks like an upside-down frying pan. The image is inspired by something Kuitca noticed in a Hieronymus Bosch painting he saw at the Prado in Madrid. In order to render this miniscule thing, he bought a tiny brush and donned a pair of glasses, which he does not usually do while painting. He vaguely thought of the image as an olive on a stem and enjoyed the control he had in painting the |diminutive form. His expectation was that he would paint it out before the canvas | was finished, but in the end he left it in. A few inches away is another hard-to-identify and hard-to-explain detail. It looks a little like a yellow glove. In fact it was originally a chair, before Kuitca painted out its legs and made it into a kind of garment. Smaller still is a little door barely visible in the gray wall in the central panel, which looks like an enormous slab of steel.

There are very few figures in *The Family Idiot* paintings, and when they do appear they are barely present, concealing themselves from us, and perhaps from the artist. On one small canvas on a ground the color of a dusty playground, an armless, footless figure from *Nadie olvida nada* stands to the side of a Fontana cut. The slash is about the same height as the figure. One can imagine her slipping into it, or that she has just escaped from the dark zone within. In another small single-panel painting (fig.94) a figure sleeps on a bed that had been jammed up against a mirrored wall in which the sleeping figure is reflected – or is it a sheet of glass, separating two identical figures?

As I was looking at *The Family Idiot* paintings in Kuitca's studio shortly before they were shipped to an exhibition at Hauser & Wirth in Los Angeles, the artist remarked to me that they were prefigured by his *L'Enfance du Christ* House Plan paintings. The resemblance has nothing to do with any religious symbolism in *The Family Idiot*, he explained. It is because, for him, both sets of paintings are, in his words, 'about a child wandering through an empty house'. Not that Kuitca paints any such child. That would be too illustrative, too narrative, too limited. Maybe we are looking through the eyes of a child, or rather through the eyes of an adult who remembers what it was like to be a child. Or maybe the child has just stepped out of the room, or into one of those enormous mirrors. Or disappeared through a tiny door. I suddenly remembered how in his Theater Paintings he would frequently change the locations of the figures and that traces of the painted-out figures were sometimes still visible. Noticing the smudges, shadows and smoke-like patches that pervade *The Family Idiot* paintings, I wondered if these could be the pentimenti of figures who had passed through these chambers, the memories of motion, the residue of lives lived. Throughout *The Family Idiot*, Sartre pursues the impossible task of understanding how a child like Flaubert

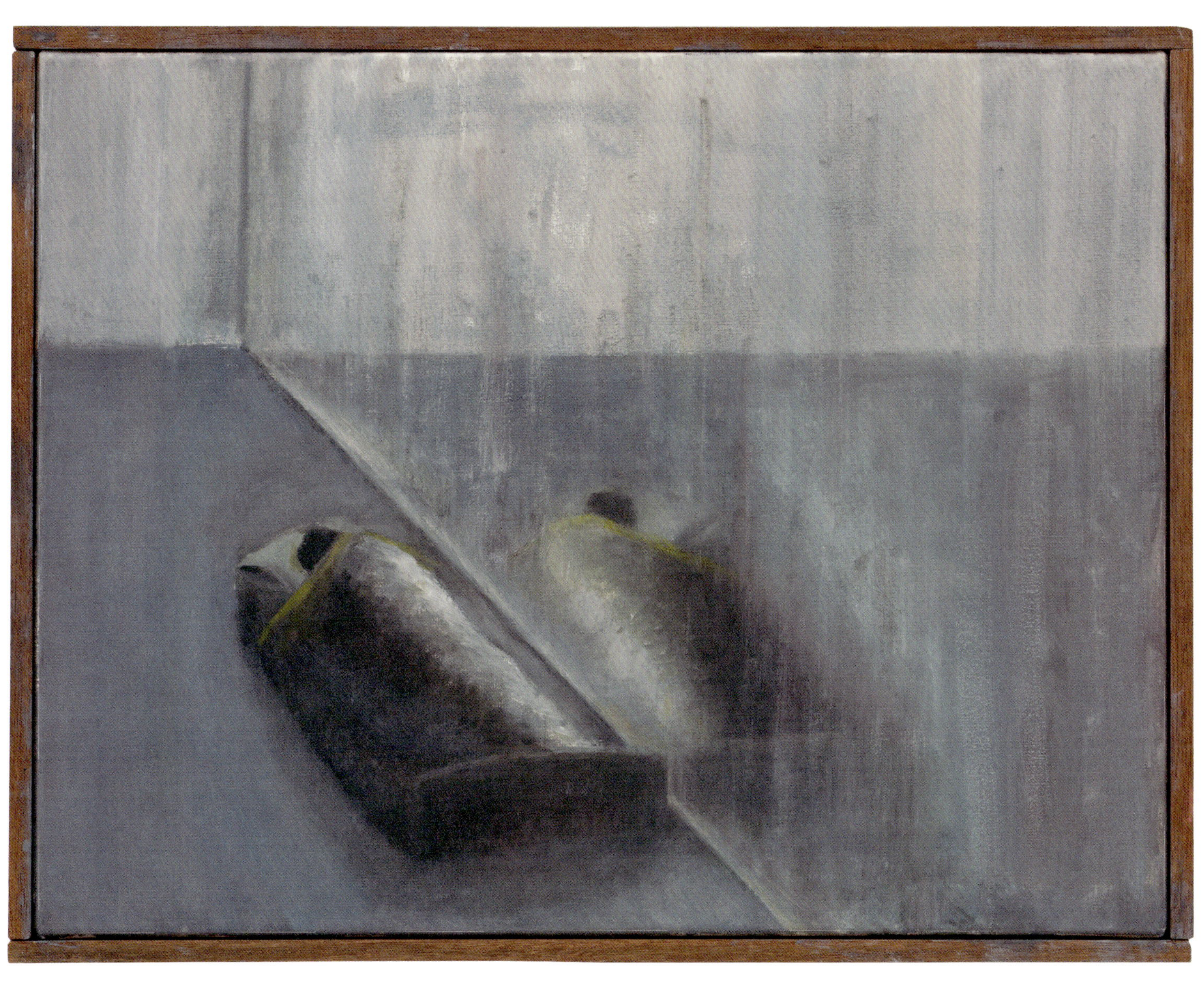

94. The Family Idiot (Sleeper in the Mirror) 2019

Oil on canvas in artist frame
35 × 45 cm (13 ¾ × 17 ¾ in)

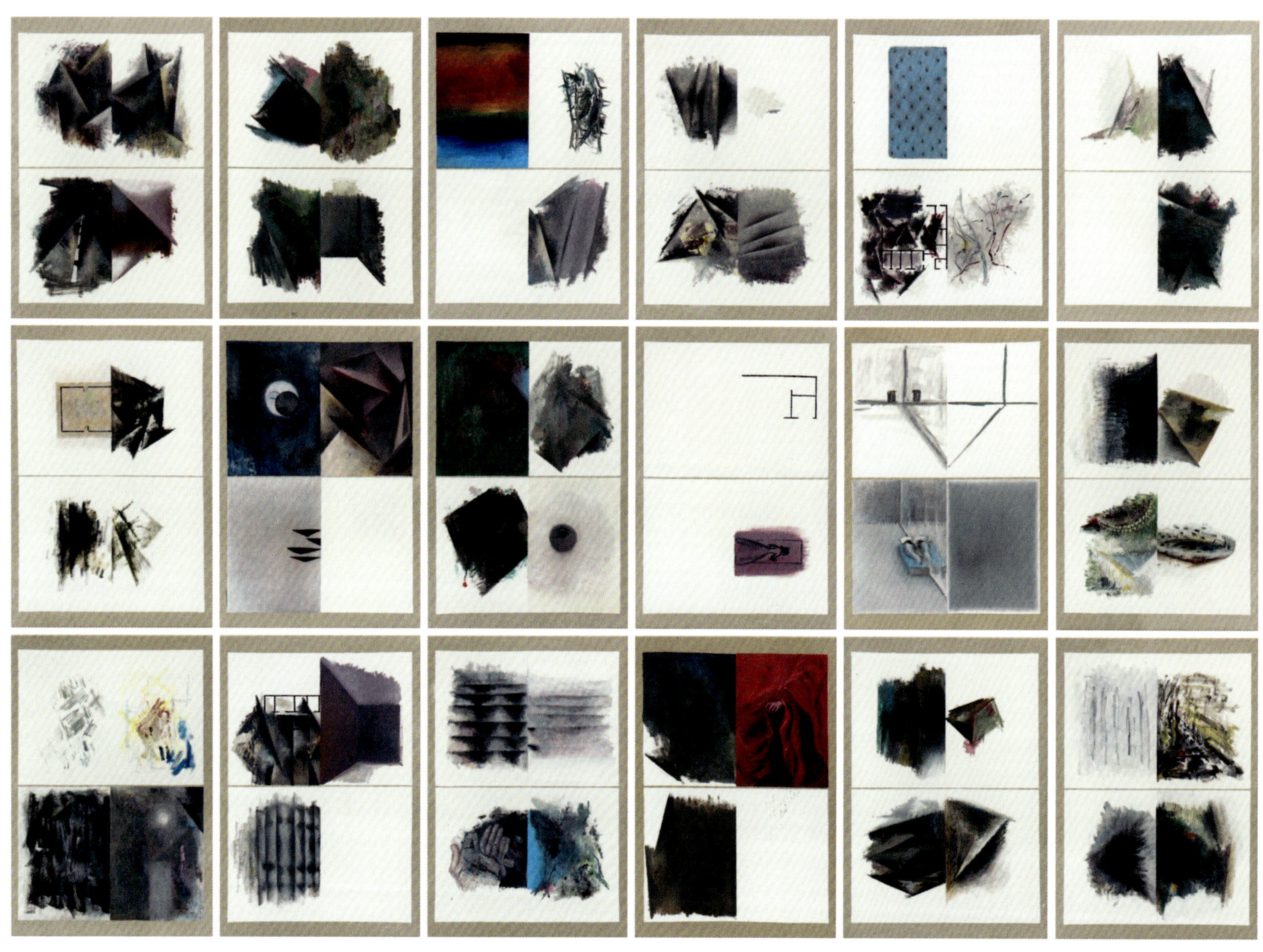

95. Missing Pages (18 parts)   2018–19

Oil on canvas
18 works, each 95 × 63 cm (37 ⅜ × 24 ¾ in)

becomes 'someone who writes, who wants to speak of the imaginary'.[68] In Kuitca's version the artist seems to be on the trace of his own evolution, summoning the scenes and desires that turned him into a lifelong devotee of the painterly imaginary. Also included in the Hauser & Wirth show was *Missing Pages*, an 18-panel painting with 72 paired images that are often abruptly cropped (the format was inspired by how reproductions sometimes are cut off in the 'gutter' of an art book). Drawn from Kuitca's own back catalogue of motifs as well as the work of other artists, the images of *Missing Pages* constitute a concise encyclopaedia of painting.

We think of Kuitca as a painter of space, and rightly so. For nearly four decades he has led us through an atlas of spaces, places of sleep and spectacle, places of death and diversion, places of tenderness and travel. His muses are to be found amid buildings and maps, in the disciplines of architecture and cartography. Yet there is something in the *The Family Idiot* that suggests how memory may drift through his spaces, that he is also a painter of time.

At the end of his book *Species of Space*, French writer Georges Perec confesses how he would 'like there to exist places that are stable, unmoving, intangible, untouched and almost untouchable, unchanging, deep-rooted'. He has in mind the place where he was born, the house he grew up in, a tree he watched grow, an attic he used to play in as a child. Unfortunately, Perec concludes, 'such places don't exist, and it's because they don't exist that space becomes a question, ceases to be self-evident, ceases to be incorporated, ceases to be appropriated. Space is a doubt. I have constantly to mark it, to designate it. It's never mine, never given to me, I have to conquer it.'[69] This seems to be exactly what Kuitca's paintings tell us, over and over again: that there is no such thing as a stable space, that our fate is to venture forward in uncertainty, always marking and designating where we have been, where we might go, and, if we are lucky, sometimes remembering something like home, the losses surrounding us and their images, the nothings that nobody forgets.

Notes

1. Conversation with the author, Buenos Aires, March 2019.

2. Quoted in Andrea Giunta, *Avant-Garde, Internationalism and Politics: Argentine Art in the Sixties*, Duke University Press, Durham, 2007, p.95.

3. Original Spanish version in *Guillermo Kuitca: Obras 1982–1998, Conversaciones con Graciela Speranza*, Grupo Editorial Norma, Buenos Aires, 1998, p.17. English translation from an unpaginated manuscript provided by Sperone Westwater Gallery, New York.

4. This summary of Pina Bausch's work is indebted to dance historian Susan Allen Manning's article 'An American Perspective on Tanztheater' in *The Drama Review (TDR)*, Spring 1986, pp 31–44.

5. Original Spanish version in *Guillermo Kuitca: Obras 1982–1998, Conversaciones con Graciela Speranza*, p.17.

6. Christos M. Joachimides, *A New Spirit in Painting*, Royal Academy of Arts, London, 1981, p.14.

7. *Guillermo Kuitca: Obras 1982–1998, Conversaciones con Graciela Speranza*, p.20.

8. Quoted in *A Book Based on Guillermo Kuitca*, Contemporary Art Foundation, Amsterdam, 1993, p.170.

9. Mari Carmen Ramírez, 'Guillermo Kuitca: The "Death of Painting": Painting as a Resistance Movement', *Literal 29*, Literalmagazine.com, posted 30 June 2012, accessed 7 July 2019.

10. Graciela Speranza, 'Conversation with Guillermo Kuitca', in *Guillermo Kuitca: Everything*, Albright-Knox Gallery, Buffalo, 2010, p.80.

11. *Guillermo Kuitca: Obras 1982–1998, Conversaciones con Graciela Speranza*, p.18.

12. Graciela Speranza, 'Conversation with Guillermo Kuitca', p.76.

13. At the time Kuitca inserted this still into his paintings he had not yet seen the film. Instead he came across the image in a book on Eisenstein published in a mass-market series of books titled *Los Hombres de la Historia*.

14. Graciela Speranza, 'Conversation with Guillermo Kuitca', p.77.

15. Nadine Meiser, 'Come Dance With Me: Interview with Pina Bausch', *Dance and Dancers*, September–October 1992, in *The Pina Bausch Sourcebook: The Making of Tanztheater*, ed. Royd Climenhaga, Routledge, London and New York, 2013, p.173.

16. Graciela Speranza, 'Conversation with Guillermo Kuitca', p.76.

17. ibid., p.79.

18. ibid., p.82.

19. See Lynn Zelevansky, 'Kuitca', in *Guillermo Kuitca*, Newport Harbor Art Museum, Newport Harbor, 1992, no pagination.

20. Interview with Josefina Ayerza, 'Guillermo Kuitca on the Map', *Flash Art*, November–December 1993, pp 45–7.

21. Lynn Zelevansky, 'Kuitca'.

22. Robert Alter, *Imagined Cities: Urban Experience and the Language of the Novel*, Yale University Press, New Haven, 2005, p.157.

23. ibid., p.159.

24. See entry for *point de capiton* in *From No Subject – Encyclopedia of Psychoanalysis*: nosubject.com/Point_de_capiton, accessed 8 July 2019.

25. One of Kuitca's crucial early supporters in Buenos Aires and in New York was Josefina Ayerza, a Lacanian therapist and publisher of the journal *Lacanian Ink*.

26. Graciela Speranza, 'Conversation with Guillermo Kuitca', p.80.

27. *Guillermo Kuitca: Obras 1982–1998, Conversaciones con Graciela Speranza*, p.84.

28. Graciela Speranza, "Conversation with Guillermo Kuitca," p.79.

29. Mari Carmen Ramírez, 'Guillermo Kuitca: The "Death of Painting" Painting as a Resistance Movement', accessed 8 July 2019.

30. 'Guillermo Kuitca: Experiences with Documenta', *Universes in Universe Magazine*, February 2017, universes.art, accessed 8 July 2019.

31. ibid.

32. Interview with Josefina Ayerza, 'Guillermo Kuitca on the Map', pp 45–7.

33. Graciela Speranza, 'Conversation with Guillermo Kuitca', p.79.

34. 'Guillermo Kuitca: Experiences with Documenta', universes.art, accessed 8 July 2019.

35. *Guillermo Kuitca: Obras 1982–1998, Conversaciones con Graciela Speranza*, p.157.

36. Kuitca himself makes this association in a letter to Lynne Cooke. See 'Iterations 15 July 1994–18 October 1994: Letters: Lynne Cooke, Guillermo Kuitca', in *Guillermo Kuitca, Burning Beds: A Survey 1982–1994*, Contemporary Art Foundation, Amsterdam, 1994, p.19.

37. Peter Halley, 'Notes on Abstraction', *Arts Magazine*, June/Summer 1987, in Peter Halley, *Collected Essays 1981–1987*, Bruno Bischofberger Gallery, Zurich, p.195.

38. In Laurie Firstenberg, 'Painting Platform in NY', *Flash Art*, November–December 2002, p.70.

39. Olga Viso, 'Resistant Painting', in *Guillermo Kuitca: Everything*, Albright-Knox Gallery, Buffalo, 2010, p.68.

40. 'Iterations: Letters Lynne Cooke Guillermo Kuitca', p.20.

41. *Guillermo Kuitca: Obras 1982–1998, Conversaciones con Graciela Speranza*, p.156.

42. Guillermo Kuitca in conversation with the author, Buenos Aires, 9 March 2019.

43. Quoted in Sonia Becce's chronology in *Guillermo Kuitca: Everything*, Albright-Knox Gallery, p.210.

44. Guillermo Kuitca, 'An Eight Day Diary', no.67, in *Guillermo Kuitca: Drawings 1981–1996*, Sperone Westwater, New York, 1998, no page numbers.

45. Graciela Speranza, 'Conversation with Guillermo Kuitca', p.84.

46. In *Guillermo Kuitca: Castle to Castle (from the Neufert Suite)*, Sperone Westwater, New York, 1998, no pagination.

47. Mike Kelley, 'Architectural Non-Memory Replaced with Psychic Reality' (1996), in

Mike Kelley, *Minor Histories: Statements, Conversations, Proposals*, ed. John C. Welchman, MIT Press, Cambridge and London, 2004, p.319.

48. 'Iterations 15 July 1994–18 October 1994: Letters: Lynne Cooke, Guillermo Kuitca', p.19.

49. Michel Foucault, 'Of Other Spaces: Utopias and Heterotopias', originally published as 'Des Espaces Autres' in *Architecture/Mouvement/ Continuité*, October 1984, pp 46–9. English version, trans. Jay Miskowicz, can be found online at web.mit.edu/allanmc/www/ foucault1.pdf Accessed 9 July 2019.

50. Guillermo Kuitca, 'An Eight Day Diary', no pagination.

51. Nonetheless, Kuitca makes no mention of the AMIA bombing in his faxed letters to Lynne Cooke between July and October 1994. The first of the artist's faxes is dated July 18, 1994, the very day of the bombing. See 'Iterations 15 July 1994 – 18 October 1994: Letters: Lynne Cooke, Guillermo Kuitca', p.14.

52. Graciela Speranza, 'Conversation with Guillermo Kuitca', pp 91–2.

53. ibid., p.91.

54. Quoted in François Cheng, *Empty and Full: The Language of Chinese Painting*, trans. Michael H. Kohn, Shambala, Boston and London, 1994, p.76.

55. Around the same time, another artist, David Hammons, began a series of Basketball Drawings made by repeatedly bouncing a basketball covered with 'Harlem earth' and graphite against sheets of paper. What appear to be the earliest of Hammons's Basketball Drawings are dated 2001.

56. See, for instance, 'Guillermo Kuitca: Experiences with Documenta', universes.art, accessed 6 July 2019.

57. Douglas Dreishpoon, 'Sometimes Walking is Enough', in *Guillermo Kuitca: Everything*, Albright-Knox Gallery, p.47.

58. Graciela Speranza, 'Conversation with Guillermo Kuitca', p.95.

59. ibid., p.97.

60. Douglas Dreishpoon, 'Sometimes Walking is Enough', p.36.

61. In a 2007 conversation Kuitca tells Graciela Speranza that it was a book she wrote about Argentine novelist Manuel Puig that inspired his Lichtenstein homage. See Graciela Speranza, 'Conversation with Guillermo Kuitca', pp 93–4.

62. Andreas Huyssen, 'Guillermo Kuitca: Painter of Space', in *Guillermo Kuitca: Everything*, Albright-Knox Gallery, p.24.

63. Clement Greenberg, 'After Abstract Expressionism', *Art International*, 25 October 1962, reprinted in Clement Greenberg, *The Collected Essays and Criticism*, vol.4, ed. John O'Brian, University of Chicago Press, Chicago, 1993, p.124.

64. Michael Fitzgerald, 'Guillermo Kuitca's Journey', in *Guillermo Kuitca*, Snoeck and Hauser & Wirth Publishers, London, 2016, p.16.

65. Graciela Speranza, 'Conversation with Guillermo Kuitca', p.97.

66. ibid., p.98.

67. Aina Pomar, interview with Guillermo Kuitca, *Artdependence Magazine*, June 2016.

68. Jean-Paul Sartre, quoted in Judith Butler, 'Desire and Recognition in Sartre's *Saint Genet* and *The Family Idiot, Vol. 1*', *International Philosophical Quarterly*, vol.26, issue 4, December 1986, p.371.

69. Georges Perec, *Species of Space and Other Pieces*, ed. and trans. John Sturrock, Penguin Books, London, 1997, pp 90–1.

Alter, Robert, *Imagined Cities: Urban Experience and the Language of the Novel*, London and New Haven: Yale University Press, 2005

Ayerza, Josefina, 'Guillermo Kuitca on the Map', *Flash Art*, November–December, 1993, pp 45–7

Butler, Judith, 'Desire and Recognition in Sartre's *Saint Genet* and *The Family Idiot, Vol. 1*', *International Philosophical Quarterly*, December, no.26, issue 4, 1986, pp 359–74

Cheng, François, *Empty and Full: The Language of Chinese Painting*, trans. Michael H. Kohn, Boston and London: Shambhala, 1994

Foucault, Michel, 'Of Other Spaces: Utopias and Heterotopias', originally published as 'Des Espaces Autres' in *Architecture/Mouvement/ Continuité*, October 1984

Giunta, Andrea, *Avant-Garde, Internationalism, and Politics: Argentine Art in the Sixties*, Duke University Press, Durham, NC, 2007

Halley, Peter, 'Notes on Abstraction', *Arts Magazine*, June/Summer, vol.61, 1987, in Peter Halley, *Collected Essays 1981–1987*, Bruno Bischofberger Gallery, Zurich, 1988, pp 168–95

Kelley, Mike, 'Architectural Non-Memory Replaced with Psychic Reality', in Mike Kelley, *Minor Histories: Statements, Conversations, Proposals*, ed. John C. Welchman, Cambridge, MA, and London: MIT Press, 2004, pp 316–23

Joachimides, Christos M., *A New Spirit in Painting*, London: Royal Academy of Arts, London, 1981

Kuitca, Guillermo, 'An Eight Day Diary', no.67, in *Guillermo Kuitca: Drawings 1981–1996*, exh. cat., New York: Sperone Westwater, 1998, unpaginated

—— *Guillermo Kuitca, Burning Beds: A Survey 1982–1994*, exh.cat., Amsterdam: Contemporary Art Foundation, 1994

—— *Guillermo Kuitca: Castle to Castle (from the Neufert Suite)*, exh.cat., New York: Sperone Westwater, 1999

—— *Guillermo Kuitca: Everything*, exh.cat., Buffalo, NY: Albright-Knox Gallery, 2010

—— 'Guillermo Kuitca: Experiences with Documenta', *Universes in Universe Magazine*, February 2017, universes.art

—— *Guillermo Kuitca: Obras 1982–1998, Conversaciones con Graciela Speranza*, Buenos Aires: Grupo Editorial Norma, 1998

—— *A Book Based on Guillermo Kuitca*, Amsterdam: Contemporary Art Foundation, 1993

Manning, Susan Allene, 'An American Perspective on Tanztheater', *The Drama Review (TDR)*, vol.30, no.2, Spring 1986, pp 57–79

Meisner, Nadine, 'Come Dance With Me: Interview with Pina Bausch', *Dance and Dancers*, September–October, 1992, in *The Pina Bausch Sourcebook: The Making of Tanztheater*, ed. Royd Climenhaga, London and New York: Routledge, 2013, pp 167–76

Perec, Georges, *Species of Space and Other Pieces*, ed. and trans. John Sturrock, London and New York: Penguin Books, 1997

Pomar, Aina, interview with Guillermo Kuitca, *Artdependence Magazine*, June 2016

Ramírez, Mari Carmen, 'Guillermo Kuitca: The 'Death of Painting' Painting as a Resistance Movement', *Literal 29*, Literalmagazine.com, 30 June 2012

Zelevansky, Lynn, 'Kuitca', in *Guillermo Kuitca*, California: Newport Harbor Art Museum, 1992, unpaginated

Biography

1961
Born 22 January in Buenos Aires to Maria Kuperman, a doctor specializing in child psychoanalysis, and Jaime Kuitca, an accountant. Both his parents are children of Russian Jews who immigrated to Argentina in the early 20th century.

1967
Begins attending art workshops.

1970
Kuitca tells his parents that he wants 'a more rigorous training'. He begins a nine-year course of studies with Surrealist painter Ahuva Szlimowicz.

1975
He studies drawing with Victor Chab until 1978.

1980
Admitted to the art history department at the University of Buenos Aires, but never attends classes.
Solo exhibition at Fundación San Telmo in Buenos Aires.
Attends performance of *Café Müller* by Pina Bausch's Tanztheater at Teatro San Martín, travels to Europe for the first time, spends time in Wuppertal, Germany, where he befriends dancers from Bausch's company and sees more of her work.

1982
Stages *Nadie olvida nada*, a theater production in Buenos Aires, in collaboration with his friend Carlos Ianni, and begins a series of related paintings on wood scraps and old doors.

1984
Stages *El mar dulce*, a play he co-authors with Ianni, in Buenos Aires at Teatro Planeta. Works on series of paintings titled *El mar dulce* inspired by Bausch and by his own theater pieces.

1986
Exhibits paintings from *Siete últimas canciones* series at Galeria del Retiro-Julia Lublin in Buenos Aires. This is his last show in Buenos Aires for 17 years.

1987–8
Begins making paintings based on city maps and road maps; first apartment-floor-plan paintings.

1989
First map-mattress works.

1990
First solo exhibition in New York at Annina Nosei Gallery.

1991
Exhibits at Project Room at Museum of Modern Art, New York; inaugurates annual workshop/seminar for young Argentine artists.
Begins *The Tablada Suite*, paintings based on architectural plans.

1992
Participates in *documenta IX* in Kassel, Germany, where he shows an installation of 20 mattress paintings.

1993
Moves to studio in Belgrano neighborhood of Buenos Aires.
First solo exhibition at Sperone Westwater, New York.
First retrospective, *Guillermo Kuitca, Works 1982–1993*, at Instituto Valenciano de Arte Moderno (IVAM), Spain, and in Mexico at the Museo de Monterrey and the Museo Rufino Tamayo.
Makes first *Diarios* paintings by mounting an unfinished discarded canvas on a round table in his studio and letting drawings and notes accumulate on it over a period of months.

1995
Presents *The Tablada Suite* at the 52nd Carnegie International.

1996
Begins *Poema Pedagógico* series of paintings, which he makes while blindfolded.

1998
Neufert Suite based on diagrams in Ernst Neufert's architectural reference book.

2001
Presents two large-scale realist paintings of airport luggage conveyor belts at Hauser & Wirth, Zurich.
Begins work on a series of paintings based on Wagner's *Ring Cycle*.

2002
Creates set designs for a production of Federico García Lorca's *La casa de Bernarda Alba* at Teatro San Martín in Buenos Aires.
Concentrates on large-scale collages based on theater seating charts.

2003
Retrospective travels from Reina Sofía in Madrid to Museo de Arte Latinoamericano de Buenos Aires (MALBA), his first exhibition in Buenos Aires since 1986.

2006
Begins *Desenlace (Dénouement)* paintings that incorporate 'cubistoid' motifs.

2007
Represents Argentina at the Venice Biennale with *Desenlace (Dénouement)* series.

2010
The artist's first retrospective exhibition in the United States, *Guillermo Kuitca: Everything, Paintings and Works on Paper 1980–2008*, opens at the Miami Art Museum and travels to the Albright-Knox Art Gallery in Buffalo, NY, the Walker Art Center in Minneapolis and the Hirshhorn Museum and Sculpture Garden in Washington, D.C.

2013
Paints murals using cubistoid motifs on the walls of his home-studio in Buenos Aires.
Spends five weeks creating a permanent mural, commissioned by Hauser & Wirth, in a restored farmhouse in southwest England.

2014
Creates *Les Habitants* at the Cartier Foundation in Paris, an immersive installation inspired by the films of David Lynch and Artavazd Pelechian.
Shows *L'Encyclopédie* series at Hauser & Wirth, Zurich.

2019
Unveils *The Family Idiot*, a new series of paintings of interior spaces at Hauser & Wirth, Los Angeles.

Exhibitions

Selected Solo Exhibitions

2019
Guillermo Kuitca, Hauser & Wirth Los Angeles,
  South Gallery, Los Angeles
Guillermo Kuitca, Galería Elba Benítez, Madrid

2017
Guillermo Kuitca, Kunsthaus Pasquart, Biel,
  Switzerland

2016
Guillermo Kuitca, Hauser & Wirth, London

2014
Doble Eclipse, Mendes Wood DM, São Paulo
Diarios, Galeria Fortes Vilaça, São Paulo
Guillermo Kuitca: Filosofia para princesas
  (Philosophy for Princesses), Pinacoteca do
  Estado de São Paulo, Brazil
*Guillermo Kuitca: L'Encyclopédie Nos. I, II, III,
  IV, V, VI*, Hauser & Wirth, Zurich
This Way, Sperone Westwater, New York

2013
Diarios, Eli and Edythe Broad Art Museum
  at Michigan State University, Minnesota.
  Traveled to Museum of Contemporary Art
  Denver, Colorado

2012
Diarios, The Drawing Center, New York
Guillermo Kuitca, Hauser & Wirth, London

2010
Guillermo Kuitca, Hauser & Wirth, Zurich
*Guillermo Kuitca: Paintings 2008–2010, Le Sacre
  1992*, Sperone Westwater, New York

2009
*Guillermo Kuitca. Everything—Paintings and Works
  on Paper, 1980–2008*, Miami Art Museum,
  Florida. Traveled to Albright-Knox Art Gallery,
  Buffalo, New York, 2010; Hirshhorn Museum
  and Sculpture Garden, Washington D.C.,
  2010; and Walker Art Center, Minneapolis,
  Minnesota, 2010

2008
Guillermo Kuitca, Hauser & Wirth, London

2007
Guillermo Kuitca: Si yo fuera el invierno mismo (If I
  Were Winter Itself), Argentine Pavilion, Venice
  Biennale
The Ring, Galerie Daniel Templon, Paris
Stage Fright, Gallery Met at The Metropolitan
  Opera House, New York

2006
Das Lied von der Erde (The Song of the Earth),
  Daros Exhibitions, Zurich
Obras Puntuales, El Museo de Arte del Banco de
  la República, Bogota, Colombia. Traveled to
  National Fine Arts Museum, Santiago, Chile

2005
Theatre Collages, Hauser & Wirth, London
Acoustic Mass, Sperone Westwater, New York

2003
Guillermo Kuitca: Obras 1982 / 2002, Museo
  de Arte Latinoamericano de Buenos Aires
  (MALBA), Coleccion Constantini. Traveled to
  Museo National Centro de Arte Reina Sofía,
  Madrid

2002
Galleria Cardi, Milan
Galeria Enrique Guerrero, Mexico City
LA Louver Gallery, Venice, California
The Ring, Sperone Westwater, New York

2001
Hauser & Wirth, Zurich

2000
Oeuvres récentes, Fondation Cartier pour l'art
  contemporain, Paris

1999
Guillermo Kuitca: Beds, Theaters & Drawings, The
  Arts Club of Chicago
Centro de Arte Hélio Oiticica, Rio de Janeiro
Galerie Barbara Farber – La Serre, Trets, France
LA Louver Gallery, Venice, California

Castle to Castle (From the Neufert Suite), Sperone
  Westwater, New York

1998
Galerie Thaddaeus Ropac, Paris

1997
Guillermo Kuitca en Caracas, Museo Alejandro
  Otero, Caracas
Guillermo Kuitca – Poema Pedagógico, Sperone
  Westwater, New York
Timothy Taylor Gallery, London

1996
Galleria Gian Enzo Sperone, Rome

1995
The Douglas Hyde Gallery, Trinity College,
  Dublin
Galerie Barbara Farber, Amsterdam
Guillermo Kuitca: Puro Teatro, Sperone Westwater,
  New York

1994
Guillermo Kuitca – The Tablada Suite, Sperone
  Westwater, New York
*Guillermo Kuitca. Burning Beds: A Survey 1982–
  1994*, Wexner Center for the Arts, Columbus,
  Ohio. Traveled to Center for the Fine Arts,
  Miami, Florida, 1995; and Whitechapel Art
  Gallery, London, 1995

1993
Guillermo Kuitca, Center for the Fine Arts.
  Traveled to Museo Rufino Tamayo, Mexico
  City; and Centre Georges Pompidou, Paris
Guillermo Kuitca, Works 1982–1993, Instituto
  Valenciano de Arte Moderno (IVAM), Valencia,
  Spain. Traveled to Museo de Monterrey, Mexico
Guillermo Kuitca – Les Lieux de l'Errance, Musée
  d'Art Contemporain de Montréal, Canada
Sperone Westwater, New York

1991
Annina Nosei Gallery, New York
Galerie Barbara Farber, Amsterdam

Projects 30 – Guillermo Kuitca, Museum of
Modern Art (MOMA), New York. Traveled
to Newport Harbor Art Museum, California,
1992; The Corcoran Gallery of Art,
Washington D.C., 1993; and Contemporary
Arts Museum, Houston, Texas, 1993

1990
Kunsthalle Basel, Switzerland
Guillermo Kuitca, Städtisches Museum, Mulheim,
Germany. Traveled to Witte de With Center for
Contemporary Art, Rotterdam
Galleria Gian Enzo Sperone, Rome
Thomas Solomon's Garage, Los Angeles

1986
Guillermo Kuitca – Siete últimas canciones, Galeria
del Retiro-Julia Lublin, Buenos Aires
Thomas Cohn Arte Contemporanea, Rio de
Janeiro

1985
Elisabeth Franck Gallery, Knokke-Le-Zoute,
Belgium

1984
Galeria del Retiro, Buenos Aires

1980
Guillermo Kuitca: Obras 1978–80, Fundación San
Telmo, Buenos Aires

1978
Guillermo Kuitca: Dibujos 1978, Galeria Christel
K., Buenos Aires

1974
Galeria Lirolay, Buenos Aires

Selected Group Exhibitions

2019
Opéra Monde, Centre Pompidou-Metz, Metz,
France
Art_Latin_America. Against the Survey, Davis
Museum at Wellesley College, Massachusetts

2018
Géométries Sud, du Mexique à la Terre de Feu,
Fondation Cartier pour l'art contemporain,
Paris
Chaos and Awe: Painting for the 21st Century, Frist
Art Museum, Nashville

2017
Home—So Different, So Appealing, Los Angeles
County Museum of Art

2015
My Buenos Aires, La Maison Rouge, Paris
*Contingent Beauty: Contemporary Art from Latin
America*, Museum of Fine Arts, Houston
Picasso in Contemporary Art, Deichtorhallen
Hamburg. Traveled to Wexner Center for the
Arts, Columbus, Ohio
Dark Mirror – Art from Latinamerica since 1968,
Kunstmuseum Wolfsburg, Germany
Species of Spaces, Museu d'Art Contemporani de
Barcelona (MACBA)

2014
Les Habitants, Fondation Cartier pour l'art
contemporain, Paris
*Permission To Be Global/Prácticas Globales: Latin
American Art from the Ella Fontanals-Cisneros
Collection* (traveling exhibition), Museum of
Fine Arts, Boston
Guillermo Kuitca & Eduardo Berliner – Pinturas,
Casa Daros, Rio de Janeiro
Pressed, Sicardi Gallery, Houston

2011
*Radical Shift. Political and Social Upheaval in
Argentinian Art since the 1960s*, Museum
Morsbroich, Leverkusen, Germany

2010
Performance/Art, Dallas Museum of Art, Texas

2008
Face to Face: The Daros Collection. Part 2, Daros
Exhibitions, Zurich
Daros Exhibitions, *Painted! New Acquisitions of the
Daros Collections: Beate Gunther*,

2007
*Think with the Senses – Feel with the Mind. Art in the
Present Tense*, 52nd Venice Biennale
*New Perspectives in Latin American Art, 1930–
2006: Selections from a Decade of Acquisitions*,
Museum of Modern Art (MOMA), New York

2006
Altered, Stitched and Gathered, PS1 Contemporary
Art Center, New York

2005
Looking at Words, Andrea Rosen Gallery, New York
Inverting the Map, Tate Liverpool

2004
Être. Les droits de l`homme à travers de l'art, Palais
des Nations, Geneva

2003
*Drawing Modern. Works from the Agnes Gund
Collection*, Cleveland Museum of Art, Ohio
Gesellschaftsbilder/Images of Society, Kunstmuseum
Thun, Switzerland

2002
Time to Consider: The Arts Respond to 9.11,
Deutsche Bank Lobby Gallery, New York
Tempo, Museum of Modern Art (MOMA), New
York
Trauma, Museum of Modern Art, Oxford

2001
7th International Istanbul Biennial

2000
*Architecture and Memory: Kevin Appel, Guillermo
Kuitca, Julie Mehretu*, CRG Art Incorporated,
New York

1998
Wounds: Between Democracy and Redemption in Contemporary Art, Moderna Museet, Stockholm
Cartographers: Geo-Gnostic Projection for the 21st Century, XXIV Bienal de São Paulo

1996
Distemper: Dissonant Themes in Art of the 1990's, Hirshhorn Museum and Sculpture Garden, Washington D.C.
Sin Fronteras: Arte Latinamericano Actual, Museo Alejandro Otero, Caracas
Painting: The Extended Field (traveling exhibition), Rooseum, Malmö, Sweden

1995
52nd Carnegie International, Carnegie Museum of Art, Pittsburgh, Pennsylvania
Cartographies – 14 Artists from Latin America (traveling exhibition), Fundación La Caixa, Madrid
Kwangju Biennale, Kwang Ju Museum of Contemporary Art, Gwangju, Korea

1994
La Ville, Centre Georges Pompidou, Paris
Mapping, Museum of Modern Art (MOMA), New York
Written/Spoken/Drawn in Lacanian Ink, Thread Waxing Space, New York
Burnt Whole: Contemporary Artists Reflect on the Holocaust (traveling exhibition), Washington Project for the Arts, Washington, D.C.

1993
Drawing the Line Against AIDS (traveling exhibition), Solomon R. Guggenheim Museum, New York

1992
Latin American Artists of the Twentieth Century, Centre Georges Pompidou/Hôtel des Arts, Fondation Nationale des Arts, Paris. Traveled to Museum of Modern Art (MOMA), New York, 1993
Documenta IX, Kassel, Germany

1991
Mito y Magia de los '80, Museo de Arte Contemporáneo (MARCO), Monterrey, Mexico
Metropolis, Martin Gropius Bau, Berlin

1990
Hommage to Van Gogh (poster design), Fundacion Van Gogh, Amsterdam

1989
XX Bienal, São Paulo
New Image Painting, Argentina in the Eighties, America's Society Art Gallery, New York

1988
Salon Internacional Bienal, San José, Costa Rica

1987
Art of the Fantastic, Latin-America, 1920–1987, Center for the Fine Arts, Miami. Traveled to Centro Cultural de Arte Contemporaneo, Mexico City; Indianapolis Museum of Art; and The Queens Museum, New York

1985
XVIII Bienal, São Paulo, Brazil
Latinoamericanos en Nueva York, M13 Gallery, New York

1984
Cambre–Kuitca–Marcaccio, Galeria Sala de la Pequeña Muestra, Rosario, Argentina

1983
Buenos Aires a travers de sus Artistas (traveling exhibition), Akademie der Kunst, Berlin
Sieben Maler aus Buenos Aires, DAAD Galerie, Berlin
Intergrafik '83, Berlin

1981
25 anos, Museo de Arte Moderno, Buenos Aires

Selected Theater Works

2011
Co-author Permanent stage curtain design, Teatro Colón, Buenos Aires

2009
Permanent stage curtain design, Winspear Opera House, Dallas, Texas

2003
Der Fliegende Holländer (stage design), Teatro Colón, Buenos Aires

2002
La casa de Bernarda Alba (stage design), Teatro San Martín, Buenos Aires

1984
El mar dulce. Un espectáculo de Carlos Ianni y Guillermo Kuitca (direction), Teatro Planeta, Buenos Aires

1983
Besos brujos. Performance en Expresiones 83 (direction in collaboration with Carlos Ianni), Centro Cultural Recoleta, Buenos Aires

1982
Nadie olvida nada. Un espectáculo de Carlos Ianni y Guillermo Kuitca (direction), Teatro Planeta, Buenos Aires

Public Collections

21st Century Museum of Contemporary Art,
  Kanazawa, Japan
Albright-Knox Art Gallery, Buffalo, New York
Art Gallery of Ontario, Toronto
Art Gallery of Western Australia, Perth
Art Institute of Chicago, Illinois
Center for Curatorial Studies, Bard College,
  Annandale-on-Hudson, New York
Centro Galego de Arte Comtemporánea,
  Santiago de Compostela, Spain
Cleveland Museum of Art, Cleveland, Ohio
Dallas Museum of Art, Texas
Daros Latinamerica Collection, Zurich
Fonds national d'art contemporain, France
Fondation Cartier pour l'art contemporain, Paris
Hirshhorn Museum and Sculpture Garden,
  Washington D.C.
Instituto Valenciano de Arte Moderno (IVAM),
  Valencia, Spain
Museo Jumex, Mexico City
Los Angeles County Museum of Art, California
Milwaukee Art Museum, Milwaukee, Wisconsin
Musée d'Art Contemporain de Montréal, Quebec
Musée d'Art Moderne Grand-Duc Jean
  (MUDAM), Luxembourg
Museo de Arte Contemporáneo de Rosario,
  Argentina
Museo de Arte Latinoamericano de Buenos Aires
  – Colección Costantini
Museo de Arte Moderno de Buenos Aires
Museo de Monterrey, Mexico
Museo Extremeño e Iberoamericano de Arte
  Contemporáneo, Badajoz, Spain
Museo Nacional Centro de Arte Reina Sofía,
  Madrid
Museo Nacional de Bellas Artes, Buenos Aires
Museu d'Art Contemporani de Barcelona
  (MACBA)
Museu de Arte Moderna, Rio de Janeiro
Museu Serralves, Porto, Portugal
Museum Boijmans Van Beuningen, Rotterdam
Museum of Fine Arts, Boston, Massachusetts
Museum of Fine Arts, Houston, Texas
Museum of Modern Art, New York
Museum Voorlinden, Wassenaar, the Netherlands
National Gallery of Victoria, Melbourne
Pérez Art Museum, Miami
Smithsonian Institution, Washington, D.C.
Stedelijk Museum, Amsterdam
Tate, London
The Jewish Museum, New York
The Metropolitan Museum of Art, New York
Walker Art Center, Minneapolis, Minnesota

Acknowledgements

The author would like to thank the following people: Katherine Borkowski at Sperone Westwater for her invaluable assistance in tracking down images and documentation, Martín Touzón at Guillermo Kuitca's studio for instantly providing whatever images and information were needed, Sonia Becce for sharing her deep knowledge of Kuitca's career during a 2019 conversation in Buenos Aires, Josefina Ayerza for first introducing me to the artist in New York in the early 1990s, my wife Heather Bause Rubinstein for her constant encouragement and painter's insight during the writing of the book, and, most of all, Guillermo Kuitca, for welcoming me into his studio day after day, patiently answering all my questions with thoughtfulness and precision, and generously sharing his always enlightening ideas about his own work while never seeking to impose them.

I would also like to thank the wonderful editorial team at Lund Humphries, including Lucy Clark, Rochelle Roberts, Anna Norman and, last but not least, series editor Barry Schwabsky. Thanks as well to Catherine Serrano at Hauser & Wirth, New York.

Image Credits

The numbers listed below refer to figure numbers.

Nina Subin (photo): Frontispiece.

Courtesy of the artist and Sperone Westwater, New York: 5, 7, 8, 9, 11, 12, 16, 17, 18, 20, 22, 23, 24, 26, 31, 39, 41, 42, 43, 44, 45, 46, 49, 50, 51, 53, 56, 74, 77, 79; and A. Burger Fotographie, Zurich (photo) 63; and Jorge Miño (photo) 64; and Tom Powel (photo) 71, 72, 73.

Courtesy of Hauser & Wirth collection services: 70.

Courtesy of the artist and Hauser & Wirth: 62, 75, 80, 84, 87, 88, 89, 90, 91, 92, 93, 94, 95.

Courtesy of Sperone Westwater and Hauser & Wirth: 81.

Alex Delfanne (photo): 81.

Aaron Schuman (photo): 85.

The Estate of Francis Bacon. All rights reserved. DACS 2019: 4.

Pina Bausch Foundation (photo Ulla Weiss): 3.

First published in 2020 by Lund Humphries

Lund Humphries
Office 3, Book House
261a City Road
London
EC1V 1JX
www.lundhumphries.com

ISBN: 978-1-84822-373-8

A Cataloguing-in-Publication record for this book is available
from the British Library.

Copy-edited by Catherine Hooper
Designed by Mark Thomson
Set in Custodia (Fred Smeijers)
Printed in Italy

Frontispiece: Photograph of Guillermo Kuitca by Nina Subin
Cover: *Untitled* (2003–15) (detail), oil on canvas, 196.5 x 196.3 cm
(77 ⅜ x 77 ¼ in), private collection.